THREE WOMEN

Die Windsbraut (The Tempest) by Oskar Kokoschka, 1914.

Walter Sorell

THREE WOMEN

LIVES OF SEX AND GENIUS

OSWALD WOLFF

LONDON

Excerpts from AND THE BRIDGE IS LOVE by Alma Mahler-Werfel with E. B. Ashton reprinted by permission of Harcourt Brace Jovanovich, Inc.

Excerpts from SIGMUND FREUD AND LOU ANDREAS-SALOMÉ LETTERS edited by Ernst Pfeiffer reprinted by permission of Harcourt Brace Jovanovich, Inc.

Excerpts from THE AUTOBIOGRAPHY OF ALICE B. TOKLAS by Gertrude Stein copyright © 1933 and renewed 1961 by Alice B. Toklas. Reprinted by permission of Random House, Inc.

Excerpts from EVERYBODY'S AUTOBIOGRAPHY by Gertrude Stein copyright © 1937 by Random House, Inc. and renewed 1965 by Alice B. Toklas. Reprinted by permission of Random House, Inc.

Excerpts from MY LIFE by Oskar Kokoschka copyright © 1974 by Thames and Hudson Ltd. Reprinted by permission of Macmillan Publishing Co., Inc.

Excerpts from THE FREUD JOURNAL OF LOU ANDREAS-SALOMÉ, translated and with an Introduction by Stanley A. Leavy, © 1964 by Basic Books, Inc., Publishers, New York.

Selections from Rudolph Binion, FRAU LOU: NIETZSCHE'S WAYWARD DISCIPLE (copyright © 1968 by Princeton University Press; Princeton Paperback, 1974), pp. 12–113. Reprinted by permission of Princeton University Press.

Excerpts from MY SISTER, MY SPOUSE by H. F. Peters copyright © 1962 by H. F. Peters. Reprinted by permission of W. W. Norton and Company, Inc.

ISBN 0 85496 258 1

Copyright © 1975 by Walter Sorell

First published in the United States of America
Published in Great Britain by
Oswald Wolff (Publishers) Ltd., London 1977

Made and printed in Great Britain by
Billing & Sons Ltd., Guildford, London and Worcester.

For Suzanne Naville

Acknowledgments

For the last few decades I have read all of the books and most of the published material in periodicals and newspapers on Alma Mahler-Werfel, Gertrude Stein and Lou Andreas-Salomé as far as it was available to me, and I have spoken to many people who knew them or about them. Their published testimonies and oral information have helped to maintain my interest and increase my enthusiasm for the "three women," and I wish to thank all of them for their direct or indirect assistance.

My particular gratitude goes to E. B. Ashton, who collaborated with Alma Mahler-Werfel on her autobiography, and to Harcourt Brace Jovanovich as well as to Princeton University Press, publishers of Rudolph Binion's *Frau Lou*, for their generous attitudes, as well as to several other publishers listed in the Bibliography.

My special thanks goes to Barnard College for having assisted me with a grant that made it possible for me to spend some time in Switzerland, where I finished this book. I also want to express my gratitude to my editor, Stefanie Tashjian-Woodbridge, whose counsel was of great help to me. Last, but hardly least, I wish to thank my wife, Gertrude Maria, for her infinite patience, criticism and encouragement.

Contents

Contents

By Way of Confession

This is not a preface but a confession. Like the twentieth century, I am now in my seventh decade. Thus, I have the perspective of someone who has matured as our century has developed. I spent my youth in Vienna. As luck had it, I was young when Vienna was one of the major focal points of European culture. So, at an early age, I became aware of the various creative forces that were about to give the twentieth century its unmistakable face of boldness and beauty, of uproars and upheavals. During my formative years many vestiges of the nineteenth century were stored in my mental rucksack; they helped to make the past, as much as the present, a living experience for me.

Centuries never begin and end with the years of their calendrical dates. In the endless flow of time what is new is signaled and prepared long before it happens. In my personal history book the twentieth century began in the 1880s and came to an end with the incineration of Hiroshima. These decades brought forth momentous innovations. We witnessed the impressive labor of a dying culture giving birth to a new civilization, one whose path and direction may be surmised and perhaps feared, but one we cannot yet fully envision. We witnessed then, as we do today, man struggling with himself. And no other human activity but the arts could better mirror and register man's battle with himself, against himself; his drifting hopes and faltering dreams. To capture some of the highlights of this era, I have thus chosen to describe three women whose lives were uniquely involved with the arts. Their stories are the story of their time. In the cast of characters making up the private drama of their lives we find some of the most significant architects of new ideas, men who earned their reputations as traitors to the past and fighters for the future.

These three women were contemporaries. Although they moved in similar spheres, indeed the same sphere, they never met one another. But some of the supporting characters in my triptych played a role in the lives of more than one of these women, and did meet and know one another on their own. Even though it is no longer true—if it ever was—that culture is made by twelve people, as Ezra Pound once arrogantly said, it still was made by a select company whose paths had to cross in Vienna or Paris, in Rome, Munich or Berlin, and whose paths crossed those of my three women: Alma Mahler-Werfel, Gertrude Stein, and Lou Andreas-Salomé.

I have chosen these three women in particular for several reasons. First, they inspired some of the greatest artists of this century. They attracted genius because they themselves could freely enter its kingdom, even though, to posterity, their passports may have been limited in scope and validity. We are accustomed to measure genius or great talent with tapes showing the length, height, and depth of creative output and its effect on civilization. But this "method" defeats itself by excluding many people: for instance, someone who has the genius to awaken genius and, in this ecstatic process, becomes creative. To this "scientific" day, artistic creativity has remained man's greatest marvel, the wonder eluding and defying definition and description. Three women who were intimately involved with creativity thus seem to me worthy of attention.

All three women were atypical of women of their time and quite different from each other (although one can detect similarities). What they had in common was a sort of spell-binding intensity and the effortless ability to fascinate gifted—literally extraordinary—personalities. Together with vision, they had an unfathomable sensitivity to

people and situations; they exhibited an intuitive sense that sometimes reached the frontiers of extrasensory perception. As a man, I
wanted to understand these qualities as much as I could, and even
learn from them, if possible.

Moreover, all three dared to be true to themselves. They were
feminists long before the movement had caught the imagination of
womanhood; yet it would be unthinkable to imagine any of the three
as card-carrying members of an organization. They were unorthodox
in every respect.

Alma Mahler-Werfel's life paralleled Lou Salomé's, even though
Alma was her junior by eighteen years. Their experiences seem to
complement one another. But Alma was less ambitious than Lou, and
no one can say how far her creative powers would have reached had
she not willingly—however grudgingly—exchanged them for the
total use of her femininity as a weapon and creative tool. In many
ways she took a rather passive attitude toward wielding her artistic
powers, channeling them in favor of her relationships with men. In
comparison to her two contemporaries, Lou Salomé and Gertrude
Stein, she seems least fulfilled and most ambivalent about herself.
Though she often tried to rebel, and to run away from the role of the
"inspiring" woman, a role she fully enjoyed yet furtively resented,
she always returned to it out of fear of being alone in the world and
because she had a compulsive need to be surrounded by famous men.

Alma was far more the victim of her own charms than Lou ever
was. As a collector of famous men, she paid the price for her passion.
Alma delighted in her "possessions," never wanting to be possessed.
She basked in the sun of fame, surrounding herself with names that
lit up her void and the world's. She played the driving motor for the
genius of other people, but her ultimate gratification always remained
vicarious. Her lot was to be needed by men about to unfold their own
genius.

At the end of her life Alma could walk through the gallery of her
memory admiring her collection of famous men. She thought she
possessed and possessed and possessed when, in fact, she was the one
possessed. She was the handmaiden to creative minds. Sometimes she

played the part of midwife; on other occasions, she stood at the cradle of great works. To whatever function destiny called her, she fulfilled a signal task.

Lou Salomé played the game of the male in a male world with great skill because of her personality's magnetism. Her amazing willpower was an intimidating weapon not only of her mind but also of her genitals. A woman of extremes and a calculating woman to boot, she asked her mind to rule her emotions time and again and defended her virginity as long as it pleased her—only, in a complete turnabout, to suddenly open the cornucopia of her female beauty for, as much as against, man.

Lou possessed great creative potentialities. In the 1890s and at the beginning of this century, she was considered one of the respected women of letters; later in her life she became a vital force in the psychoanalytic movement. Lou was as fascinating as she was controversial; put on a pedestal by some, she was aspersed and denigrated by others, particularly by those eager to reduce Freud's significance. It was too often said facetiously that no woman could help being mentioned in the annals of history when a man like Friedrich Nietzsche was ready to marry her—Nietzsche, the philosopher who did not want us to forget the whip when going to the woman (and this thought was, after all, directed against Lou); when Rainer Maria Rilke loved her as a woman and as the tree on which the complexities of his thoughts ripened; and when Sigmund Freud saw in the reflection of her eyes the realization of his great dream, especially at a time when his psychoanalysis was fighting through schisms for its very life.

However, to picture Lou simply as a catalyst for the achievements of these great men, who signify major developmental stages in our age, would reduce her real significance. She was never a reflective mirror only. Nietzsche was the first to recognize that even her way of listening, by itself, had a creative quality beyond all inspiration. And her spirit and some of her thoughts have certainly found their way into the works of those with whom she was intimate. In her own right she was a powerful and constructive force in the intellectual edifice of our time—a period stretching from Nietzsche's trumpet calls, warning man of the destructiveness of his own averageness, to the days when the wounds caused by this same destructiveness had to be healed.

In many ways, Gertrude Stein was the most unorthodox of these three women. She did not hesitate to let the world know that she preferred to live with another woman. How much the "otherness" of her sexual inclinations in a heterosexual world contributed to or was in concord with her stubbornly personal and willful way of combining words and phrasing thoughts has not yet been sufficiently considered.

Together with James Joyce, Gertrude Stein has often been named as one of the important iconoclasts of twentieth-century literature. Even though their points of departure, their methods and the final results were different, both tried to liberate literature from its dead sleep in the arms of conventionality. "Joyce is an incomprehensible that anyone can understand," she believed with Picasso. Is her work more—or less—comprehensible? A great deal of criticism has been leveled at her, and many writers have tried to capsule the essence of her message, to assess the meaning of her wordscape; for instance, William Carlos Williams likened it to crowds at Coney Island as seen from a plane at high altitude.

She cared little about exact descriptions or about being true to facts. With her compelling sense of geometrizing relationships and events, she was closest to Cubism in literature. She wanted to rediscover the poetry of simplicity, the depth of ordinariness which she caught in the rhythm of repetition, in the recurring patterns of psychological types. Like Jean Cocteau—and essentially very much unlike him, as she rightly would say—she captured the ecstasy of banality; in the last analysis, it is the ultimate expression of so much of our time and perhaps of man's existence.

Gertrude Stein was a compulsive writer whose improvisations grew out of the many daily annotations written on the margin of her life. Most of her writing is a true reflection of her being, meditating and moving around, bent to a telescopic vision of depth in distortion. What may appear as lightly conceived sentences or asyntactical patterns of trivia, obviously inspired and yet disconnected, were the result of labored compositions. The notoriety she acquired—it always annoyed her to be better known than her work—makes it more difficult to see beyond her linguistic acrobatics and stylistic sleight-of-hand to her importance as a lady of letters. She will always be read and appreciated by a small group of people who are fed up with expected, patterned experiences and seek the surprise of poetic innovation. Is she, therefore, more a writer's writer? Perhaps. But it matters little to us here. She is an appropriate contrast to Lou Salomé and Alma Mahler-Werfel: different, to be sure, but a personality of similar volcanic intensity and magnitude. Moreover, Gertrude Stein became a focal point for some of the great minds and artistic rebels of her time. In discussing her life and her new word-mysticism, I am trying to find some meaning in the being she was, the being behind her protective and aggressive mask, and to capture the artists who passed through her life to make great lives of their own, a feat that might have been impossible had they not touched Gertrude Stein's.

Lou Salomé, all mind and body, used her feminism with subtle skill; Alma Mahler-Werfel, all body and mind, seduced a world that desired to capitulate and wonder why; Gertrude Stein, all mind, stood outside the ring in which the heterosexual games took place. She extolled the oneness of twoness after her permanent alliance with Alice B. Toklas and the freedom of being there for whoever found the way to her.

Despite their differences, all three women attracted some of the most powerful pioneers of a world to come, men whose magnitude of mind and boldness of vision changed the direction and meaning of our existence. In their own ways, they are wonderful examples of liberated women, fighting traditions and taboos, struggling against the ordinary and orthodox. They were such individualists that, in their freedom, they could afford to retain the essence of their being and to replenish their own and others' creative powers in a play of give and take.

Finally, I have chosen these three women for one more, and a very personal, reason. I had the opportunity to meet both Alma Mahler-Werfel and Gertrude Stein, and I would have given my life—as some men virtually did—to meet Lou Salomé. All three made a deep impression on me, and I have lived with their images, with their fascinating life stories, for many decades.

Some people may find fault with their behavior and attitudes. They may see only their excessive egocentricities and rhapsodic eccentricities where I see human beings with many strong qualities organized into mysterious wholes. People cannot be explained like machines; they must always elude us, and extraordinary people attract—and elude—us all the more. Whatever its dimension and radiance, the halo of extraordinariness invites and evokes criteria of measurement different from those applied to average people. I see in these women humanity and exceptional individuality. In looking behind mere surfaces, we may encounter a total image of a woman as herself; of a woman fulfilling herself; of a woman at the same time fighting and fulfilling her traditional role of being source and motivation for the creative man.

The faces of these three women have often accompanied me on my imaginary journeys into the past. I still see them in the midst of those many other faces that have become an inseparable part of their lives as much as of the story of mankind. To allow other people to see these three women as I have seen them—my three women—I tell their stories.

W. S.

New York,
January, 1975

Before her marriage in 1902
to Gustav Mahler.

Lithograph (1913) by
Oskar Kokoschka from his
Der gefesselte Kolumbus.

The Granger Collection

Alma Mahler-Werfel
Body and Mind

A Life of Fairy Tales

ALMA MAHLER-WERFEL was still an incurable romantic when I met her in New York in the early 1960s. She was then a very old lady, having passed eighty, with an expressive face still beautiful and beautifully framed by her yellowish-gray hair. When she entered the restaurant where I waited for her, she attracted everyone's attention. She had a way of commanding all eyes to pay homage to the radiance of her personality. She was immaculately dressed, the colors of her tailored suit stressing her fair complexion.

As the child of an era when Vienna was one of the most important cultural centers of the world, she had never lost her sincere nostalgic feeling for the days of her youth. In a tone of protest: "I'm not conservative now because my rich life has turned my hair grayish. Probably I have always clung to another world than the one we now live in. How much marvelous work was accomplished by candlelight! And how much darkness is so often around us now when at the flip of a thought we can illuminate our life with electric light. Does it really electrify us? And all this happens to us on all levels of existence. I do not mind being called a sentimentalist. But I say, man is the flower of God. I have always regretted the sad decline of religiousness, even though I grew up as an agnostic."

We spoke of inner conflicts created by pressures from the outside world and how they lead to compromises all through life. "I was brought up as a Catholic. Mahler and Werfel, my first and last husbands, were Jews. I spent some of my most exciting and rewarding years with them." After a short pause, "Of course, they both were radicals in their own ways. Perhaps there is no greatness without fanaticism. And it was on that point only that I was never wholly with them. In the name of many a dream I have seen so much wrong done in this world." She loathed radicalism, pretending to have no understanding of revolutions, regardless of what needs gave birth to them. She spoke of Werfel, the man she may have loved most and with whom she lived longest. She never understood his radical attitudes after the First World War. "Everything was so different from how our literary ideologists saw the world. They recognized too late how their ideals were murdered and turned against them."

Perhaps Alma Mahler-Werfel never fully realized that she was a radical herself, a fact proved by her own life. In defending her own private rights as a woman she fought for the rights and the assertion of all women. She remembered a discussion with Arthur Schnitzler in Vienna in what must have been the late twenties. They debated the odd fact that women in contrast to men are so often turned away from their own selves after their marriage. "I told Schnitzler of my wonderful talks with Mahler during our secret courtship, and how from one day to the next I no longer understood his language the moment our wedding day was set. It seems that at certain points men and women cannot understand one another. I've always been attuned to the same wavelength as Schnitzler. And yet at one point in our friendship it seemed that the man was stronger in him than the philosopher, poet, physician and friend. I remember our long daily walks through the beautiful Belvedere Park in Vienna. On one of those walks Schnitzler talked and talked and I had remained silent all the time. Finally, my silence astonished him. I told him, 'You could have spoken Chinese just as well. I did not understand!' "

Before anything else and above all, she was a woman. She recalled laughingly that Gerhart Hauptmann, who was very fond of her, once dropped all pretense and said to her: " 'At least in our afterlife we must become lovers.' Whereupon his wife, Grete, injected: 'Even then Alma will no longer be free!' Hauptmann and I looked at one

another smilingly. We both knew that at least for that fleeting
moment we were lovers."

Alma often lived in a world all by herself in which she thirsted for
her childhood dream. Life reduced to its simple humdrum existence
had never interested her. It was what she called, with disdain, a life
without fairy tales. In all the fairy tales she experienced, the prince
was a genius, endowed with powers beyond ordinary perception.
There were many princes and probably many more than we know of.
But there were also many fairy tales she could invent and live,
although the stories did not seem to be so different from one another
when one looks closer. But the princes were. Or was it only so in her
imagination?

She was always the same and never quite the same. Had she not
always been the center of attention wherever she went? When I
asked this question she blushed smilingly, as if a thousand and one
incidents of her life could be remembered in a moment: "I could not
help it. I suppose this is how everything happened. Also, perhaps I
have always been ambitious. When I was young I saw myself as one
of the first great women composers. But then I also began to realize
the tremendous impression I could make on men, what an important
role I could play in some of their lives, becoming literally the creator
of creators. Would you want me to recall the works in music,
literature, in painting and architecture which would never have been
done without my having been there? No, let's not think back. I have
had a wonderful life for which I sacrificed my becoming the first
great woman composer." She closed her blue-gray eyes for a
moment: "At any rate it's nice to think I might have been that great
artist I was not."

She certainly loved and needed to be loved. And yet, she said that
even then she was very much alone with herself, in a secret world of
her own, while listening to others or to the music she constantly
seemed to hear.

Later that day I thumbed through her autobiography. When I
came across one of her diary notes, I stopped. Perhaps at a moment
when she was angry with the world and herself she caught a glimpse
of her real self. Then, in a calculated mood of self-assertion and

unashamed pride of having been the woman she was, she boldly confessed in print:

What do you earth-bound morons know of the vast happiness I derive from my imagination, in the intoxication of love, of music, of wine—and of my strong religious feelings underneath? With iron claws I claw my way up to my nest. . . . Any genius is the right straw for me to clutch at, the right prey to feather my nest!

Gustav Mahler:
The Struggle of a Genius with Himself

How Destiny plays games with chance and circumstance will always remain one of her impenetrable secrets. She does so either in a most obvious and blunt manner or in a most intriguing and intricate one. Any step taken is destined to move us in a certain direction; it creates unexpected possibilities and complexities for us which, in retrospect, may appear as self-evident experiences in our lives.

Gustav Mahler left Hamburg more or less to escape a love affair with a singer who was everything but happy. He gladly accepted the position of a first conductor in Vienna with the prospect of becoming the *Direktor* of the then most important opera house in Europe. Moreover, a few of his best friends lived in Vienna, and he had also settled the rest of his family there a few years previously. Hence, there were sufficient reasons for him to accept the challenge.

Only a handful of people knew this small, thin and energetic man and the wonders he had worked at the opera houses in Budapest, Leipzig and Hamburg. When he was appointed *Direktor* of the Viennese Opera he was determined to create more wonders. He knew of the intrigues that lurk in all corners of such an institution as Europe's first opera house; he knew of all the difficulties that his power would bring about. But he was determined to create conditions in the theater that would make it possible for him to give all his thought to the artistic side of his work: the claque had to disappear since it only corrupted art and accomplishment; for the first time the house lights were dimmed to aid concentration; latecomers could no longer be seated until intermission. Even the Emperor's objection that opera should be pleasure was overruled; to Mahler, opera was more—dedication, a devotional rite—and he recognized no rule but his own. He was a man ready to fight for his convictions.

Once his authority and the quality of his work had been firmly established, Mahler's circle of friends widened considerably. By chance, Mahler had met Berta Zuckerkandl at the Austrian Embassy in Paris. She was the wife of one of the important physicians and anatomists of the day, Emil Zuckerkandl, who contributed a great deal to the fame of the medical school in Vienna at that time. Berta was a well-known society lady who not only loved music and the arts in general, but had also made a name for herself as a journalist. Mahler became one of the many artists who were often seen in the home of the Zuckerkandls. They also knew the painter Emil J. Schindler, an Austrian landscape painter of repute. He had once shared his studio with the flamboyant historical painter Hans Makart, a Renaissance figure with a flair for the Baroque, who happened to live in the Vienna of the Biedermeier period and gave the mid-nineteenth century his personal stamp. In many art and history books, there is a very specific image of the Makart period. In fact, Emil Schindler never got rid of the Makart gesture. He loved music and the beauty of life wherever he found it and managed to live in castles but always in debt. There was a grand style about everything he did. He could, for instance, say with an air of importance: "People who play in the locks of God . . ." He painted well. He was the Schubert of the Austrian landscape painters, and anyone interested in Vienna and its environment at that time has only to acquaint himself with Schindler's work. His greatest achievement, however, was his daughter Alma Maria, who inherited quite a few of her father's characteristic features. When Schindler died, her mother married another Viennese painter, Carl Moll, a man of great culture but minor talent.

Berta Zuckerkandl was also on friendly terms with Carl Moll and his stepdaughter Alma Maria. One day she invited the young woman to meet Mahler, since the Zukerkandls knew of Alma's interest in music. But Alma did not wish to accept the invitation and could only be persuaded to join the party when she heard that Max Burckhardt and Gustav Klimt would be there as well.

There is an account of Burckhardt and Klimt that needs to be told since their relationship to the seventeen-year-old Alma anticipated much that would become part of the pattern of her life. Burckhardt was *Direktor* of the Burgtheater, the court playhouse and pendant to the Opera. In other words, he was a colleague of Mahler, who detested him. But the disdain was mutual. It was fed and funneled by jealousy when Burckhardt noticed that Mahler had become interested in Alma and had succeeded in his advances.

For many months Burckhardt had felt drawn to young Alma who, in turn, admired him, but without responding to his amorous intentions. For her he was, and remained, a mentor who brought Nietzsche and Schopenhauer closer to her understanding. But from time to time he simply could not help making this beautiful girl feel that his interest in her was not just spiritual. Apparently he did not know that Alma was emotionally attached to the painter Gustav Klimt at the time. And yet Burckhardt played a more important role in her process of growing up than anyone else. His love of life was as intense as hers, and he strengthened in her the insatiable lust for experience. He would say: "Death does not exist, it is an invention of man." He loved nature as much as books. He was a minor poet, but he made his name in the theater and did for the legitimate theater of his time as much as Gustav Mahler did for the opera. Against the protests of the court clique he gave Ibsen and Hauptmann a chance to be heard. He never took no for an answer, and thus he could never quite accept that Alma loved to be with him without loving him as a man.

She had met Klimt before she met Burckhardt, when she was present at the secret meetings of a few painters in her stepfather's house. She was then hardly seventeen years old and had a unique touch of innocence and awakening; she was just as excited as she was exciting. The chief conspirator, Gustav Klimt, who rebelled against the stifling atmosphere of the old *Künstlerhaus* and founded the Viennese *Sezession* at these meetings, fell in love with Alma. World-famous by then, he passed through her life at a most vulnerable moment, as the entries in her diary reveal. "His looks," she wrote later, "and my young charm, his genius and my talents, our common, deeply vital musicality found us attuned to one another. My ignorance in matters of love was appalling, and he sensed it intuitively and found me wherever I went."

Klimt was twenty years older and much experienced in playing with emotions. He was not his own free agent, being married and having children and sisters to support. When Alma went to Italy with her family in 1897, Klimt followed her. In Genoa her mother got hold of Alma's diary and, learning about her first gropings amidst the confusion of her feelings, killed the hesitant beginnings of love. Very few mothers can bear the vision of their young daughters being kissed. Klimt was told not to talk to her anymore. Only in the bustling crowd on the Piazza San Marco in Venice, hidden from Moll and his wife by the gaily milling multitude, could Klimt reach and keep Alma long enough by his side for his hasty whispers of love, to implore her to wait for him, to assure her he would divorce himself from his past. Surrounded by Renaissance ambience, what young girl would not accept such a moment as a secret betrothal, a sweet and sweeping folly within a perfect Romeo-and-Juliet setting? Some of this experience later found its way into Klimt's most famous painting, *The Kiss*.

Faced with the conflict between her feelings and her mother's authority, Alma felt crushed, her feelings crucified. "For months I was close to suicide. As an embittered human being I began my life as a woman." Although she resented her parents' feeling that they had the right to play Destiny, she bowed to the morals of her environment. ("I believed in a virginal purity in need of preservation. It was not only a trait of the period, it was a trait of mine"). Klimt often tried to get in touch with her; he wanted her to come to his studio. Several years later when they met again he would say: "The spell you have cast upon me never vanishes, it only grows stronger and stronger"; or even much later: "We have looked for one another an entire life and never have really found the way."

For a few years Alma lived as if she were bound by their clandestine betrothal. She thought in those years that he was her ideal, that he functioned as the matinee idol of her awakening feelings. For his part, he may have needed her to move artistically in a different direction from the one he actually took, one marked by a Byzantine delicacy and the playfulness of the art nouveau (or *Jugendstil*) with his artistic vision lost to gold mosaics and decorative ornaments. Indeed, later Alma felt that she had missed the opportunity to make a greater artist of Klimt than the one he became. Although her good upbringing may have crushed Alma's first experience of love, in fact, it only saved her from inevitable disillusionment and kept her free for a destiny with greater demands on her and seemingly greater fulfillment.

She never forgot Klimt. When he died on February 6, 1918, she wrote: "A great piece of my youth vanished with him from my life. How I understood him! And I have never stopped loving him—even though in a different way. He was an extremely fine colorist. His large paintings for the University in Vienna were rejected. They were then too modern, off the beaten path, briefly: too important!"

Some people can turn chance into destiny. In her suffering she discovered that there was music in her. She began to compose and never seemed to stop composing. She took her talent seriously and so did her teacher, Alexander von Zemlinsky, a then famous musician, composer and teacher. He was as ugly as Klimt was handsome, but it was at that time that Alma began to realize that it was the indefinable something, the genius in man, that most attracted her. Many decades later she described Zemlinsky as "a horrifying gnome. Short, toothless and without chin, unwashed and always having that coffeehouse smell . . ." But one day after he had played *Tristan* for her, her knees began to tremble, and she fell into his arms. Only her foolishness, as she described it, her insistence on preserving her virginal purity, kept her from becoming his at that very moment.

When she told her mother that she wanted to marry Zemlinsky, her mother was not angry, nor did she keep Alma from seeing and working with Zemlinsky. She only laughed at the idea. Alma found great satisfaction in her compositions and in working with her teacher. In his house she met other students of his who, later, were to make music history. One of them was Arnold Schönberg, who was Zemlinsky's favorite student. Zemlinsky was convinced that one day Schönberg would astonish the world with his radical ideas. Schönberg's own students, Alban Berg and Anton von Webern, went further than their master. Berg became one of Alma's close friends; he dedicated the score of his opera *Wozzeck* to her. Schönberg once complained how much he suffered from the dangerous influence of Webern and that he needed much strength to withstand it. As Alma recalled, Schönberg was sometimes unbearable, but even then whatever he did had the stamp of genius. He once addressed a professor of music at a meeting of teachers: "Does anyone exist who could know less than you do?" Or: "If no longer anything occurs to a composer, he promptly falls back on the folksong." (Mahler never felt at ease with Schönberg, the man or composer. Once Mahler said: "Even if I often do not understand him: I am old and he is young, therefore he is right.")

Alma was quite certain she wanted to be a composer when she met Gustav Mahler. He could not resist courting her. Music brought them together, but it was the re-creating of music that complicated their lives. Alma met Mahler at Berta Zuckerkandl's house. He urged her to see him at the Opera the following day. She said she didn't know whether she would have time. But she found it and went. He visited her parents a few days later and that same day he asked her to come with him for a walk. When he said that it was not simple to marry a man like him who had to be free for his work and who also could not guarantee a secure income, it seemed to her as if everything was a foregone conclusion. Everything seemed to flow with the relentless rhythm of a river: she had allowed herself to be kissed without really wanting to, and agreed on a wedding date without knowing what had happened to her—except that she knew "she no longer wished to live without him." And when Mahler said, "To give rings to one another is a vulgar gesture," she agreed that such a custom struck her as idiotic, although she had not thought of it before nor really thought he was right.

During the short time of their betrothal, Mahler was in Berlin and Dresden to fulfill assignments as guest conductor while Alma continued her studies with Zemlinsky. Once, with the excuse that she had to work on her compositions, she wrote Mahler a somewhat shorter letter than he expected. This brought about a decisive change in her life. Mahler replied that she would have to give up any attempt at composing; she had to live for nobody else's music but his. He simply would not tolerate a ridiculous marriage like the one between Robert and Klara Schumann.

Without ever having heard any of her compositions, he had made up his mind. He was not only egotistical to want someone by his side who would serve his genius and copy his music; he was also a perfectionist and feared he would have to live under the same roof with a blown-up nobody or, at best, a conceited mediocrity. In his eyes nothing was more arrogant and unbearable than the little talent.

What Alma had achieved by then was nothing that promised a great creative future, but it was also nothing she had to be ashamed of. At the time she met Mahler she had composed nine lieder to poems by Heine, Rilke, Dehmel and others. Some time later her lieder were published; the critical consensus was that they revealed great musical understanding and technical skill. It was only human— and perhaps all-too-human—that she believed in herself and, at the same time, may have had doubts about the scope of her abilities. Thus when she had to face this unexpected demand of her husband-to-be, she felt there was no other choice but to leave him or to give up composing forever. "I buried my dream then," she wrote. "Perhaps it has been for the better." And looking back on her life she could say: "Whatever my productive gifts were, I could relive them in other more important minds. Nevertheless, somewhere burnt a wound in me whose scars never quite disappeared."

Her marriage with Mahler was difficult from the very beginning, and Alma's ambivalence made her feelings soar to the heights of great happiness one minute and throw her into pits of unbearable disgust the next. Mahler's jealousy cost her most of her old friends. She had to learn to live someone else's life, to share someone else's interests while giving up the demands and aspirations of her own personality. Naturally, the strong, self-willed Alma suffered from such a sacrifice. At the beginning of their marriage they had particularly painful clashes that had to be resolved through serious and painful discussions; the discussions usually ended with her giving in to the needs of his genius. She noticed how immediately the tone of lover changed to that of mentor after their marriage. Twenty years old, she often accepted the word of her forty-year-old husband as the advice of the more mature partner. But this in no way altered the smoldering resentment that the most obedient child subconsciously harbors against his parent. The seesaw of her emotions may best be pictured through a few of her experiences with the composer.

Immediately after their wedding Gustav Mahler had to journey to St. Petersburg where he was engaged to conduct three concerts. Two experiences during that first trip stayed with Alma throughout her married life. One was the early realization that Gustav was a sick man, destined to suffer physically and mentally, but also that his vision of himself as a creative giant had instilled in him tremendous willpower to overcome his many handicaps. All his life he suffered from torturous migraines. On this particular occasion it was caused by the bad air in an overheated compartment of the Russian train. In raging madness he ran up and down the corridor of the train; at each station he jumped from the car and ran back and forth on the platform without a hat or overcoat—in freezing temperatures—to fight the headache. He arrived in St. Petersburg with laryngitis, coughing and chilblains, but he conducted as if nothing were wrong. Standing behind the orchestra, Alma saw his face from the front for the first time while conducting. "I saw his face which—while he conducted—assumed a divinely beautiful expression." Reminiscing about this experience, she said: "This face was so incomparable that I felt in a frightening way and knew as if forever and with certainty it would be my mission to keep all evils away from him and to live only for him."

No doubt, in the early years of their marriage she was very much in love with him, or perhaps with his accomplishments, because what she always adored in men was their achievements. This is the aspect from which we must see the ecstatic entries in her diary at that time: "I have a wise guide and . . . I am filled to the brim with my mission of smoothing the path of this genius!"

At the age of twenty-two, Alma was not ready to have children. After the birth of her first child she realized that she had not yet the right love for her child. She could still proudly confess: "Everything in me belongs to Gustav." And Gustav? Having married a beautiful young girl, he was utterly confused in his feelings. He treated her with dictatorial strictness, more often than not like a student of his. Alma could never free herself from the impression that, even as a passionate lover, he was basically afraid of youth and beauty. He often made strange remarks to the effect that he could only really show how much he loved her if she were somehow disfigured and ugly. This young girl hardly understood the deep and very involved feelings of this older man, strong to the point of overbearance on one level, weak and anxiety-ridden on the other.

Totally engrossed in his own work, he ignored and, as we have seen, suppressed any of her artistic aspirations. It took her a long time and great effort before she forced herself to resume playing the piano again. "My knowledge of music," she wrote in her diary, "suits him only as long as I use it for him." Whenever she complained that he slighted her abilities—and with the years those complaints were uttered less and less frequently—he used to say, as we read in her notes: "Is it my fault that your budding dreams have not material- ized?" Her reaction was one of suppressed outrage and helpless fury. But realizing that she had tied her life to a powerful genius, she was torn between wanting to serve him and to be recognized as a human being and artist in her own right. During their first five years of marriage she often felt stripped of everything and cried out in her diary: "He lives his own life—and I must live it, too!"

From time to time she became frighteningly aware of her life's emptiness. After she had had her second child she threw herself into the study of Greek and translated Plato, only to keep herself occupied. Another exclamation in her daily notes reflected her feelings at that time: "If he were only young—young at heart!" She had a nagging feeling that perhaps Gustav Mahler had never been more than an object of adoration, a hero and father substitute. She may have been right: was not Gustav Klimt, her first great love, like Gustav Mahler, her first husband, twenty years her senior?

In her privacy, giving vent to her grudges, she admitted that they often had bitter squabbles during which he felt that she might no longer love him. At times, she was not very wrong: "The latest scene has frozen everything in me. I realize that the man who had to spread his peacock train in public wants to relax at home. That, after all, is woman's fate. But it isn't mine!"

When she wrote these lines she was still very young and not yet quite aware that her rebellious feelings were harbingers of a different life. She was not made for the role in which Gustav Mahler saw her: nursing the children he loved; copying the manuscripts of the brain children he loved with even more passion than his own children; waiting for the tired conductor and *Direktor* to come home from the Opera to find his meals prepared, his peace to rest, his quiet to work, his wife with whom he might discuss music and the arts at any time it pleased him. "This was all he needed," she wrote in anger and disgust, "all he wanted. It never occurred to him that I might have expected something else of life."

Alma always wanted to be of use but without being used. One of her great goals in life was to inspire. But it always had to be of her own choosing and of her own will. Dreading the ordinary and commonplace in life, she always hoped for the unexpected, the miracle waiting for her. Reflecting on the year 1917, when she was at a crossroads and feeling very sick, she wrote:

I felt no regrets at the prospect of leaving this world that had given me so much true, genuine life. For what would come now? At best, an hourly repetition of all that had gone before. Should I become a housewife with all the tricks and quirks of one—I, who dreaded possessions because they possess us?

It was nothing but a variation on a theme she deeply felt. It had come to mean a great deal in her life, and she found it best expressed when a few years later she came across the opening phrases of Franz Werfel's poem:

> Nothing is mine to own;
> I possess alone
> This awareness. . . .

Alma gave birth to four children in all, and there can be no doubt that she loved them all. Yet she never was the prototype of a mother. If Otto Weininger, a famous Viennese philosopher, was right in his assumption that a woman is basically either a mother or a hetaera, then Alma Mahler belonged to the latter category. She was convinced that she could not occupy herself exclusively with her children, and often said so. She always had the help of a governess.

In the early years of her marriage she often felt "used" without being gratified. She then looked into herself with brutal frankness; once in a while she concluded that her children and a suddenly awakening sense of duty could play tricks with her feelings, as this diary note confirms:

My children are sick. . . . Sad as it is, it's giving me my strength back. I have not been so cheerful in a long time. I suddenly know again why I'm here: my children need me. Mahler needs me, too. But I can't give him all of my love. Why can't I?

As so often happens in marriage, the two children Alma had with Mahler seemed to improve their relationship, at least at certain times. Alma felt the great effect the little girls had on their lives, with Mahler being strongly attached to each child in an intimate and highly individual relationship. His love for his children made him appear in her eyes more human and certainly more communicative.

The children absorbed his emotions and, although she had reason enough to feel happy as a mother, her need for attention as a woman was rarely satisfied. Some of her diary notes not only reflect the romantic feelings of a young girl, but their style betrays the flamboyant echo of a period marked by the flowery *Jugendstil:*

I often feel as though my wings had been clipped. Gustav, why did you tie me to yourself—me, a soaring, glittering bird—when you'd be so much better off with a gray, lumbering one?

But then, when she had doubts about her own abilities (which she was not allowed to put to the test) and when she came to realize Mahler's inner strength, she could jot down such lines as: "I feel so often how little I am and have in comparison with his immeasurable riches." It was particularly difficult for her to understand and accept how a man could be possessed by his mission in life, while she remained unfulfilled as a woman, both in her desire to do something with herself and to know how far that desire could carry her.

When she was in labor with her second daughter, Anna, Mahler was with her trying to help her forget the pain, which lasted for many hours. He held her hands and sought means of alleviating her ordeal. In his own despair he hit upon the odd idea of reading aloud to her passages from Kant's work. She did not understand a single word, and having to listen to his monotonous voice only drove her crazy. It never occurred to her, not even much later when she reminisced about this incident, that Mahler chose to read to her from Kant mainly to calm his own excitement.

When Anna was a year old, Mahler finished his *Kindertotenlieder (Children's Death Songs)*, based on poems by Friedrich Rückert. This German romantic lyricist could not help writing these sad verses after having buried his children who were victims of an epidemic. But how, Alma asked herself, could Mahler sing about the death of children when, a few minutes earlier, he had hugged and kissed his two girls before they ran down the stairs to play in the garden? How could he throw himself into such tragic feeling in his study when Maria and Anna were the incarnation of living joy?

Mahler had started to compose these songs a year before Maria, his first child, was born. Carrying the thought of death with him all the time, he was deeply impressed when he came across the poems and put three of them to music. When Maria came, he stopped working on them. Was he now asking for punishment, as Alma felt, when, three years later, he finished them?

The summer of 1905 was one of their most beautiful and rewarding ones. Mahler had completed his *Sixth Symphony*. He was happy. Their marriage was free of conflict. Alma and he walked arm in arm to the little chalet where he worked, and he played the symphony for her alone. "I have tried to capture you in the theme of the first movement," he told her.

He often talked to her about what he intended to compose. But he only played for her or anyone else what he considered completed. The perfectionist and puritan in him considered it unchaste to show an unfinished work. His *Sixth Symphony* reflected his life—for instance, in the first movement, his inner joy. But in the third movement he caught a great deal of his little children playing in an arhythmic way, blissfully running through sand, until their voices had something tragic about them; finally, a thin voice faded away. With the final movement Mahler described himself and his end. "The hero who had to bear three fateful blows, with the third felling him like a tree." Alma could never forget these words.

Why was she then horrified that he completed the *Kindertoten-lieder*? We still know little of the strange voices and visions that plague a genius and compel him to materialize in artistic form what he himself may often create in a state of seeming unawareness. Was it so eerie, as Alma thought, to write about the death of children? The fear of death had already forced him to picture the dying voice of one of his children in his *Sixth Symphony*. Such foreboding may be the price a man pays for being blessed, or cursed, with sensitivity to things beyond all conception of the palpable, the ordinary, the real.

Two years later Maria died at the age of five. The year was 1907, a grave one in Gustav Mahler's life.

Most summers the family stayed at Lake Wörther where Gustav worked on his symphonies. But Maiernigg, a small place at this lake, was far away from a skilled physician or hospital. Maria contracted diphtheritic scarlet fever. For two weeks she struggled to stay alive. Finally, the danger of suffocation made a laryngotomy necessary. A primitive operating table was improvised for the village doctor. While Mahler hid in his room, Alma ran screaming along the lake shore. A day after the operation the child was dead.

Two days later Alma suffered a fainting spell. A temporary cardiac weakness, the doctor said, probably caused by all the excitement. On this occasion Mahler also had his heart examined, both as a matter of routine and to cheer Alma up; she had suspected for a long time that living on excess energy for years might have affected his heart. And it had. The doctor's verdict came as a severe blow to Mahler, who rushed to Vienna only to have a specialist confirm the village doctor's diagnosis.

They left Maiernigg with all its bad memories to spend the rest of the summer at Toblach in the Tyrol. Neither of them mentioned the dead child. Neither of them spoke about Mahler's heart condition. He went for long and lonely walks in the mountains. He began to sketch music to a few sad Chinese poems that culminated in a breathtaking Farewell. These lieder for orchestra had all the makings of a symphony and later turned into *Das Lied von der Erde* (The Song of the Earth). His working title was more appropriate for what he felt: "The Song of Sorrow on Earth."

In those days of silent agony, Alma and Gustav discussed their future, since Mahler's resignation from his directorship at the Vienna Opera had preceded these sad events. He once said: "Others care for themselves and wear out the theater; I wear myself out and care for the theater." Every morning he was the first at his desk, and in the evening the last to leave the opera house. He tolerated no weaknesses and, loathing mediocrity, was a hard taskmaster. His dictatorial powers were only used to serve the arts. He was responsible for his actions to no one but the Emperor and his representative, Prince Montenuovo, and both respected Mahler's integrity. Alma recalled what must have been one of many similar incidents: A young singer auditioned for Mahler and presented a letter of recommendation from Archduke Franz Ferdinand. Mahler tore up the unopened letter in front of the singer and said: "Now, please, sing." Strangely enough, such effronteries in no way weakened his position.

He stumbled, however, over a minor incident. When he returned from his wedding trip to St. Petersburg in 1902, he met the painter Alfred Roller in Alma's stepfather's house. Roller impressed Mahler with his revolutionary ideas of how to stage a Wagner opera. They spoke about *Tristan and Isolde* in particular, and Mahler hired him.

Although Roller followed his own imaginative ideas, which liberated the static images of the traditional staging of operas, Adolphe Appia's spirit was noticeable in his designs; they eschewed illusion painting and achieved unexpected space concepts through simplification and architectural perspectives.

In the beginning of his engagement with the Opera, of course, Roller, the painter, felt ill at ease on the stage, and became the victim of little intrigues by the stage crew opposed to this intruder and innovator. But Mahler always stood by his side. Roller finally became production superintendent at the Opera, and Mahler's success in rejuvenating the spirit of this theater was partly due to Roller's contributions. Together they staged almost all the classic operas and some new works. It became automatic for Mahler to support Roller in whatever he undertook.

But in the spring of 1907 hubris overwhelmed Roller. He fancied that he would like to stage a ballet of his own creation, something he had never done before. With Mahler's permission he went over the head of Josef Hassreiter, who was then the ballet master at the Opera. Both scheduled a rehearsal for the same hour! Hassreiter, after facing an empty studio, complained bitterly about being slighted by Mahler, who was subsequently summoned to Prince Montenuovo. He was more than indignant about Mahler's attempt to cover up such misconduct. Mahler had no choice but to submit his resignation. It was accepted.

At that time, of course, Mahler could not know that it was the best thing that could have happened to him, for after the break with the Opera he still had time to finish *Das Lied von der Erde* and to create such monumental symphonies as his *Seventh*, *Eighth*, *Ninth*, and to begin his *Tenth*, which he had to leave behind unfinished.

Judging from his farewell letter to the members of the Opera, he realized that, although many of his hopes had been fulfilled, he had not succeeded completely in turning a repertory theater into a year-round festival. He also noticed that, with the years and some triumphs, his enemies grew in proportion to the obstacles he had to overcome. Disgust and fatigue set in—disgust at the discrepancy between ideal and reality, fatigue at continuing an apparently vain struggle. When saying good-bye, he addressed the members of the Opera with the words: "Instead of a whole, finished in itself, as I have dreamt of, I leave behind only patchwork—incomplete, as is man's destiny." On October 15, 1907, he once more conducted *Fidelio* and, for the last time, stood in front of the orchestra and stage to which he had given so much of his love and which gave him as much doubt as satisfaction. The goal of his vision was set so far that no cooperative effort could ever reach it.

What followed was anticlimactic with respect to his theatrical career. He accepted an invitation to conduct in the United States and, in his last two years, to conduct his own orchestra. He appeared in America with great success for four seasons, between 1907 and 1910. The Metropolitan paid him extremely well, and he had the greatest singers at his disposal—Caruso, Chaliapin, Farrar, and whomever else he wanted. But he was no longer the same. The frightening prognosis of his physical condition seemed to have broken his spirit. When he conducted at the Metropolitan, he accepted the usual cuts, the latecomers, everything he had fought against for so long. He no longer seemed to care. The awareness of being marked for an early death changed his attitude toward everything else. He became less intransigent in his demands on life.

As a child Mahler had replied to the question of what later in life he would like to be: "a martyr." As a man he found it difficult to come to terms with himself and to achieve inner peace. He always remained a haunted man, struggling within to silence the voices of his fears and those annoying voices of an outside world to which he was little attuned. His moments of happiness were rare and came between long stretches of self-consuming work and despair. Ecstatic happiness occurred when he felt gratified by what he composed; he also found a lightness of feeling with his family. But his inability to be diplomatic and tolerant or to say a dishonest word made life with him often difficult. At a gathering of people, he loathed small talk. If annoyed by the slightest remark or irritated by the presence of a person he disliked, he would leave early or abruptly get up from the

table to withdraw into the corner of another room where he would
be found reading. He could, however, be just as intense in showing
his preferences.

Alma observed that Mahler grew very fond of Gerhart Hauptmann, although Hauptmann's slowness in thinking and speaking
often made Mahler impatient. Hauptmann also felt very close to
Mahler and once told Alma: "Your husband voices so lucidly
everything I sense in a chaotic way. I have not profited from anyone
as much as from him." Alma recalled two characteristic scenes. After
a long and spirited dinner party at Burckhardt's house, the Mahlers
and Hauptmanns left to walk home together. It was shortly after
midnight when they set out to cross the streets of nighttime Vienna.
Hauptmann and Mahler were so intense in their discussions that they
frequently stopped at lampposts, holding each other by the lapel
while vehemently gesticulating with the other hand. Thus they would
stand and talk for ten or fifteen minutes, oblivious of their impatient
wives waiting for them to resume their walk home. At four o'clock in
the morning they were near exhaustion, and Alma insisted on being
taken home in a fiacre.

On another occasion the composer Hans Pfitzner was present.
Mahler was not too fond of him, being jealous of the man and
thinking little of the composer. The conversation turned to Wagner.
Pfitzner thought that the truest and deepest aspects of Wagner could
be found in Wagner's Teutonic stance. Mahler adored Wagner's
music so much that he could easily overlook the man's overly stressed
Germanic and anti-Semitic gestures. Mahler did not mind in the least
contradicting himself and being found on both sides of the fence;
even then he could argue his case with convincing vigor. The
conversation became unpleasant and heated. Pfitzner clumsily defended Wagner as an ideal German while slighting his greatness as a
composer, whereas both Hauptmann and Mahler would hail Richard
Wagner as a great composer despite his errors. When Mahler,
meaning Pfitzner rather than Wagner, maintained that the greatest
artists stand above and reach beyond all nationalistic boundaries,
Pfitzner got up and left.

The most contradictory notes follow one another in Alma's diaries and autobiography. Her father-fixation and hero-worship made her swear how much she belonged to Mahler and how much she lived in and through him alone. But in the same breath she could rail against his tyrannical nature. She was most seriously opposed to her own feelings for Mahler when she admitted to having been unfaithful to him in her musical appreciation of his compositions. Triumphantly she added: ". . . and he knows it." She realized of course that she could hurt him most by showing him how little she liked his music. (Only much later did she come to understand and love his work, particularly after his death, when the hurt over his suppression of her own talent was more or less gone.)

. She was also fully aware of how much it must have hurt his pride when she let Hans Pfitzner court her. Pfitzner, who was such a mediocrity in Mahler's eyes and ears! But Alma needed the attention of other men. "Of course, I am flattered that this man loves me so obviously, and I do not fight the sensuous excitement caused by his touch, an excitement I have not felt for so long." This is the admission of a girl in her twenties, that she could no longer find her husband's embrace meaningful. She liked Pfitzner; she could act more playfully with him than with the always serious-minded Mahler. Also, Pfitzner's music was closer to her own than Mahler's and, to top all her feelings, Pfitzner would play the piano and sing with her the lieder she had once composed. Thus, they often spent happy hours together while Mahler conducted at the Ópera. (Much later, after Mahler's death, Pfitzner revealed strange features to Alma's way of thinking, an egocentricity worse than Mahler's and a ridiculously dilettantish approach to lovemaking.)

Alma had always been very attractive. Men were constantly around her, reminding the wife of Gustav Mahler that she was neither romantically nor physically fulfilled. In the fateful year of 1907 Mahler brought to their home the young and gifted pianist Ossip Gabrilowitsch. He was about Alma's age and as lonesome and full of undefined longing as she was. A tender romance developed, with a single kiss that frightened them both. They loved Mahler, didn't they? They could not betray him. The young man fought valiantly within himself. Later, in New York, they met again and said a final adieu after he had played for her Brahms's little Intermezzo in A major of which she was very fond. They both agreed he had never played it so beautifully. Then he left, victorious over his deepest desires.

They thought Mahler had been asleep. But he had eavesdropped on this scene, and a serious debate ensued between him and his wife. She could easily defend herself since nothing had really happened between her and the young pianist. He believed her, but, for the first time, seemed desperate. Alma could write about this period in her life: "This strange marriage with Gustav Mahler, with this abstract being, had preserved my mental virginity throughout these first ten years of my conscious life. I loved Mahler's spirit; his body was like a shadow."

It was about a year before his death that Alma felt so worn out that she left her husband well cared for and working on his *Tenth Symphony* in Toblach while she went to a sanatorium in a Styrian spa. Her physical state of exhaustion was a part of her general depression, and the clever doctor prescribed an unorthodox treatment for her despondent condition: dancing. And to ensure a successful cure he introduced her to a few young men. One of them, with whom she danced most often, was obviously intrigued by her, and she did not dislike him. They talked a great deal together. He was a young architect and had studied with one of her father's friends. His name, then unknown, was Walter Gropius. Alma could not help noticing that he fell passionately in love with her. He saw to it that she noticed.

A few days after she had left the spa to join her husband in Toblach again, a letter arrived for *Herr Direktor* Mahler. Purposely addressed to him, it was actually a love letter to Alma from Walter Gropius. Was he intent on creating a scandal and thus winning Alma by force? Apparently. What followed was the most serious crisis in the marriage. Alma's reassurances that she would never leave Mahler calmed him but did not remove his grave doubts that perhaps he was at fault, that something was very wrong with him and his relationship with Alma. He decided to go to Holland to talk to Sigmund Freud.

Mahler's decision to seek sound counsel was preceded by a burlesque scene, according to Alma's autobiography. While in the village of Toblach she discovered Gropius hiding under a bridge. She rushed home to tell her husband about it. Mahler insisted on looking for the young man, and in the darkness, carrying a lantern, he walked back home followed by Gropius. Mahler forced a showdown. Alma had to have a talk with Gropius while Mahler waited in his room for the outcome. "In a sudden fear for Mahler," Alma broke off her talk with the daring young man and rushed into Mahler's room. There she "found him pacing the floor with a book in his hand. Two candles burned on his desk. He was reading in Holy Scripture."

However accurate her description may be, this scene has something sinister and ludicrous about it, on the one hand, and, on the other, something very credible and in keeping with Mahler's fanatic reactions. The image she pictured was like a throwback into Mahler's past: the desperate Jew, with the prayerbook in his hands, in front of an imaginary Wailing Wall. Even the words he spoke when Alma entered sounded like a prayer, "O Lord, whatever you do is well done!" turning into: "Whatever you do, Alma, will be well done. Choose!"

She put Gropius on a train, and he proceeded to send her a telegram from each station and to telephone declarations of love in cascades. Even though her eyes were opened "by the tempestuous wooing of the young man," her mind was made up: she had to stay at Mahler's side, help fulfill his destiny; there was no other choice left to her. (Of course, she could not know that Mahler had little more than a year to live.) Nevertheless, she tells us: "All of a sudden I knew that my marriage was no marriage, that my own life was utterly unfulfilled. Yet I denied this truth to Mahler, although he knew it as well as I."

In those fateful days Alma must have remembered what a deep impression Goethe's words "The Eternal Feminine leads us on!" had on Mahler. It stuck in his mind, and he often debated its possible meanings with Hauptmann and Pfitzner. There was something that frightened him about this sentence. Alma suspected that he feared Woman per se, that he was afraid of being "led on." This, in her eyes, was decisive: in being afraid he shunned the experience of Woman; but to her, experience with the opposite sex was identical with living life.

Realizing that he was at an impasse in his marriage, Mahler sought out Sigmund Freud, who at that time happened to be in Holland. We have learned from several sources, mainly from Ernest Jones's biography of Freud, that the two men spent an afternoon together at Leyden, mostly strolling through the town and talking. It was a long and certainly an unorthodox psychoanalytic session. At that time Freud had finished *Leonardo*, his study of da Vinci, in which he investigated the importance of childhood experiences for later artistic accomplishments. It was Freud's genius to recognize immediately that a great part of this marital crisis had to do with the psychology of Mahler's creativity.

There are no exact records of their probing of Mahler's mind and psyche. I deliberately say "their" because we know from Freud's own remarks that Mahler contributed a great deal of self-interpretation to their analytic discussion. Although Mahler rejected belief in such conceptions as his mother-fixation, it played a major role in his life. His unconscious identification with his mother was at the root of some hidden resentment of his wife. His mother's name was Marie, and in the beginning he insisted on calling Alma by that name, although her middle name was Maria. He was often seen limping. His mother had a birth defect: she limped. Mahler's remembrance of his mother's face was one of suffering. And he once expressed his regret that the features of Alma's radiantly beautiful face showed no trace of suffering. Freud also related Mahler's leanings toward Catholicism, toward martyrdom, to his "Marie" complex.

Freud blended the warmth of a friend's voice with that of a scientist's reasoning during this therapeutic shortcut reduced to an afternoon. The dark images of Mahler's home life; his father's outbreaks of wrath and acts of brutality, and time and again his mother's face marked by suffering; the traumatic impression of witnessing a sexual assault in the house of a friend; the need early in his life to take care of his many siblings; even in the years of accomplishment Mahler remained a man divided: there was the conductor and interpreter responsible for everything that went on in the theater, and then there was the creator, deeply resenting that he could only compose during the summer months.

Mahler returned from his trip to Freud seemingly a changed man. But his sudden self-realizations precipitated another scene, reflecting the tragic irony of life in which a marriage began, continued and ended with a thousand and one errors and fallacies, with a thousand and one moments of hope, belief and self-deception. When, shortly after his return, Alma came home from a walk with her daughter, she could hardly believe her ears. She heard her songs played on the piano and a familiar voice singing them: her forgotten lieder, the music for which she still mourned secretly, supposedly buried forever. She intended to walk in and tell Mahler that it was too late. But when she saw him full of joy she said nothing and listened to his ecstatic exclamations: "What have I done! These songs are good. You have got to go on working. They must immediately be published!" He went on playing them and was happy that he could atone for having killed her aspirations ten years before. Time can heal wounds, as the saying goes, and make us forget. But Alma's wounds had left visible scars, and she certainly had not forgotten. Now she only wondered at the change that had come over him; and she kept her thoughts to herself.

The last years of their marriage brought changes. Mahler became more and more aware of how much Alma meant to him. Berta Zuckerkandl, one of their closest friends, reveals some of it:

Taking leave [before his first journey to America] Mahler said today: "I take my home with me. My Alma, my child. And only now that I am relieved of my heavy burden of work do I know what will be my nicest task from now on. Alma sacrificed ten years of her youth. Nobody knows and can ever know with what absolute selflessness she subordinated her life to me and my work. Now I can go on my way with an easy mind."

Toward the end of their first American stay Alma and Gustav had befriended a well-known physician in New York, Dr. Joseph Fraenkel. At once they were both under his spell. He was a witty, somewhat bizarre bachelor. He admired Mahler, who adored him in return. Fraenkel became Mahler's physician in America. Mahler believed in whatever Fraenkel prescribed and said. And since Mahler was a very sick man during the last few years of his life, Fraenkel's influence was very important.

The three were very close. Alma tells us of a New Year's Eve that they spent together. They sat in their hotel room overlooking Central Park and the hazy splendor of the lighted city. When midnight arrived, the sirens rang from factories and ships, the church bells tolled. The three clasped each other's hands without saying a word and wept. They wept without knowing why. Or did they know? Perhaps all three of them were afraid; perhaps fear had a different face for each of them.

On their last American journey in 1910, when Mahler was stricken with a streptococcal infection and fell fatally ill, Fraenkel did not leave his bedside. He insisted that they immediately return to Vienna. Fraenkel repeated all his instructions once more on board ship, he named the doctors they ought to see in Paris and then those in Vienna. When he took leave of Mahler he knew he would never see him again.

It was a long and painful struggle for Mahler, and immediately after he died Alma felt a terrifying emptiness. She knew she had experienced a unique relationship and that something great had gone out of her life. During the first weeks after his death she found a great deal of time to think about those past ten years, years of becoming, years in which she gradually grasped the intricacy of feelings whose contours were often blurred. How much had she gained while being with Mahler? How would his loss affect her future? Many questions went through her mind that remained unanswered. But never before had she felt this sudden aloneness, a void that she knew how to fill only with music. It was Mahler's will that she should not mourn but see people, hear concerts, go to the theater. It was inevitable that she was soon surrounded by fascinating men who courted her.

It came to Alma as a surprise that Dr. Fraenkel should be the first serious contender for her favors. During the many years of their friendship, years in which she was utterly devoted to Mahler, she had never thought of him in any other way than as her friend. Fraenkel's life had begun much as Mahler's had. He was a Viennese Jew and about to become an army surgeon when he realized that his career as a medical man in the old Austro-Hungarian monarchy depended on his being baptized. At this point he made a different decision than Mahler, who early in his career took holy water and always thought of being closer to Christ than to Jehovah. When Fraenkel was about to enter the church door, he suddenly turned around and left for America, where he arrived as a poor immigrant. There he made the American legend come true. From a newsboy and dishwasher he rose to the rank of one of the most prominent physicians and was appointed head of the Montefiore Hospital in New York.

Twice, Fraenkel made the trip to Europe to ask Alma to marry him. Twice she refused. In this period, when she became aware of her strength as a woman, she delighted in collecting souls that had a touch of greatness. She was not ready for some time to deprive herself of her chance to make up for the ten years of longing for what she imagined as the excitement of living. She knew she would thoroughly enjoy herself and felt confident that her partners would enjoy her company. She was, however, much too serious to become a light-hearted flirt; she knew how inescapable her charm was. She was prepared to be responsible when she could sense the importance of a relationship, and particularly when the titillation came from knowing that one of the Muses had brushed the man of her choice. Even though music was closest to her heart, she felt no prejudice for or against any of the other arts. And it did not necessarily have to be any Muse at all. The heightened pulse beat of life or the poetic realization of existence were the requirements she wanted to find. In other words, she was looking for a divine spark because, as far as she was concerned, there was no humanity without divinity. She did not expect her partner to know the secret of existence, but, in awe of all life, he should hold in his hand a key that might open a door leading to the magic of Being.

Dr. Fraenkel asked her to marry him at the worst moment—the

moment when she was about to find her inner independence. She no longer needed another father substitute, another dominating brain without earthy strength. I quote her farewell letter to Fraenkel because it is a manifesto of love and existence with and for Alma:

The fate that parts us is the divergence of our own souls. Every fibre of my heart draws me back into true life, while you are striving for consummate de-materialization.

What is salvation to me is unthinkable to you, with your cerebral makeup; what is salvation to you strikes me as madness. That's how different we are!

My watchword is: *Amo—ergo sum.*

Yours: *Cogito—ergo sum.*

When it comes to living you're a miserable failure. At best, men like you are put between book covers, closed, pressed, and devoured in unrecognizable form by future generations. But such men never *live.*

Today I know the eternal source of all strength. It is in nature, in the earth, in people who don't hesitate to cast away their existence for the sake of an idea. They are the ones who can *love.*

I go on living with my face lifted high, but with my feet on the ground—where they belong.

Amo—Ergo Sum

Alma gained ten years of inner growth while married to Gustav Mahler. When he had met the twenty-year-old girl, she was not yet sure of herself. She was very diffident toward strangers, often reacting in a clumsy way with the worst answers or an embarrassed laugh. There was still something childlike in her.

She had lost her father, the hero of her childhood, at thirteen. In her autobiography she makes the point that she secretly adored him. "All I did had been to please him. All my ambition and vanity had been satisfied by a twinkle of his understanding eyes." Alma also tells us emphatically that it was her will to keep her virginity intact. Against whom? Klimt? Twenty years older? Burckhardt? Twenty-four years older? Zemlinsky? Seven years older, and, she said, as ugly as a dwarf? It was an unwritten law of Victorian morality for a young woman of that time to remain a virgin, or at least a demi-virgin, until marriage. As will become even more obvious in the chapter on Lou Salomé, the custom of preserving virginity was a strong weapon with some women. Beyond this, both Lou and Alma, with their strong father-fixation, must have unconsciously felt compelled to remain faithful to their childhood hero.

Mahler, twenty years older than Alma, was father substitute, husband and lover; but, after being sexually awakened, she gradually discounted Mahler in the role of lover. After her encounter with the dashing young Gropius, her protestations that she would never leave Mahler were true to the point of not wanting to leave her father image. Only after ten years of marriage had she gained strength and vision, the strength to say no, the vision of what she wanted. Looking back over those years of lost freedom she realized that she had been plagued by doubts and desires to which she reacted with ambivalent feelings. Immediately after Mahler's death the dramatic emptiness, the sudden silence around her, was an even greater trauma than his slow dying. But she soon recovered to find the scope and depth latent in her, both of which so many experienced and intuitive men sensed.

Even in old age she had not overcome some bitter feelings about Mahler's tyrannic temperament. As she wrote her autobiography, some nasty remarks and ugly innuendoes crept into her thoughts of those early days and her life with an older man whose real loves were his music and his mother. However, her resentment seemed far more directed against herself than against Mahler. She may have more easily pardoned her romantic feelings for the older Klimt than her youthful adoration of the older Mahler. Insecurity was deeply imbedded in her, bolstering her undying romantic need to pay homage to a matinee idol or to gratify her yearning for submission to a man in whose greatness she could bathe. With this in mind we can more aptly read the lines she wrote as an introduction to a new chapter of her life:

Unwittingly, while looking for greatness in men, I was facing life—tempting, seductive life . . . in a figurative sense I could now realize my childhood dream of filling my garden with geniuses.

She could and undoubtedly should have continued to compose despite Mahler's dictatorial "No." If she had been an artist possessed by the urge to express herself, she would not have given in so easily. Seen from the standpoint of her psychic difficulties she rightly resented that her father figure interfered with her free will and made her lose the chance of accepting creativity as a challenge. But where would it have led her? Mahler's instinct may have been right in preventing her talent from developing. Small talents have the habit of running dry after a while. They easily end as parlor entertainment, as so often was practiced in the bourgeois homes during the nineteenth century: an exercise of the *bel esprit,* of *Schöngeisterei.*

No doubt forces conspired in Alma to enable her to give her emotional being an unusual lift, to find its way into an ecstatic expression, thus creating potential powers and an atmosphere fraught with the urge to lend some form to the meaningfulness of the moment. To say briefly that she inspired gifted men to reach the peak of their abilities would minimize her share in the creative process of the other person. Her participation was, however indirect, active. She was like a painter without arms, an architect without tools, a writer without paper and pen, a composer without an instrument— but she could conjure up in all of these figures a world of fantasy through which she walked, a world that took shape because she happened to pass by and willed it to be. For those men she was not the illusive romantic image of the unattainable woman, but in her attainability she became in their eyes "the Eternal Feminine," as Goethe phrased it, leading them on to unforeseen accomplishments.

Inevitably, she was surrounded by many men who wanted her and whose achievements counted in the public eye, but her almost infallible instinct made her bow out at the right moment when she felt drawn in the wrong direction. During this transitional period between Mahler's death and her emotional entanglement with Oskar

Kokoschka her notes mention several men, but two contrasting individuals seem most significant.

There was Franz Schreker whom she recognized as "an immensely gifted composer." After Mahler's death he conducted successfully in Vienna. He had five operas to his credit, but Mahler would have called them mediocre works destined for oblivion. Alma tells us that for a while they saw much of each other. Schreker's past was as fascinating as his fate was frightening, the fate of a man who never quite made it to the top. Alma left Schreker, whom she described as "a strange mixture of a spirited and constitutionally uneducated person," at the right moment.

Paul Kammerer, "one of the oddest individuals" she ever came across, was notorious among the biologists of his time. All his discoveries were sensational but prematurely announced and insufficiently supported by research. His colleagues in London did not hesitate to call him a fraud. And Alma made it quite clear that he made use of similar methods in his courtship. As a grotesque gesture of fraudulence she mentioned his threat to shoot himself at Mahler's grave if she would not yield to his demands.

One of her great and probably most tempestuous experiences occurred when she met Oskar Kokoschka in the winter of 1912. From that time on they never lost touch with each other as long as Alma lived, but their emotional and sexual affair was, in its sweeping articulation, accented by several dramatic highlights. Although Kokoschka's story of his life differs in its presentation of some of the details from Alma's, the intensity of their involvement remains uncontested. It was with the help of mass destiny, which has so often played its assassin's role in the fate of the individual, that a natural caesura took place in their relationship. Mass destiny was the outbreak of World War I. But the caesura probably would have come then or shortly thereafter, if we can trust Alma's notes as honest confession to her daily diary and not as something concocted later with a great deal of hindsight. Accepting the former, we see Alma again torn between the reality of her world and the vision of something that would free her from male domination.

She and Oskar met in Carl Moll's house. "She was anxious to meet me," Kokoschka wrote in his autobiography, *Mein Leben* (My Life), "because she had already heard of me." Carl Moll had asked Kokoschka, that "talented terror," as he was often referred to at that time, to paint his portrait and suggested to Alma that Kokoschka, the "poor starving genius," also paint hers.

His reputation as a unique portraitist was well established by then, his style defying any conventional accuracy as to the obvious resemblance of a face. The photographic image seemed to be of little interest to him at a point in history when photography began to mature as an art form and psychoanalysis showed the way to a better understanding of the complexities of man. Kokoschka probed the puzzling mechanism of what poets once referred to as the human soul. He had to do away with man's wish-face and look instead for the inner likeness of a person. Karl Kraus, the sharp-edged Viennese satirist, whom he portrayed in 1909, epigrammatized most profoundly Kokoschka's approach in taking a face apart and re-creating the hidden face in man while putting it together again: "Kokoschka has made a portrait of me. It is quite possible that those who know me will not recognize me. But it is certain that those who do not know me will recognize me."

Alma knew his work from the *Kunstschau* exhibit "and from his unusual, grandly conceived designs. But his shoes were torn, his suit was frayed. A handsome figure, but disturbingly coarse," she thought. Kokoschka remembered: "After dinner she took me into an adjacent room where she sat down at the piano, played and sang only for me, as she said, Isolde's *Liebestod* with great expressiveness. I was fascinated by her appearance, her youth, her beauty and the touching way in which she wore her mourning and lonesomeness."

Alma recalled that "he had some sheets of paper with him and started drawing at once." Kokoschka: "When she suggested I should paint her in her apartment I was enchanted and concerned at the same time. First, never before did I paint a woman who seemed to have fallen in love with me at first sight and, on the other hand, I felt a certain reluctance: how could anyone expect happiness when shortly before someone else had gone from her forever?"

Alma: "We hardly spoke—and yet he seemed unable to draw. We got up. Suddenly, tempestuously, he swept me into his arms. To me it was a strange, almost shocking kind of embrace; I did not respond at all. And precisely that seemed to affect him."

Here are the eyewitness accounts—recalled many decades later— of the only two persons who were there when it happened. But however it may have started, they both agreed that during the next three years they entertained, as he expressed it with restraint, "a very passionate relationship." Alma was far more descriptive when she called the three years during which they were inseparable "one fierce battle of love." In one breath she admitted to having never before "tasted so much tension, so much hell, so much paradise."

That such tension and hell should cause a flood of recriminative statements years later is understandable. The discrepancy of what was and what might have been easily distorts the thought-feelings of one's memory. The experience that both had was gratifying and turbulent, but differently anchored. Alma needed Kokoschka in order to grow beyond him. He needed to grow through her.

Although Alma felt again a prisoner in her relationship with Kokoschka, she was free to go at any time. She was not legally tied to him and yet, as Kokoschka rightly maintained in his apologia, she stayed with him until he volunteered in the Austro-Hungarian army. In his old age, looking back on those days when he had not yet matured and stubbornly tried to force fate to obey his wishes, he remembered a woman who had grown through some beautiful and bitter experiences and knew rather well what she wanted from life. In those days he could not imagine a life without her. He was ready to marry her and desired nothing more than to have her for himself. He struggled to keep her from her friends. It was, however, not mere jealousy. Everything lying outside their being together seemed trivial to him. When he walked up and down in front of her window until the early hours of dawn, it was not to spy on her or to make sure she was not seeing another lover, as she suspected. It was the compulsive feeling of a passionate lover who had to hold on to some outward sign of his object of love.

For some time their relationship was an idyll. Her country house on the beautiful mountain resort, Semmering, two hours by train from Vienna, was ready, with its oversized fireplace, for Kokoschka to paint a mural above the mantel: Alma moving heavenwards in blinding brightness, Oskar thrown into hell, surrounded by serpents. (The house was destroyed when the Russians moved into Austria in 1945.) Alma's little girl watched Kokoschka at his work and once asked: "Can't you paint anything else but Mummy?" "That child hasn't got any face," he said to Alma. "She's got nothing but expression." Only love and work, the two pillars of man's existence, filled their days. The leisure hours in the evening were spent around the fireplace. They would read aloud. They would listen to music. "It was a happy, positive, forward-looking time . . . cut short by the news . . . of war . . ."

He was completely filled with her, and this accounted for his need to paint her over and over again. Yet he was sure of himself. After they had met, he wrote her: ". . . I want you to save me until I can really be the man who does not drag you down but lifts you up. . . . If you, as a woman, will strengthen and help me escape from the confusion of my mind, the beauty that we worship beyond our power to know will bless us both with happiness." But the violent struggle between these two lovers went on, she desiring more freedom, he trying to keep her for himself. At times when he felt he was losing ground, he seemed ready for a compromise: "In the daytime I don't need to take you away from your circles. That's when you are gathering—and this, I know, is as it should be. I can work all day, spending what I have absorbed at night . . ."

Their relationship seems to have been based on their different needs, which furtively kept their feelings apart, while it made them cling to each other passionately. Kokoschka must have sensed that her presence meant constant inspiration to him, the feeding of his mind with impulses that gave him strength to struggle with himself, to endure and to overcome. "I must have you for my wife soon," he cried out in a letter, "or else my great talent will perish miserably. You must revive me at night, like a magic potion . . ."

In this way, of course, he wanted her to play a role which she had resented in her marriage to Mahler and, more and more, resisted in her life with Kokoschka. He verbalized so well how strong she made him in his work when he wrote: "Don't listen to the reasons and the ways of ignorant people who cannot know what we are good for and capable of. You are the Woman, and I am the Artist . . ." It was the one word she could not take, the thought that tore up old wounds.

She was aware of how much he depended on her. One day she decided to go to the Bohemian spa Franzensbad, but not before promising Kokoschka that on her return she would marry him if he had then created a masterpiece.

He kept his side of the bargain. He completed one of his most famous paintings, *Die Windsbraut* (The Tempest), now at the Museum in Basel, Switzerland. She reneged on her promise and "insisted that we should see each other only once every three days. It was in self-protection," she apologetically explained, "that I gradually relaxed our bonds, at least the bonds of habit." It was the beginning of the end.

Given his feelings, the painting was full of premonitions and melancholy. It threw its dark shadows across their ecstasy. It was a portrait of Alma and himself on the wreck of a boat on the sea somewhere in the world. He expressed in it how "his great love as if on sandals stole away from the azure reflection of the sun into the land of shadows and chimeras."

Alma described it with other words: "The *Windsbraut* showing the two of us together in a storm-tossed boat: I lying calmly, trustfully clinging to him, expecting all help from him who, despotic of face, radiating energy, calms the mountainous waves."

It seems that in a premonition of the end he also painted the walls of his studio black, some of them covered with white crayon sketches, and illuminated two parts of the room with a red-and-blue lamp. When the painting of their shipwrecked love was finished, the Austrian poet Georg Trakl visited him. Sitting in front of the painting, his voice suddenly pierced the silence and, staring at the picture, he slowly intoned a poem, which he called *"Nacht"* (Night), and repeated the lines until he knew them by heart:

> . . . *über schwärzliche Klippen.*
> *stürzt todestrunken*

die erglühende Windsbraut. . . .
(. . . above blackish cliffs
rushes, drunken with death,
the fiery tempest. . . .)

When he saw the poet's hand pointing at the picture and heard him reiterating the word: *Die Windsbraut*, Kokoschka took it for the title of his painting.

When he had joined the army at the outbreak of World War I, everything came to an end for her, despite her own attempts to loosen the bonds of the relationship. Kokoschka, she felt, had fulfilled her life and destroyed it at the same time. Where had she gone wrong? She did not know, except that she was called upon to care while, in her weariness, she would have loved to be cared for. She instinctively felt Kokoschka's genius, but at that stage he was still a man of promise, or maybe's.

"Why do I need male tormentors?" she asked herself in a diary note written during the early days of the war. When she wrote this, she had spent "an independent, happy evening full of music. . . . For a long time, though, I will be sick of the artistic Bohemia. I'd like to caution my soul: 'Hide your emotional silver spoons—the artists are coming!' "

But we know as much as she knew then: she could not help forgetting to hide those emotional silver spoons in time, or she would conveniently have kept them in the upper right-hand drawer where every thief would look first. The thieves came in quick succession.

When Kokoschka was seriously wounded on the Russian front in 1915, his transport back home became one of the great traumas of his life. His head injury made him feel as though he were isolated. He had lost all sense of time. Sometimes he remembered his past with unusual clarity, particularly his times with Alma. He had visions of her strong enough to make her appear right before him. "I thought," he wrote, "I would succumb to her attractiveness, I would be unable to separate from her." He held long dialogues with this phantom, and the imaginary verbal exchange was so intense that he retained every word of it. Out of these hallucinations emerged his play *Orpheus and Eurydice*.

He sent his old friend Adolf Loos to Alma. Adolf was supposed to urge her to come and see him in the hospital. Later Kokoschka admitted that it was too late, too late for anything. But it was not easy for Kokoschka to tear himself away from her; he could not help stirring the ashes of his pain. He would suddenly write her a letter begging her to forget the past and to begin anew, or he would send her a telegram or flowers or an invitation to the premiere of *Orpheus and Eurydice.*

Kokoschka often tried to reassure himself that this chapter in his life had to be ended. It was in the early twenties in Dresden where he then lived that he had a puppet made out of cloth and sawdust, an effigy of Alma. "I tried in vain to recognize in it Alma Mahler, 'The Blue Woman,' as I now called her. . . . Theories led nowhere. Why has no one forgotten the name of Pygmalion while the names of statesmen and theoreticians are mostly preserved only through their own memories?" But doesn't this statement imply that somewhere in a hidden corner of his heart Kokoschka may still have hoped that the puppet would come to life? It did not, according to all theories and the vulgar facts of life. Indeed, the effigy came to a bad end.

Kokoschka arranged a sumptuous party in honor of his puppet, which he also nicknamed "The Silent Woman." He invited all his friends. In their presence, and with many bottles of champagne, he wanted to end the existence of his "life companion" by the light of many torches. He also invited a famous Venetian courtesan in Renaissance style who, facing her mock rival, was nonplused when the puppet was paraded as in a floor show. "The courtesan asked me," Kokoschka reported, "how expensive the puppet was . . . and that I would be welcome in her bed whenever I should get fed up with warming a puppet. During the feast the puppet lost her head, and red wine was poured all over her." Poor Alma and even poorer Oskar! How hard it must have been for him to rid himself of his feelings for her. He ended the chapter: "At early dawn the garbage van took away the dream of Eurydice's return. The puppet was an effigy which no Pygmalion could awake to life."

It seems that he never forgot the scars of his pain, nor the woman who had meant more to him than anyone else. He set up a most beautiful monument to his love for her in a simple letter of finality which he wrote her on the occasion of her seventieth birthday on August 31, 1949:

My dear Alma,

You're still a wild brat, just as when you were first carried away by *Tristan and Isolde* and used a quill to scrawl your comments on Nietzsche in your diary, in the same flying, illegible hand that I can make out only because I know your rhythm. Ask your friends, who are preparing to celebrate your birthday, not to tie you down to a silly, accidental, ephemeral calendar year. Tell them instead to give you a living, imperishable monument, by discovering a real American poet with a sixth sense for language, implication, rhythm and timbre—one who knows the emotional scale from tenderness to the most vicious sensuality, can extract it from my *Orpheus and Eurydice*, and will translate it into American (not modern English)—so we may tell the world what the two of us have done with and to each other, and may pass the living message of our love on to posterity. . . . We'll always be on the stage of life, we two, when disgusting banality, the trivial visage of the contemporary world, will yield to a passion-born splendour. Look at the dull and prosaic faces about you—not one has known the thrill of playing with life, of relishing even death, of smiling at the bullet in your skull, the knife in your lungs. Not one—except your lover whom you once initiated into your mysteries. Remember that this love play is the only child we have. Take care of yourself, and spend your birthday without a hangover.

Your Oskar.

In Search of Love Through Passion

The inconsistencies of Alma Mahler's notes are less puzzling when we envision her as a person determined and realistic in the pursuit of her goals as much as depending on the indefinite and undefinable rumblings of her subconscious. She could experience things in the light of the moment and see them differently afterwards. She believed that nothing happens by chance, that there is nothing accidental in life. Events are most often linked in a mysterious manner, and the way in which she met men destined to play a great role in her life proved her right. She felt that her subconscious would dream up someone who would then suddenly stand in front of her and make their "chance" meeting meaningful. "Consciousness swept me along through life," she once noted, "but what really mattered emerged as if by a miracle from deep within."

The more her marriage with Mahler became a thing of the past, the brighter she saw her life with him, fulfilled because she had accomplished a mission. She never felt the same about Kokoschka, although she could state at one point that he had everything that makes a human being great. But, immediately after having left him, she thought she had been less successful with him because he always tried to keep the upper hand. He had a different style of living; his temper differed from Mahler's, and he was easily irritated and vehemently outspoken in his demands. He certainly had none of Mahler's century-old burden of Jewish introversion. When he gave himself, he gave with the fury of giving. Before he left for the front, Alma received from him a farewell present "of unimaginable beauty," as she described it: seven fans. "In glowing colors, with a delicacy of which the art experts would not have thought him capable, he had painted our love story on seven bits of folded paper."

Shortly before destiny made her meet Gropius again, she was full of anxieties and fears. She felt lonely: "No man's hand in mine. I know nothing anymore and am wasting away disconsolately. I long to offer my life, but my offering hand trembles with fear." Now with Kokoschka gone to the wars she averred that she had conjured herself away from him (to use her phrase) and that she could no longer find him in herself. With men of minor interest around her now, Alma felt forsaken. Berta Zuckerkandl, who had meanwhile made her reputation as an international journalist and in whose house she had met Gustav Mahler more than a dozen years ago, told her about an exhibition in Cologne at which a yet unknown architect had made a deep impression on everyone.

The young architect happened to be the same Walter Gropius who had fallen in love with her in a Styrian spa some years previously. Spontaneously, Alma sat down to write him a letter of congratulation, adding innuendoes that could not be mistaken: a plea to see him again and to renew their friendship more seriously. Although she knew many people, as she admitted, she felt strangely lost at the moment: "I am seldom alone, too much among people. I long for a will that would wisely guide me away from what I have acquired, back to what is inborn. I know I could get there by myself, too, but I would so much like to thank someone for it!"

It may have been difficult for any man to resist this plea, let alone Gropius, who well remembered his love for her. She had rebelled against Mahler and Kokoschka because she felt suppressed and treated like a student by the former, bullied and isolated by the latter—yet here again she was asking for another will to direct her. Did she not best express her own difficulties when she conceded that "everything in my life seems enigmatic to me"?

However, there was no immediate reply to her letter, since Gropius was at the Russian front. Then, in early January, 1915, he wrote that he had been buried under the dead somewhere, had had a nervous breakdown and was now on convalescent leave in Berlin. She took the next train to Berlin, but not before writing in her diary what her sixth sense dictated (or was it her preconceived decision?): "I feel or rather surmise that he will mean something in my life."

They spent two weeks together in Berlin, but Kokoschka's shadow hovered over them. "Days were spent in tearful questions, nights in tearful answers. He could not get over my relation with Oskar Kokoschka . . ." Gropius emerges from her diary and tales as a perfect human being (even though he tore one of Kokoschka's seven fans to pieces in a fit of jealousy), decent and full of understanding for Alma's emotional and sexual confusion, as he later proved when Alma was helplessly and totally entangled with Franz Werfel. Gropius had accepted her need to send him off while she was still married to Mahler. But why did she not get in touch with him after Mahler's death? This question must have occurred to him. He must have known of Mahler's death, too. Yet, through the years, he had not tried to find his way back to her.

Undoubtedly, Alma was banished from his mind as a passing episode. When she got in touch with him and when he saw her again, his buried feelings for her reawakened with the same tempestuousness with which he had demanded her five years previously. She accompanied him to the station. He had to leave for Hannover to see his mother. When the train started to move Gropius pulled her up, and she could not help going with him. It was the prelude to their marriage which, as Gropius could not foresee, would be fragmentary and short-lived.

The days before her decision to marry Gropius were confusing and exciting for her. Was it mere coincidence, she asked herself, that Mahler died on May 18th, which was Gropius's birthday? Whatever the subliminal process that caused her to connect these two events, it was symptomatic of her reactions, which were so often prompted by mystical phenomena, or, we could also say, by irrelevancies that she raised to meaningfulness.

In those days a letter arrived from Kokoschka—a sad, long note in which he expressed his disbelief that everything between them could be over forever; it ended with the remark: "I love you and hold on to you—what do you know who you are, and where? We do not carry our limits within ourselves."

She felt puzzled and intrigued when she realized how responses to her will called forth events that got out of hand and yet only seemed to brush the surface. The enigma of her existence, with which she struggled valiantly, grew to a frightening specter. At that point in her life she could no longer comprehend what was happening to her. She tried to calm herself by going to church. Finally, in the despair of her own *angst*, she spent many hours with one of Vienna's famous psychiatrists, Professor Julius von Wagner-Jauregg. She needed to be reassured that it was her way of being to ask for storm and conflict, for the ultimate in greatness and gratification, and that she had to learn that even the greatest of men were only human, on one or another level as human as she herself or even more so.

Then she married Walter Gropius. Meanwhile, the war continued relentlessly. Gropius, nursed to renewed strength, had to go back to the front. Alma wrote in her diary: "Nothing shall deflect me from my course. My will is clear: I want nothing but to make this man happy. May God preserve my love . . ." These resolutions and vows sounded similar to those made during her marriage to Mahler; they had a touch of naïveté and the longing for fulfillment and inner peace.

In those early war years too many Germans were swept along by patriotic slogans. An ugly war cry—in the form of a manifesto of Germany's intellectuals and artists—was denounced and satirized by Karl Kraus in his periodical *Die Fackel* (The Torch). It bore the names of such famous men as Max Reinhardt and Gerhart Hauptmann. Although his three sons served in the army, Hauptmann's nationalistic feelings went overboard: "Nothing is uglier than an unaired room. The people become fresher, stronger, rejuvenated." Most of the German and Austrian officers bought their own equipment. Kokoschka had to borrow money so that he could have his own horse and be accepted as a cavalry officer. Gropius also went to a military-equipment store to choose the leather for his riding boots. Alma accompanied him, but the strong odor of leather nauseated her, and she returned to the cab to wait for him.

While idly sitting there, she bought a monthly magazine, *Die Weissen Blätter* (The White Pages), and thumbed through it. Her eyes fell upon a poem that she read and reread: *"Der Erkennende"* (The Knowing One). The author's name was Franz Werfel. The poem captivated her, it engulfed her and stayed with her. She took the magazine along to her chalet on the Semmering after Walter Gropius had left to go on fighting in the first cataclysmic event of the century, and she proceeded to set Werfel's poem to music.

"A Marriage of Beauty and Significance"

In Alma's life, Gropius played the thankless role of the kindest man she had ever met. They hardly ever lived together, and her passion for Franz Werfel whom she met in the fall of 1917—about two years after having married Gropius—overshadowed their relationship. Her feelings for the young architect could never fully develop in two years of a marriage lived at a distance most of the time. She was not cast for the part of a Penelope; she did not have the stuff of which war brides are made who sit and wait and, while sitting and waiting, live with the remote image of a person whom they have had little opportunity to know. Alma soon became convinced that a marriage from furlough to furlough is doomed.

She sensed the genius in Gropius, and she had taken vows and made resolutions, but she did not have the patience to wait for him and for his greatness to unfold, even though she recognized his charming and disarming human qualities during their short intervals together. Perhaps her most revealing reaction to her relationship with Gropius is her thought that she had always wanted a child from a handsome man. She gave birth to a lovely girl who was called Manon. But then, she admitted, "my curiosity was at an end."

Four years after her marriage to Gropius, in the summer of 1919, when she went to Berlin and then to Weimar to ask him for a divorce and for the custody of her child Manon, she still wondered about the reasons for the failure of this marriage. She was then enduring some turbulent experiences. A baby boy, born prematurely and sickly—her child by Franz Werfel—had died. Gropius had been at her bedside, only concerned about her and the child's life. There were no scenes, no reproaches. It was also Gropius who gave her the news of the child's death while she was with him in Berlin. "I'd rather have died myself," he is reported to have said. It may seem somewhat strange that she was pleading for a divorce in Berlin, while the child was dying in a hospital in Vienna. But she was in a state of compulsive despair. She was madly in love with Werfel, frantic both about the child who had no chance to live and about her legal tie with Gropius. In her ecstatic feelings of having found the man whom she believed to be her hope and salvation, she played with the adolescent thought of running away from everything and herself, of taking the next boat to travel around the world, of escaping a sterile life and "the coming of a non-culture," of trying to begin life anew, somewhere at a hidden place on earth, "and so perhaps to experience a rich artistic life and happiness."

At that point she was as confused as the events in her life. Kokoschka was still sending emissaries who tried to convince her that he could neither work nor go on living without her. (Even Gropius still wrote to her many years after their divorce about how much he needed her.) There must have been something about Alma that could not be defined and was only felt and experienced by those to whom it revealed itself.

Gropius was always wonderful to her without being able to reach her. When he saw her again after the war, the day she had come for her divorce, his very first words were: "There is a new expression in your face." He immediately sensed how far she had moved away from him. In trying to find the reason for her change of heart, she mainly blamed his lack of musical understanding for separating them. She also admitted that, on the other hand, she could not muster sufficient interest in his work and ideals, his desire to give the world a new architectural face.

He was the only one of Alma's lovers for whom the realities of life were weightier than any dream about them, whatever great work of art this dream might ultimately produce. He was a teacher and in some ways a preacher. He loved to experiment, and as one of the driving forces of the *Bauhaus* which, in the mid-twenties, was to change the concept of architecture, he sought a new synthesis of art and modern technology. Was all this too sober for Alma? Gropius could instinctively foresee and perceive problems that he then subjected to logical thinking and exact calculations in order to make their realization possible, but apparently he could not master his emotional problems with Alma.

It was not so much the music, to which he was undoubtedly less attuned than to any other art form, that separated them. What really stood between them was her way of dreaming and his way of thinking.

The final separation from Gropius was preceded by one of Alma's great emotional experiences, one destined to last the longest in her life and to give her the gratification she needed and desired. Franz Blei, a minor German writer of the postwar period, but a great wit and conversationalist with an impressive well-founded knowledge, was introduced to her almost against her will. She disliked his books and transferred this antipathy to him as a person. She found his brilliance exhausting, his protestations of love hollow-sounding.

One day, in the winter of 1917, he brought a friend of his along. She described him as "a stocky man with sensuous lips and large, beautiful eyes under a Goethean forehead." He was Franz Werfel.

It seemed to Alma that she was predestined to meet the man whose poems had impressed her so much that she felt compelled to compose music for one of them. To her this had been a mystic act, the unification of two minds that did not know of one another and yet were merged in a mysterious manner. When she then sat opposite that man, alone—after Blei had left hastily since he soon realized he was eclipsed by Werfel's profundity—she understood why she had had to give in, against her better feelings, to meet Blei. There was no doubt in her mind that she would have met Werfel some other time, that her love for his poems and his love for Mahler's music, for music per se, would have brought them together.

The first evening they spent together, he read aloud Schönberg's *Jacob's Ladder*. He read beautifully and dramatically. His soft and expressive voice, his gift for oratory, captivated her. He knew how to tell stories. By way of interpreting Schönberg's dilemma as the Jew suffering from his Jewishness, he explained his own dilemma. At that moment, Alma only heard the magic sound in the musical cadences of his words.

Werfel, who was then twenty-six, often came to visit her. They talked for hours; he recited poetry; he sang to her accompaniment. Sometimes Franz Blei and other friends joined them. The war was still raging. Gropius dropped in during short furloughs. He stayed with Alma during the Christmas holidays of 1917. When he had to rejoin his regiment, she "strove to put on" her "brightest smile to help him over the sad departure." In her autobiography Alma maintained that in those days Gropius was still jealous of Kokoschka, although she was miles away from the painter, heading for a new star.

Saying farewell to her, Gropius told her that he had no longer the desire and strength to fight her past. By then, she had not yet admitted to herself that Gropius should have started to fight her future instead.

At that time Alma and Werfel went to hear many concerts together. William Mengelberg conducted Mahler's *Fourth Symphony*. These days were made full for her by Mahler's music and Werfel's presence; it was all a song of love to her ears, and, shaken by her romantic and sentimental feelings, she stammered in her diary:

It had to happen. It was inevitable that he would take my hand and kiss it, that our lips would find each other . . . Where will this godlike experience lead me? I love my life. I repent nothing . . . I am out of my mind. And so is Werfel. If I were twenty years younger, I would leave everything and follow him.

She was his senior by twelve years and left everything—that is, Walter Gropius—to follow Franz Werfel. She could not help breaking out into her war cry: "I love my life. I repent nothing!" which always contained the premonition of a great love affair dictated by the law of chance that she administered, interpreted and judged. By then she had written off her marriage with Gropius. She may have denied regrets, but her conscience searched for a justification of what she knew she was about to do: "This deep musical and mental bond with Franz Werfel is almost fatal. It had to happen that I would fall in love with him, and music will protect us," she reiterated time and again.

As we might expect, there were many moments of ecstasy and many days and weeks of agony before they were married on July 6, 1929. Werfel had been on active duty in the army for three years. In 1917 an aristocratic patron of the arts, Harry Count Kessler, a lover of literature, made it possible for Sergeant Franz Werfel to be recalled from the Russian front to serve in mufti at the Army Press Section in Vienna. (Some of his compatriots there were Rilke, Hofmannsthal, Musil, Altenberg and Blei. Kessler saved the lives of many Austrian literati.)

In May 1918 he was sent to Switzerland on an official lecture tour to promote the image of Austrian culture. It was five months before the collapse of the monarchy and the outbreak of the revolution. Wherever he read his poetry he was very successful, but he could not refrain from lampooning the diplomats in Berne, where his lecture was attended by the ministers of the Austro-Hungarian and German legations, and making revolutionary remarks on other occasions. He wrote to Alma from Zürich:

I only think of you, Alma. I am here very unhappy. I can hardly stand it any longer!!—Every day I am away from you I feel full of guilt of which I am innocent, after all.—I suffer from palpitation, bad dreams wake me out of my sleep. What is it??—Is it an occult sign that you suffer? I am tied to you. I sense a holy shudder gripping my soul when I can talk about you.—Yesterday Ehrenstein, K's best friend, spoke to me about O.K., told me how he got crying fits when you did not permit him to visit you, told me the same as Dirzstay said that K. is tied to you out and out. This conversation excited me very much. . . .

While on his lecture tour he loved Alma with a feeling of nostalgia from which, as he said, his love for her was never free. In the month of July, 1918, he often visited her at her house on the Semmering, stayed there for days, his room adjoining her bedroom. Previously, he felt, he only imagined women. Now for the first time he found a woman who was as real and passionate as none he had ever known. Perhaps his descriptive statement of Alma's lovemaking may explain her fatal attraction for men: he thought of having discovered "something suicidal, a self-destructive urge in her climactic surrender."

Werfel blamed his violent lovemaking for a series of hemorrhages from which Alma suffered and which were dangerous in her pregnant condition. Werfel's diary of those days tells us of the ordeal both lovers went through, Alma in frightful pain and danger of losing the child and her own life, Werfel in painful fear, ready to sacrifice whatever he could think of, from stopping smoking to bellowing all kinds of vows to the gods. He could stay with her only in the very beginning of her collapse. He was "almost tearfully conscious of her great beauty," as she lay in bed, very pale and sick. ("She spoke in a low voice, and in everything she said there was a glorious enthusiasm such as only great souls can have in suffering. She is a powerful creature . . .")

Gropius—to whom she was then still officially married—was called to her sickbed. He arrived with a Viennese physician and stayed with Alma until the danger was over. She had to be moved to a hospital in Vienna where she was under special care of Dr. Friedrich Pineles, who had been not only an intimate friend of Lou Salomé and Vienna's most beloved society doctor, but the medical friend of the city's intelligentsia.

Werfel received some notes from Alma, but was not allowed to see her. When he called the hospital one August morning, Gropius was there. "It was a bad night," he said in a shaken voice, as it seemed to Werfel. "The child is alive. Alma is doing well under the circumstances. We'll have to wait and see for a few days." Werfel, too, was shaken and thanked God. He wrote a paean on the birth of his son. Days later he cried out in his diary: "Is it my child? Her letter says it is. . . ." Still under the impression of "my son" he wrote another poem: *"Nicht Wir"* (Not We). When he was allowed to visit Alma in the hospital, Gropius was there. It was only then that Gropius found out they were lovers. In the afternoon he came to see Werfel, who, however, was asleep. Gropius left a note for him: "I am here to love you with all the strength at my command. Spare Alma! The worst might happen. The excitement, the milk—if our child should die!"

There was a nobility in Gropius's pain that neither of the lovers could match. They could only wonder at it and admire him.

"How shall I get away from this man?" her diary says. "He does not hound me like others, he is restlessly calm like the sea, as unpredictable, as vacillating, as universally dirigible as myself."

Who was this man from whom Alma could not get away and with whom, after a stormy beginning, she finally found inner peace and happiness? One could not think of two more different personalities. She, a Wagnerian figure in the disguise of a Viennese Catholic. He, a Jew from Prague with a message of brotherhood behind the mask of an eternal rebel. In her constant flight from herself, Alma found the realization of her dreams in the opposite of everything she was.

To understand better this man who—so much younger than herself—was as unpredictable as she was, but who could give her the feeling of being at home with him, we must consider the environment which produced him.

Werfel was the son of a wealthy industrialist with a calculating mind, interested in business only, and of a superficial and extravagant mother. The boy was strongly attached to his Czech nurse Babi; it was an attachment that accounted for his fondness for the Czech nation. Forced to work at his father's factory, which he was to take over one day, he had a short and ignominious business career. He fled to Leipzig, where the publisher Kurt Wolff employed him as a reader.

Besides Vienna, Prague—Werfel's home—had always been a cultural center in the midst of which—for about a thousand years until the end of the thirties—a German community existed mainly of Jewish families. From this cultural German enclave within the Czechoslovakian people emerged an amazing literature that enriched the world of letters immensely. Three authors from this group achieved international reputations: Rainer Maria Rilke, Franz Kafka and Franz Werfel. Others, Max Brod, Willy Haas and Johannes Urzidil, became well known. These and many other literary figures often met at the Café Arco in Prague. It is a historic phenomenon that this ambiance of isolation and linguistic lostness created an explosive atmosphere of creativity.

With his first volume of poetry Werfel established himself as a literary person of great promise. Another volume soon followed. Rilke, impressed by Werfel's poetry, wrote him the first of four letters in 1913 in which he spoke of himself as one who was "long grown-up" (Rilke was Werfel's senior by fifteen years) and as one "lost in God that tries us out."

Werfel's early lyric poems already showed a trend toward a strange mysticism and a strong religious feeling in which the creation of the world must be accepted as sin and man can only liberate himself from his guilt through compassion and love. The sweep of his cadences was reminiscent of the poetry of Walt Whitman, of whom the young Werfel was very fond. Spiritually he was closer to Rilke, writing to him, ". . . but now I surmise that, in God's lap, we are not so far apart," and he felt comforted that his poems reached Rilke's sentiments. Their few personal meetings were less successful. Once or twice Lou Salomé was present when the older and by then famous Rilke met Werfel, and she too noticed the hidden antagonism between the two poets. Rilke, with his aristocratic leanings, was undoubtedly disappointed in Werfel's personality, perhaps in Werfel's unwillingness to play the role of the disciple paying homage to Rilke's halo. Rilke best described his feeling of repulsion in a letter addressed to Hugo von Hofmannsthal, writing of Werfel that, ". . . there is, in the final analysis, attached to [him] a touch of strangeness, a smell as if of another species, something insurmountable . . ." And Werfel similarly pictured his meetings with Rilke: "His aura had something strange for me, something sapless-refined which strained and tired me."

In contrast to Rilke, whom the war silenced for four long years, Werfel reacted poetically to the cruelty of chance and the man-made madness. On any kind of paper he could get hold of, he scribbled his verses and thoughts and sent them to his publisher Kurt Wolff from the front post office.

Alma's love for the old collapsed Austro-Hungarian monarchy and Werfel's enthusiasm for the revolution separated them, but only for a short time. On November 12, 1918, the revolution broke out in Vienna's streets. Werfel, in his old uniform, came to her to ask her blessing. He was to join the revolutionaries, the Red Guard, in order to enforce the illusion of a better world, as Alma thought. To her, it was a meretricious revolution and Werfel's attitude and behavior more than repulsive. He stood on the ramps of the University, tearing his decorations from his chest, delivering wild speeches in which he incited the mob to storm the banks. When he returned to Alma, she was aghast to see his eyes "red and bloodshot, his face bloated and filthy, his hands, his uniform—there was a blight on everything . . ." and she threw him out. If she quoted herself correctly in her autobiography (and we can hardly doubt it since she was more than candid in every respect), then her words were as spurious as his revolution: "If you had done something beautiful, you would be beautiful now." When she saw in what squalor he lived, in the "furnished atrocity" of his flat which "reeked of vices," she cried out in her diary: "Is this how it will be? I'm sure I would never live with a loose individual. The more I love him, the less I could live with him."

In those few frightful days in which the Austro-Hungarian monarchy fell apart and Austria became a republic, Alma did not know where Werfel was sleeping. He was in hiding because the police were looking for the man who had tried to incite the crowd to storm the banks. She feared for his safety—even though she pretended to be horrified by what he had done; he needed to be told he would be in danger should he return to his room or come to see her. It was Gropius who drove to all places and living quarters where Werfel could have been hiding, so that he could warn him. It seems, however, that the Austrian police did not take this poet-turned-rebel too seriously. They probably realized that this revolutionary gesture was for Werfel a one-night performance and finally wrote it off under the heading of "poetic license."

And so apparently did Alma, for in mid-December her diary reflected a total change of attitude: "A glorious night! Werfel was with me. We clung to each other and felt the deepest oneness of our loving souls. He is the resolving chord of my life . . ."

There were one or two dissonant sounds in their relationship before they married. Werfel, becoming jealous and possessive, urged her to go to Gropius to ask for her divorce; he insisted on marrying her. By the same token he was manifesting a Bohemianism that frightened her. "A man of his sensitivity," she sounded off, "turned suddenly into a beast of prey that held me in its clutches—and this I could not stand! Was it not just what I resented in marriage?" Although she went to Germany to ask Gropius for a divorce, grave doubts accompanied her. She felt she could not and should not try to tame Werfel. But was she not asking for punishment when attaching herself to a man of such an explosive temperament, a sense-intoxicated and younger man who found whatever he sought and sought whatever he found?

An incident of minor importance once called forth a reaction of major scope. They had been to the theater and had seen a bad and vulgar play. She wanted to leave during the intermission, "but Werfel had one of his tantrums and publicly insulted me in the street." She hailed a taxi while he yelled after her: "Just remember I'm not coming home tonight! I'll fix you!"

When she reached her home, she threw herself on her bed, fully dressed, and thought about their relationship and cried with fury. She felt humiliated and abused: "I was fed up with the slavery called 'man' . . . and burst into tears." It took her weeks to get over this shock. Werfel, on one of his lecture tours, sent her telegrams "full of love while I sat in Vienna, recovering from 'man as such.' "

There was one other thing that never caused fights and friction but existed as an undercurrent moving in two different directions. He loved music and was deeply immersed in Italian opera, particularly in Verdi. She said of herself that her only lover was music and that she found consolation in his arms during moments of depression and despair. Her ideal, however, was Richard Wagner. She listened to Wagner's music as often as she could. How often did she lose herself over *Tristan and Isolde* or shed tears of happiness over the prelude to *Die Meistersinger*! When speaking of her eroticism Werfel described her "self-destructive urge at the climax" as "the living image of her Wagnerianism, justified by an erotic-musical nature." Here, at least, one facet of her fascination is made clear to us by Werfel: Alma was a total woman when in bed with a man. Did not Kokoschka insinuate the same thing when he remembered as an old man how she had initiated him into her mysteries?

Werfel's enthusiasm for Verdi made him rewrite the librettos to three of his operas and create a novel in which he tried to shape "the mythical truth" of the man and artist Giuseppe Verdi. Werfel juxtaposed dramatically the ten years of dearth in Verdi's creativity with the advent of Richard Wagner and the momentous power of Wagner's musical unfolding. Here Werfel succeeded in re-creating the most traumatic experience of any artist fearing his creative impotence.

Wagner as Verdi's antipode remains a remote character in the novel and yet his omnipresence casts a huge shadow over the hero's existence. Italo, the fanatic Wagnerian of the novel, feels pleasantly exhausted after playing Wagner on the piano as if having spent himself in coital excitement. Werfel saw the strongly suggestive power in Wagner's music which, with its erotic component, fanaticized his followers. Alma's Wagnerianism helped him paint this shade onto his verbal canvas. And how much of a psychological undercurrent colored his picture of the German who, with few traditions to lean on, must prove himself through originality? In this novel Werfel says of Wagner: "He was a German. And to be German means: You are permitted to do whatever you wish because no form, no past, no relation ties you down."

In contrast to the Alma-Wagnerian counterplayers, Werfel identified with Verdi, his hero. Verdi is not obsessed by the notion of being the chosen artist who must convince through his ideology and disseminate it. His melodies are humanized apotheoses, rooted in the past and pointing into the future, emerging from musical and not, as is the case with Wagner, from dramatic sources. In contrast to Wagner's personal behavior and seamy affairs, Verdi is pictured as a dignified figure, composed in his days of triumph, nobly resigned in his defeat. Werfel, burdened by his Jewish past and feeling uprooted in his isolation as an intellectual from Prague in the German linguistic landscape, could relate to the dramatic situation of Verdi's exile from his own creative sources.

Another character in the novel, the musician Mathias Fischböck, had features of the composer Ernst Krenek who, in the summer of 1922, joined Alma and Werfel on the Semmering, since he was about to marry Alma's daughter Anna. The figure of Fischböck may, in fact, be a composite modeled after Anton von Webern and Krenek. The presence of the latter helped Werfel cast a modern musician whose incentives were mathematical formulae rather than melodies.

Alma wrote about Werfel's *Verdi*: "I absolutely disagreed with the views expressed in the novel—to me, Richard Wagner had been and would always be greater than Verdi—but I felt I had no right to influence him." On the contrary, she encouraged him several times to go on with it when he was not sure of himself and wanted to burn his manuscript. In hours of doubt and despair she stayed close to him, giving him all the strength he needed to endure.

In the twenties, which, despite the galloping inflation, roared and spat with creative imagination, Werfel was carried by the wave of expressionism into the foreground of literary interest. He then published several volumes of poetry and prose, mainly short stories and novels. He became a successful dramatist who was produced by Max Reinhardt, by then the most recognized of all stage directors in Central Europe. Werfel established his reputation as a dramatist with the play *Spiegelmensch* (Mirrorman), which was first staged in 1921. From the vantage point of our own time, it can best be compared with Bertolt Brecht's *Baal*, which was also written about that time and is, like *Spiegelmensch*, a bad puerile play of magnificent scope. Both plays liberated their authors and prepared them for greater things to come.

The poets of the Prague circle remained in touch with each other, regardless of the different paths their lives seemed to follow. Rilke was the only exception. Werfel was often seen in Prague, together with Franz Kafka, who showed an ambivalent attitude toward Werfel's work. Strangely enough, Kafka was impressed by *Spiegelmensch*. "What an abundance of vital power," he wrote. "Only at one spot a bit sickish, but everywhere else all the more exuberant and even the sickness full of exuberance. I read it avidly in one afternoon." But, on another occasion, after the premiere of Werfel's *Schweiger* (The Silent One)—a play with a strange mixture of socialism, psychiatry and mysticism—their meeting turned into an ugly scene when Kafka expressed his disgust at the play's basic thesis and resolution. Prior to Werfel's visit with him, Kafka had written him a letter which Werfel never received or, rather, Kafka never mailed. It was found later and, among other things, said: "You are certainly a leader of this generation which is no flattery and cannot be interpreted as a flattery, because anyone can lead this society in its morasses. This is why you are not only a leader but more than that . . . and one follows your road with wild interest. And now this play. It may have many fine features . . . but it is a step back from leadership, in fact, there is no leadership in it, rather the betrayal of a generation, a mystification, a kind of anecdoting, in other words, a degradation of its suffering."

Werfel never resented Kafka's criticism. When Kafka was waiting to die in a sanatorium near Vienna, it was Werfel who made it possible for Kafka to stay in a private room, it was Werfel who sent him flowers and often visited him. Among the very few books Kafka permitted himself to read during his last days was Werfel's novel on Verdi.

Alma Mahler-Gropius did not legally become Alma Mahler-Werfel until July 6, 1929. The divorce took a long time to reach its legal finale. Gropius often delayed action on this formality since he felt he needed Alma and may, furtively, have hoped against all hope. She was in no hurry. She had all the freedom she wanted and felt spiritually wedded to Werfel. They traveled together, they lived together. When in Rome, she wrote in her diary: ". . . I am unalterably committed to my present life. It is a marriage, a marriage of beauty and significance . . ." They rarely went different ways. Once in a while he would go on a lecture tour, and she would not accompany him; on another occasion when she felt she had to escape from herself, she went with her daughter Anna from Rome to Sicily while Werfel stayed back to work. There were moments during such separations from him when "I dreaded any thought of being unfaithful to him," she wrote. Then why was this thought in the back of her mind?

These were productive years for Werfel and, more often than not, Alma fed his mind and set his imagination afire; when she heard stories of other people, she recognized at once the fictionally exploitable aspects and reported them to Werfel; at other times she silently sat by, giving him the feeling of security that his self-doubting mind so often needed.

They spent most of their time in Italy, in Venice, where Alma bought a house and tried to avoid seeing Kokoschka (who happened to be there quite often); or in Santa Margherita where they were often together with Gerhart Hauptmann and his wife (Hauptmann and Werfel were fond of one another, although the latter often had reason to be suspicious of a mild form of anti-Semitism on Hauptmann's part); or in Rome—but all summers were spent together on the Semmering which both of them loved. From this mountain retreat she wrote on July 5, 1929, in her diary:

Tomorrow we are to be married . . . I could not sleep. I was too restless. I did not know whether I, with my love of freedom, was doing the right thing.

She was assuring herself that she was not doing it for "the neighbors" nor for her own sake. Perhaps she had done it for her daughter Manon who had told in school about "Uncle Werfel who is living with us." Then a strange, resigned tone crept into her notes:

My freedom, which I have preserved in spite of everything, would receive a jolt. My love had already given way to a close, intimate friendship. I had read Kokoschka's post cards of the past months over again and found him quietly at rest within me. . . .

In a few weeks I would be fifty. And Franz Werfel was young. I had to keep in step, to feign youth. I had to devote all my interest in life to his growth . . . I could not afford the great attractions of aging, of withdrawing upon oneself, of gradually refusing to play the game. Frequent separations, as we had been having recently, would be my only escape.

With "I am ready," she closed her self-analysis. Ready she was, and she married Franz Werfel the next day.

She might have reminded herself that she *had* put down her credo only the year before, saying that she was unalterably committed to her present life and this *was* a marriage, a marriage of beauty and significance. She had even said more than once that she resented marriage as an institution, calling it "a tyranny sanctioned by the state." She always feared the feeling of being trapped, that uncertain sensation of being in someone's clutches. But the outward freedom of which Alma dreamt "presupposed an inner freedom," to use her words. She must have felt that Werfel gave her that inner freedom. And their marriage probably was the best of all possible marriages.

In the late twenties Alma and Werfel undertook several journeys to Egypt, Palestine and Turkey. They inspired Werfel to write a play, *Paul among the Jews,* and one of his best novels, *The Forty Days of Musa Dagh.*

In Damascus he was shaken by the sight of half-starved Armenians. He was fascinated by the topic, but it took some time before it crystallized into a great triptych novel, a work of signal importance when it was published in 1933, the year Hitler took over. Werfel began to labor on the idea in July, 1932, when the growing chaos in Germany opened the way for Hitler. Alma admitted that he wanted to convert her "by presenting an involuntary hero." In their discussions they often clashed, and Alma thought that a "yes-woman" would have been a great danger to him. It was obvious to everyone that with Hitler's final victory the Jews would be perse-cuted, even though no one could foresee the scope of Hitler's mania. Alma explained: ". . . now the final impulse [to write *The Forty Days of Musa Dagh*] was provided by the clash of our personalities."

Musa Dagh means the Mount of Moses, and when at that point of history and his life Werfel wanted to set a monument to the Armenian people, he actually wanted to tell the world through a simile about the fate of another people persecuted for centuries because of their religious beliefs. The constant historic repetition of the fatal destiny of the Jews was thus linked to the Armenians, Christian people living among the Moslems in the Near East. Turkey was an ally of Germany and Austria during World War I. In those years the Turkish government persecuted, slaughtered or exiled their minority of Armenians. The whole civilized world was aghast but too occupied with fighting a savage war to take much notice of this incident. The German officials were aware of what was happening there, but kept the monstrous events from reaching the people, who learned only the official wording, namely: that the Turks were "resettling" the Armenians.

A small group of Armenians succeeded in escaping and gathering their forces on an inaccessible mountain where they began a heroic struggle to survive. According to the Armenian people, they were beleaguered fifty-three days. A German version speaks of thirty-six. Werfel chose the figure of forty, because for forty years the people of Israel wandered through the desert, forty days and forty nights God made it rain during the deluge, forty days Moses fasted before nearing God on Mount Sinai, and forty days Christ spent in the desert. Finally, when salvation came to the Armenians, their leader remained on the mountain and died.

While staying in Santa Margherita, where Gerhart Hauptmann had headquarters nearby, Werfel wrote to Alma on February 17, 1934, about his realization of how prophetic his book was and how the most frightful danger signs gained in momentum. He thought that everyone should "immediately join ranks behind Dollfuss [the Austrian chancellor, a few months later murdered because he dared resist Nazism], who must no longer be weakened. It becomes more and more obvious that history is a dark encroachment of supernature in nature. Hitler is favored by a lucky star. It is a matter of no consequence that a historic figure is right or ought to represent any particular value; Attila was a belching savage and yet God's rod of chastisement."

Whenever Hitler belched, the world shook in fear. The years before the Austrians danced joyfully in the streets to welcome the conquering liberator were frightful years for Alma. Her daughter with Gropius, Manon, was stricken by polio, and her paralyzed body had only a short time to live. "She had the best I had to give," Alma noted, "and she had very much from her father." When the child sensed she would have to die—it was on Easter Monday in 1935—she said to her mother: "Let me die. I'll never get well. . . . You'll get over it, Mummy, as you get over everything—I mean," she corrected herself, "as everyone gets over everything."

They were her last words. Had the child such deep insight into her mother's psyche? Certainly, Manon had her father's gentle disposition. When she died, Alban Berg—who could not realize that the curtain was soon to fall over his own life—interrupted work on his opera *Lulu* in order to write a violin sonata in her memory, a work he called "In Memory of an Angel." Manon was wrong. Alma could never get over the death of her third child, the one she loved most, because Manon was the image of everything she herself was not. Alma sold her house in Venice where she had spent many happy months with Manon. How could she be gay there, or tolerate anyone's laughter? "In every corner I saw Manon, and burst into tears." Since Werfel also felt very close to the child, not a day passed in which he and Alma did not talk about Manon and weep.

Overshadowed by the feeling of something frightful to come, life went on. Werfel's books were among the books burned in Hitler's *Reich*. Alma recalled that in the twenties Hans Pfitzner and Werfel had had fierce arguments about the political situation in Germany. Pfitzner, always weak in debating a point, had finally shouted at Werfel: "Hitler will show you!" But when Hitler began to show the world what National Socialism meant, Pfitzner, one of his earliest followers, renounced Nazism.

There was no way of staying neutral. Richard Strauss bowed and was honored. Arnold Schönberg had already encountered difficulties in the Bauhaus, which became infected by Nazism in the late twenties. He then wrote to Kandinsky:

. . . And you join in that sort of thing and "reject me as a Jew" . . . How can a Kandinsky approve of my being insulted . . . how can he refrain from combating a view of the world whose aim is St. Bartholomew's nights in the darkness of which no one will be able to read the little placard saying that I'm exempt!

And in 1933 he wrote Anton von Webern:

I—though with difficulty and much wavering—have cut my ties with the West. I have resolved to be a Jew. . . .

Alma, having felt like an agnostic since her childhood, returned to Catholicism. "Confession came hard, after so long a time," she noted. Then a few months later: "Franz makes mistakes now. Today he would not let me go to Church! It is the wrong kind of jealousy: there I am not unfaithful to him. Or perhaps precisely there—?"

Dorothy Thompson and Sinclair Lewis came to visit the Werfels. In those early days of Nazism such men as Thomas Mann chose voluntary exile. Max Reinhardt—in spite of being the most celebrated German stage director—lost his two theaters in Berlin and, as a Jew, became an outcast overnight. Erwin Piscator, son of a pastor, had created a new political theater together with Bertolt Brecht. Both had to flee Germany at once. The list of known and unknown names grew from day to day. Those who were not quick enough to escape filled the concentration camps; those who were not lucky enough, the gas chambers. Wotan awoke. Medieval barbarism was applied with German thoroughness.

Reinhardt asked Werfel to write a panoramic play for him, "a kind of St. Matthew's Passion," as he described it, a sequence of biblical scenes from the Old Testament. The play was to be produced in America. Werfel called it *The Eternal Road*, and Kurt Weill wrote the score. For Alma the journey to New York was a repetition of an old story relived with another man under different circumstances. Werfel, whose novel *The Forty Days of Musa Dagh* had been published in America shortly before their arrival, was celebrated by the Armenian colony. But the production of the play ran into financial difficulties. The Werfels left before opening night, which was a great success. They left the New World hastily, tired from sleepless nights, rewrites, rehearsals, and festivities. Gustav Mahler's image must have appeared now and then before Alma while she moved about Manhattan. When she was back in Europe, she could not have imagined how quickly America would see her again, destined as it was to be a coveted haven of refuge.

During the days of Austria's moral capitulation, Alma returned alone to Vienna. There were ominous signs wherever one looked. A huge picture of Adolf Hitler was mounted on the famed Kärntner-strasse in front of the German Tourist Office. When Alma witnessed the Viennese women standing in long lines, then kneeling in front of the Führer's effigy in order to bestow their floral offerings, she knew her beloved Vienna was no longer her Vienna. Wisely she had insisted that Werfel stay in Italy for the time being. She left him in Naples where he had long and enjoyable talks with Benedetto Croce. When she joined Werfel in Capri again, she took with her all the belongings she could save in two suitcases. Austria had become a part of the German *Reich* of a thousand years.

"Exile is a terrible disease," she jotted down.

There are moments in one's life that one cannot fully understand while they are happening. Only later—and often much later—they suddenly return in flashes, as shreds of memory, magnified or even distorted but, nevertheless, projecting past images onto the present in proportion to their significance. Alma tried to convince herself that her own mother, who remained in her house in Vienna, did not really sympathize with the Nazis, but was only a victim of her environment. On the other hand, however, there were the long farewells. Alma knew she would never see her mother again, a mother who did not seem to understand why her only daughter left when Hitler was about to usher in a new era of happiness for everyone. Also there was Gerhart Hauptmann who, a few months before Hitler swallowed Austria, found it more convenient not to be seen with Franz Werfel, the Jew.

Alma and Werfel fled from Italy to Zürich and from there to Paris. They shared the fate of many illustrious refugees. There was a long list with some of the best names of German provenience. Uprooted, the names suddenly had a hollow sound. To be without papers meant to be without rights wherever one was; wherever one went, exposed to the wanton will of a minor clerk. People without a home and country were nowhere desired; they were huddled together in camps, left with a minimum of food and clothes. Or they were chased from city to city, from place to place. There were the bravadoes and the meek: those who in their hopelessness became hardened and ready to risk their lives at any turn of their fate, and those who died so many deaths of fear that one day the slightest gust of apprehension broke their will to go on.

The worst for all of them were the hours, weeks and months of waiting: waiting for a passport, for a visa, for any piece of paper with an official stamp. German and Austrian passports were suspect. Werfel was envied by his friends for having been born in Prague, but it took much skill and luck and persuasion to receive a Czech passport. Inventiveness, circumspection and cunning became the greatest virtues possessed by Werfel's hero Jacobowsky in his tragicomedy *Jacobowsky and the Colonel*.

The Werfels first stayed at the Hotel Royal Madeleine in Paris along with many refugees; their plight inspired the poet to write this play, which later became a world-wide success. Inspiration was bought at the high price of frightful anxieties. When Belgium capitulated in May, 1940, the Werfels wanted to reach the South of France. The trains were overcrowded with people who wanted to escape the advancing German army. The roads were clogged with caravans of cars fleeing south. There were no rooms to be had at any inn, no means of tolerable conveyance. Hitler's army entered Paris more quickly than one could have thought possible. The French army fled southward. Under great duress, with many detours, Alma and Werfel finally reached Bordeaux, went from there to Biarritz and Pau and stopped at Lourdes for some time. The nearest American consul had his seat at Marseilles. Their only hope was to get to Marseilles.

It was not a journey but variations of hell that waited for them at every turn. Wherever they stopped they heard the warning cries: Get away as fast as you can! The Germans are coming! But the getting-away was never easy. When they tried to take a train, it was always the last one, hours late, crammed with luggage, and so crowded with people, sweating out of fear, that they had to stand packed like sardines or sit huddled on some trunks. Wherever they could, they took taxis and paid small fortunes. They spent several nights in a broken-down hospital and one night in a brothel which the girls had left in dread of bombings. Since the refugees had to have permission to move from one city to another, they stood in long lines in front of police stations. The coveted visa to enter the United States was not yet in sight, but rumors thickened that a man would arrive from America to take them with him to the desired haven of freedom. Any such rumor containing only a bit of hope was something to which they could cling with a smile of despair.

Late in June, 1940, they arrived in Lourdes where they found a cell-like room with a single small bed. "After weeks in the same clothes, unable to wash properly, much less to bathe, we buried our vanity and lapsed into general indifference." It was in Lourdes that they became intimately acquainted with the story of Bernadette Soubirous. And it was there that Werfel vowed he would write a story about Saint Bernadette should he ever reach America. It became his most popular book: *The Song of Bernadette.*

At last they reached Marseilles and received their American visas. But their ordeal was not yet over. They had to travel via Spain to

Lisbon. The Spanish and Portuguese visas were not too difficult to obtain, but the French authorities refused to give them an exit visa, even though the Werfels had a Czech passport containing the genuine stamp of an American immigration visa. A quick decision was necessary. There was no other chance for them but to illegally cross the mountain passes separating France from Spain. It was a long and difficult climb. Alma was almost sixty years old.

The newspaper reports circulated in England and America at that time saying that Werfel was shot were of course incorrect. He was, however, on the Nazi list of those to be shot if caught alive. But the Werfels succeeded in reaching Lisbon and the Greek steamer *Nea Hellas* that brought them to New York.

They entered New York harbor on January 3, 1941. Almost three years had passed since they had begun their long journey to freedom. Alma's feelings were ambivalent. She proved to have more stamina, composure and endurance than Werfel and most of the other refugees whose fate she had shared. During the first months of their stay in France Werfel had suffered a heart attack. For weeks Alma was at his bedside day and night, nursing him back to life. The doctor's diagnoses were pessimistic. The ugly specters of fear, of not knowing tomorrow's quirks of fate, were in no way helpful in his condition. The hardships and anxieties during the latter part of their flight had been a severe strain on his heart.

Alma realized that so much more was at stake for him than for her. She was also fully aware of the need to help him and the other refugees. Werfel often broke down and threw himself on the bed, sobbing and crying. He needed the warmth of her hand, her words of encouragement. In such moments of despair she saw to it that her love embraced him and kept him safe.

Whatever help she was able to give, she gave. After all, she had cast her lot with these people, as she expressed it. But she was divided in her feelings. She was with them, yet not wholeheartedly. She often felt offended by the extreme elements among them; she did not always understand or approve of their biting wit with its self-castigating points, their gallows humor. She felt a world apart from them while being with them, chained to their destiny. There was an outward excuse for her hidden contempt: too many of them had communistic or leftist leanings that she despised. Fortunately, she thought, Werfel had altogether forsworn his puerile stance of wanting to overthrow the bourgeois world by force. Alma's influence had strengthened in him his feelings for mysticism and, based on their harrowing and hallowing experiences at Lourdes, he gave articulate expression to the strength and effectiveness of believing in God (whatever God it may be), when he wrote *The Song of Bernadette*. She praised God every day for having won him over to her side: to the side of Catholicism, though he never took holy water.

There was a touch of self-pity in her note: "The whole world is grey and dismal . . . we are homeless . . . not knowing the language of the land, and to be thrown into a most foreign foreignness . . . I'm longing for 'home' . . ." But where was her home? The old Vienna of which she was a part, but which no longer existed? In all this senseless suffering she had experienced and witnessed, she felt more and more drawn to Christ the Saviour. A suspect alien in the Gallic world, she had realized how her Germanic blood rebelled against her environment. To be exiled is a serious disease, she stressed over and over again, and was not aware of how sick her mind was when she expressed Wagnerian thoughts with a dash of Catholic apotheosis in her diary:

Most Jewish melodies begin with a dissonance: A Midsummer Night's Dream—Wedding March—The Tales of Hoffmann—Barcarole, etc. This is because they have not yet experienced their Messiah. Therefore, their finales rise to promises. We begin with a C-Major chord (Prelude to *Die Meistersinger*), show conflicts and end in Christ.

What is most revealing in this note is not only the rejection of everything Jewish and its juxtaposition to the Wagner-Christ image, but mainly the harsh, discrepant tone of "they" and "we." How Alma must have suffered in those days of anxieties from the discord between "belonging" and "being"!

The years that followed in America were somewhat anticlimactic for both Alma and Werfel, even though their reception in the New World was impressive and Werfel's success with *The Song of Bernadette* and his play *Jacobowsky and the Colonel* stupendous. Friends had found a lovely little house for them in Los Angeles, and had provided for everything, even a butler, who stayed with the Werfels for many years. They were immediately surrounded by the cream of the European intelligentsia that gathered in Hollywood and New York—from Thomas Mann and his children to Erich Maria Remarque, from Max Reinhardt to such actors as Ernst Deutsch, Oskar Homolka and Oscar Karlweis (who enacted the little wise Jew in Werfel's play on Broadway). Vicky Baum, Arnold Schönberg, Bruno Frank, Lotte Lehmann, and Werfel's best friend, Friedrich Torberg, and many others helped them reshape the memory of a world and era lost forever. Ludwig Bemelmans added a new touch to their lives.

Werfel's physical condition, however, remained poor and worsened. Too much excitement had to be endured by writing and rewriting the play. He was dissatisfied with the various adaptations: first, for instance, with Clifford Odets's version; later he fell into fits of fury about S. N. Behrman's attempt to turn his lofty ideas into something sentimental. He was especially incensed about Behrman's insistence on omitting an imaginary scene in which Saint Francis of Assisi met with the Eternal Jew. Werfel was still too much of the old German school of playwriting in which the literary aspect reigned supreme and messages had to be underlined. Behrman, on the other hand, knew how to ensure a Broadway success.

Misunderstandings about his theme and intentions in *The Song of Bernadette* had already caused Werfel many difficulties and left him with a feeling of tired resignation. The book was dedicated to Manon's spirit, a dedication with which Werfel wanted to pay homage not only to the memory of this lovely girl, but also to Alma, who had endured much for his sake. She of course accepted this work as a justification for everything it stood for. The Book-of-the-Month Club was at first afraid of Werfel's avowed Catholic tendency in Bernadette's story, but finally published it. They profited handsomely.

Some of the criticism hurt Werfel severely, particularly that coming from his best friends. Thomas Mann said—in a somewhat condescending tone—that he never begrudged Werfel his little flirt with Rome. In his introduction Werfel explained that since his early youth, when he had written his first verses, he had vowed to glorify in all his writings the divine secret and human holiness regardless of our age, which blatantly shuns and derides the ultimate values of life. Also among the friends who chided him for what he had done with the story of Bernadette was Erich von Kahler, who said that Werfel turned a very private vow into a "sensational lead-horse," or Joachim Maass, who called the poet "a genius of piety who had lost his way into literature." Werfel protested in letters: what he had intended to create was the mystery of the final truth and innocence that seemed too difficult for most people to accept. He did not realize—or did not want to have it true—how great Alma's influence on him was, how her return to Christ helped him find his own way.

In the year 1943, when Werfel was fifty-three years old, he suffered several heart attacks. He was still able to finish his last novel, *Star of the Unborn*, a utopian story, a travelogue through tomorrow's time and history, but he did not live to see it published. On August 26, 1945, he died. He was then in his fifty-fifth year.

The last two years of his life in America were a constant struggle with death. Every minute that he was strong enough he felt compelled to write. Alma was extremely worried about him all this time, and in those months she lived only to make life possible for him. "Those months," she wrote, "were a permanent torture. I wept through many days and nights . . ." He often fled Beverly Hills in order to work in the quiet atmosphere of Santa Barbara, but every goodbye and every separation were painful experiences for both.

After his death Alma wrote: "Our life is so provisional that every word seems too stable." The death of the man with whom she was happiest gave her a poet's strength and vision when she wrote these lines. But only a few days later her diary shows how she reverted to sentimentalizing and how becoming her mourning was:

Why am I still alive?
A week ago I lost my sweet man-child, I still can't grasp it. I keep

thinking that he must come home from Santa Barbara. But he will never come home. . . .

She spent her last years in a two-room apartment in New York. One room was dedicated to music, the other to literature, both to her past. A few paintings by Kokoschka, one by Bemelmans (which Werfel had loved), three Viennese landscape paintings by her father, Emil Schindler, and a few photographs held music and literature together. She traveled sometimes, mostly in the summer months, and then, in spite of her age, she still added admiring men to the long list of well-known names. Thus, she tells us, on a return trip from Rome a man approached her and interrupted her reading. "I'm Thornton Wilder," he said, and after a voyage-long conversation they became friends.

She reached the ripe old age of eighty-four years, surrounded by friends and music, by books and memories. She could close her autobiography with the gratifying words: "My life was beautiful. God gave me to know the works of genius in our time before they left the hands of their creators. . . . I believe that any man can well recognize the paths of his destiny, if he is only attentive enough. He is also warned by an inner voice. But he must hear it and be able to listen to it. Every human being can do whatever he wants—but he must also be ready for everything."

In 1942.

In southeastern France
with her companion (left),
Alice B. Toklas, 1944.

Gertrude Stein
A Mind Is A Mind Is A Mind

"What Is the Answer?"

I walked through the Père Lachaise Cemetery where Gertrude Stein lies buried. I had passed some names which are indelibly written into the memory of man: Proust, Balzac and Musset, Chopin, Bizet, Delacroix, Seurat, Modigliani, Sarah Bernhardt, Isadora Duncan, and Oscar Wilde. The names of Molière and La Fontaine appeared on stones more timeworn than others, but there are strong doubts that their bodies were put to rest there. To walk through this cemetery is to brush the face of eternity. Of course, many more are buried there whose names are imprinted on stone, but without weight in the wind of time. In the nineteenth century the Père Lachaise Cemetery was fashionable. To be buried there together with so many great ones was a bourgeois status symbol, or as Victor Hugo expressed it, "To be buried at Père Lachaise is like having mahogany furniture."

Gertrude Stein came from a very bourgeois background. Her father was vice-president of the Omnibus Cable Company in San Francisco, and his family could enjoy any comfort desired, from governesses to extensive travels in Europe. Not as a bourgeois but as a rebel, perhaps an eccentric of literary stature, was she put to rest in Père Lachaise Cemetery. Standing in front of her grave made me re-feel some of the feelings she must have felt—to imitate the way she liked to express herself—while living the writing she wrote and writing the life she had lived. Time fell suddenly apart, was neither sequential nor consequential.

The early decades of the century came to mind: around the World War I era, when man began to enumerate the major stations of his madness; the twenties, roaring, groping, stammering, a time when artists were thrown into paroxysms of "isms"; the thirties, threatening the hope for man's sanity. Through it all I envisioned Paris, 27 rue de Fleurus, the famous Stein salon where the greatest artists of the time were her daily guests, coming to listen to her as often as they came to speak to her; the salon with a collection of precious pictures that almost anyone could come to see if he could only name someone who had recommended him. Since almost all those paintings still had little value on the art market then, Gertrude Stein knew that only those who were interested in the new art would come. I could hear her laugh and say she knew of three geniuses only: Gertrude Stein, Pablo Picasso and Alfred Whitehead; she knew she was unique in contemporary English literature, she had always known it, and after some time she did not mind saying it. I imagined myself taking a piece of paper from my breast pocket, with a poem on it, a poem I had written for Gertrude Stein:

> And yet
> it was a rose to which you had
> to add
> with emphasis
> another other rose to let
> us see
> the rose and what a rose could be.
>
> You stood aloof, you stepped aside
> to have the better better view
> because you knew time would abide,
>
> would you not cling to any tide.
> You were yourself, yourself and true,
> and true to no one else but you,
>
> when others tried all masks to hide.
> How wise a fool had said adieu
> and stepped aside! We said she died . . .

How rare
such roses are such roses where
we share
a world of words—
and do not care how much we err!
A rose
rose to the fragrance of your prose.

Of course, I had no piece of paper in my breast pocket, and if there had been one,. there would have been no poem written on it. But this reminded me of a lecture Gertrude Stein delivered at the University of Chicago. A student asked her about the meaning of "a rose is a rose is a rose." Thornton Wilder quoted her reply in his introduction to her *Four in America* and I am quoting him:

Now listen. Can't you see when the language was new—as it was with Chaucer and Homer—the poet could use the name of a thing and the thing was really there. He could say "O moon," "O sea," "O love," and the moon and the sea and love were really there. And can't you see that after hundreds of years had gone by and thousands of poems had been written, he could call on those words and find that they were just wornout literary words. . . . Now the poet has to work in the excitingness of pure being; he has to get back that intensity into the language . . . we know that you have to put some strangeness, as something unexpected, into the structure of the sentence in order to bring back vitality to the noun. . . . Now you all have seen hundreds of poems about roses and you know in your bones that the rose is not there. . . . Now listen! I'm no fool. I know that in daily life we don't go around saying ". . . is a . . . is a . . . is a . . ." Yes, I'm no fool; but I think that in that line the rose is red for the first time in English poetry for a hundred years.

Reading through her anecdotal sayings—and she remains the richest source of living anecdotes about Gertrude Stein—one realizes that she was hardly ever at a loss to find the most precise answer to any question. She rarely referred to her Jewish heritage, but through one of her characters, Adele, in *Things As They Are*, she said: "I have the failing of my tribe. I believe in the sacred rites of conversation even when it is a monologue." There was something strangely involved about her compulsive attitude toward questions and answers. Even before her training in school, she developed a questioning, probing mind, asking for, demanding answers. Yet it seems she disliked people who asked too many questions. When she found herself surrounded by journalists upon her arrival in New York for her first lecture tour, she perplexed them with the question: "Suppose there were no questions, what would the answer be?" Her answers, however, were always witty and to the point, sometimes shooting beyond it. When one of the journalists asked: "Why don't you write the way you talk?" her masterly repartee was: "Why don't you read the way I write?" She began one of her famous lectures, "What Is English Literature?" with the statement: "One cannot come back too often to the question what is knowledge and to the answer knowledge is what one knows."

Standing in front of her grave, I couldn't help thinking of her well-known last words; today they have already become so threadbare that one can only wish for a new version by her, for something strange and unexpected. "What is the answer?" she asked on her deathbed. Since no one replied, she said: "Then what is the question?"

Gertrude Stein was not fond of the idea that anyone wrote about her and her work. She was sure of herself and of the way she was, and she felt that she explained herself best in her writings and lectures, and that one simply had to listen to what one read. By once saying that even well-meaning people did her work more harm than good by writing about it, she embarrassed anyone writing about her. Surrounding whatever she spoke or wrote was a highly personal and personalized way of seeing the world. If we relate the world in which she breathed and thought to her life and work, the world, as much as Gertrude Stein as a symbol of her time, may come into clearer focus and be more understandable.

The era that gave her spiritual birth was conducive to that spectacular sensitivity of many artists who, in rebelling against and negating their environment, somersaulted into excess and eccentricity. Artistic experimentation in general and linguistic experimentation in particular were rampant. Long in preparation, this trend was a natural reaction to a time that had run itself ragged and had gone beyond its saturation point politically, socially, and culturally.

Pointers reach back to the last mid-century when Baudelaire and Gautier took as a critical starting point the shock of pleasure as an immediate reaction; then, probing their reasoning for it, they turned the shock of pleasure into critical realization. Gautier wrote in one of his feuilletons in 1843 that when painting he "could hear the sound of colors. The green, red, blue, yellow reached me perfectly clear as if coming to me on waves." When Apollinaire later used the word "music" to describe imagery negating all likeness with reality, he paralleled one of Gertrude Stein's basic concepts: rhythm as linguistic expression echoing the rhythm of personality, creating an acoustic image of the printed word.

Rimbaud, godfather to symbolism, not only invented the colors of the vowels ("A black, E white, I red, O blue, U green"), he thought he "was inventing a poetic language accessible . . . to all the senses." Did not Gertrude Stein's creative approach try to bombard all our senses? (Some artists in the sixties practiced her scheme to excess; it is undoubtedly related to the advertising method of the mass media, which finds commercial salvation in the act of repetition.) Her *Tender Buttons* was often called cubist literature and compared to Juan Gris's collages because, like his work, her style lacked apparent cohesiveness and continuity.

For Mallarmé a significant step for the poet was to create a world of allusion leading to many new dreams from dream-transformed words. He said, it is even more significant to transcend the ordinariness of existence and to penetrate "the mysterious world of essences." In trying to achieve "pure poetry" he rejected all conventional reality, the obvious and concrete, any syntactic arrangement, at the risk of avoiding intelligibility. Didn't Mallarmé thus issue the passport for Gertrude Stein's own stylistic freedom?

Antonin Artaud, who went back to myth and magic, decrying any ordinary narrative, best described Paul Klee when he said that Klee searched "for the hidden sense," for "an illumination of visions in the mind." Klee ushered in a deceptive simplicity that was to play a great role in Gertrude Stein's work. Their different personalities and media make them appear to be worlds apart, but in their essentials, their goals and approaches, they are not. Both are playful and philosophic in their way, cryptic and mystical. They are humorous, but while Klee is gently ironic, her laughter is explosive. They were both chided for childishness and even stupidity. True, they went to extremes, but, in our visual world, Klee is far more accessible than Gertrude Stein. She used words as if they had no etymological history, as if never before envisioned in literary contexts; and she used them without any punctuation to indicate the rhythm of their mental breath. In this she had her counterpart in Paul Klee who said: "I want to be as though newborn. . . . Knowing no pictures, entirely without impulses, almost in an original state." In the final analysis, the rhythm of her repetitive word paintings is tiring to the eye—more so than to the ear—whereas the objects of Klee's world fall into order, to paraphrase Artaud; ultimately, of course, both their nonsense makes sense. "I cannot be grasped in the here and now," reads the opening line of Klee's epitaph, which he wrote for himself.

The two major assaults on the use of conventional language came from James Joyce and the dadaists, both differently motivated. Joyce re-invented the stream-of-consciousness technique to perfection and hammered out new images in a multilingual style whose connotative meanings exist on many levels for those who can grasp them. Both Joyce and Stein proved that they could also write easily readable prose. But it is mainly their experimental work, even though limited to a minority of readers, that holds together a thousand dreams in one and reveals the road to the ever-clouded mystery of life.

Dadaism was a collective expression of artistic hostility, negating any aesthetic laws. It was the most aggressive reaction to the twentieth century's trauma. Dada's distorted laughter aimed at total destruction and, at best, withdrew in disgust to an attitude of defiant detachment. This movement started its attacks on a deeply wounded world in the Cabaret Voltaire in Zürich, while similar attempts were simultaneously made in New York. Hugo Ball concocted verses without words and Tristan Tzara wrote poetry by cutting out words, mixing them in a paper bag and at random putting them together and presenting them as a poem.

These extravagant excesses led dada master Kurt Schwitters to go beyond Ball's intentions "to penetrate the alchemy of the word" and to rescue the language from its threadbareness. Schwitters's *Ursonate* began with the line:

Fümms bö wö tää zää Uu. . . .

Schwitters explained himself and the furor of his time best when he wrote: ". . . the whole fraud people call war came to an end. I felt free and had to shout my jubilant feelings into the world. . . . One can also shout with garbage, and that's what I did, glued and nailed refuse together. I called it Merz [so that it can rhyme with *Schmerz* and *Herz*] . . . everything was kaputt, and now we had to rebuild something out of bits and broken pieces . . ."

The general tenor of Schwitters's outcry or the attempts of the surrealist painter Max Ernst were to violate ordinary language in order to give it new meaning. The artists who perceived the oscillations and rumblings of the political, economic and sociocultural events like a seismograph, reacted with a furor of fright to the happenings of their days. The spiritual wrecking of the world was an easy job since it fell apart physically. But weren't these same self-appointed wreckers charged with building a new world? Some intellectual magicians glorified the void, as Jean Cocteau did when he put the banality of reality onstage. Others hallowed their own sleight of hand, like Luigi Pirandello, who taught the world the indistinctness of reality and illusion, of to *be* or to *seem*. Others feared their own visions. Franz Kafka comes to mind, he who nailed the nightmares and obsessions of lostness onto the wall of our consciousness. Probably the greatest magician of them all was Pablo Picasso.

Picasso believed in Gertrude Stein and listened to her advice. Françoise Gilot, one of Picasso's wives, was told by him when she was about to meet Gertrude Stein, "By the way, I think rather highly of her judgment." Respect and understanding were mutual. She pinpointed both their aims when she explained that she and Picasso sought "to express things seen not as one knows them but as they are

when one sees them without remembering having looked at them."
His daimon and dynamism compelled him to explore, to discover and
unravel the unknown. His curiosity and the inner strength to satisfy it
had to lead to writing as another way of painting—painting with
words. During the Nazi occupation of Paris he wrote a play, *Desire
Caught by the Tail*, full of Dadaist crudeness and surrealistic shades
of colorful irony. It is probably closest to Alfred Jarry's *Ubu Roi*, a
play written as a juvenile prank at the end of the last century and
now considered a forerunner to the twentieth-century explosion of
experimental playwriting. *Ubu Roi* influenced Guillaume Apollinaire
to create his surrealistic play, *Tiresias's Breasts*, which, in turn, can
be seen as a link to Picasso's playlet, preceding The Theatre of the
Absurd.

That Picasso's poetry would break all tradition and circumvent the
obvious is to be expected. One day he told Braque that "punctuation
is a *cache-sexe* which hides the private parts of literature." He threw
the traditional rules of punctuation overboard and created monolithic
entities made up of words that can best be described as Picassoesque
images of plastic poetry. André Breton, writing in the *Cahier d'Art*,
expressed with enthusiasm: ". . . it is a poetry that cannot help
being plastic to the same degree that [his] painting is poetic."

Picasso may have thought he wrote good poetry and Breton may
have thought so too, but Gertrude Stein did not and, when she had
seen some of his poems, she was supposed to have said to him:
"Pablo, go home and paint." She worded it in a more Steinian way in
her book, *Everybody's Autobiography*:

You see I said continuing to Pablo you can't stand looking at Jean Cocteau's
drawings, it does something to you, they are more offensive than drawings
that are just bad drawings now that's the way it is with your poetry it is
more offensive than just bad poetry . . . words annoy you more than they do
anything else so how can you write you know better . . . well he said
getting truculent, you yourself always said I was an extraordinary person
well then an extraordinary person can do anything, ah I said catching him
by the lapels of his coat and shaking him, you are extraordinary within your
limits . . . you know it as well as I know it, it is all right you are doing this to
get rid of everything that has been too much for you all right all right go on

doing it but don't go on trying to make me tell you it is poetry and I shook him again, well he said supposing I do know it, what will I do, what will you do said I and I kissed him, you will go on until you are more cheerful or less dismal and then you will, yes he said, and then you will paint a very beautiful picture and then more of them, and I kissed him again, yes said he.

"I Liked Thinking . . . I Liked Looking . . . and Talking and Listening"

Gertrude Stein was born in Allegheny, Pennsylvania, now a part of Pittsburgh, on February 3, 1874. All her life she resented the fact that she and her brother Leo were afterthoughts. Her parents had decided to have five children, and only because two previous Stein children had died were Leo and then Gertrude conceived. They felt "funny" about it, she said.

She had all the advantages and disadvantages of being the youngest child, being cared for by everyone and knowing no daily duties or responsibilities since there always were servants, a governess and a tutor. Because of a quarrel with his relatives, her father moved to Vienna with his family when Gertrude was a year old. The family traveled a great deal during her first seven years, from Vienna to France and from there to Oakland, California.

Against a rather well-to-do background, the family's life was clearly defined by the character of her parents. Her mother, whom Gertrude lost when she was fourteen, was a pale figure. Mothers rarely appear in her works. When they do, they always play ineffectual parts and are rather unhappy creatures in contrast to the domineering male. The father type, often characterized by her in her fiction, is of a strong temper, willful, impatient, a dreamer of fantastic projects, restlessly moving from one plan to another, from one place to another, cold and calculating, an authoritarian who needs to be loved without really being able to return love or warmth. The children often had to submit to the father's tyrannical mood, so that

Gertrude came to the conclusion that "fathers are depressing." But there can be no doubt that her entire makeup was much closer to her father's than to her mother's. The only person in the family to whom she was very close was her brother Leo, who played a great part in her early life, particularly after her father's death, when she was seventeen, three years after her mother had died of cancer.

The outward security in which Gertrude grew up gave her the freedom of indulging herself in whatever pleased her. She openly rebelled against her father as an image of meretricious authority. On the other hand, the two youngest children "loved the freedom . . . that their father had in his queer way won for them." The way she treated the father figure in her writings indicates that, as a child growing into adolescence, he played a most important role in her imagination.

Whereas Lou Salomé could openly indulge in her father-fixation and grow beyond it, whereas Alma Mahler attached herself to older men in order to find the lost father in her lovers, Gertrude Stein seems to have suppressed her Electra complex altogether. Working herself out of the debris of frustrated feelings, she found herself deviated into channels where she could live with the authoritarian father figure in herself and find gratification in defiance of the established order of things. In her days of early womanhood, male aggressiveness occupied her mind—not the secret longing for deliverance by a princely creature.

How real her imagination was for her is indicated by two incidents that may have been partly imaginary, partly imagined reality of such intensity that they became living images for her. In the hardly veiled autobiographical writing, *The Making of Americans*, picturing the life of her family, Gertrude portrayed herself as Martha Hersland. An umbrella figures in a decisive way, and its symbolism is obvious. Furious about having been abandoned by the older children, she threatens to throw her umbrella into the mud, and finally does. The wicked things one is not supposed to do loom over Martha Hersland's early experiences: when encouraged by a little boy to do "things they should not be doing," nothing happens because of her awkward attitude, passivity, fear and uncertainty of what was being asked of her. Later on, there is the frank admission that she "was then not really very interesting to anyone" because of her innocence, lack of comprehension and physical plainness.

The other umbrella story is of greater psychological meaning and occurs when Martha-Gertrude begins a new life with her college career. On her way to a singing lesson, she witnesses a street scene in which a man strikes a woman with an umbrella. The woman whose face was red "partly in anger and partly in asking" undoubtedly wanted to be with the man—she may have been his wife or a prostitute accosting him—while the man hitting her with his umbrella rejected her and wanted "her to leave him alone."

It was a decisive moment in the girl's life. On a mental level, this incident created in her the desire to study the psyche of the animal in man; she wanted to know more about the motivations, reactions and hidden passions of people (". . . She would go to college, she knew it then and understand everything and know the meaning of the living and the feeling in men and in women . . .") On a more physical level, it revolted her and brought her close to the realization of feminist sentiments. It was a pivotal point in her life: there was always in front of her mind the umbrella threatening her.

Gertrude needed a father substitute. It was not her oldest brother Michael who, after the father's death, took over the role as breadwinner for the family and signed the checks to guarantee their carefree existence. It was Leo. What Leo did, she did. She followed him to Harvard and later to Johns Hopkins, and when Leo, possessed by his father's restlessness, eventually gave up his studies to travel in Europe, Gertrude went with him.

In college she was not what one could call a good student, being completely oblivious to any duties and routine work. She preserved a natural freedom often so daring that the positive outcome was most surprising to herself as well as to others. It mostly infuriated Leo that she could get away with everything.

At Radcliffe College, her great experience was the "Psychological Seminary," listed as Philosophy 20B, and taught by William James. During the winter semester she did very well, receiving an A, but her interest flagged in the spring. Was it the study of consciousness, knowledge, and the relation of the mind to the body? Was it spring fever, her inherited impatience, her growing interest in the opera, or was it all of them together? The sad result was a C on her term paper.

In telling her story in *The Autobiography of Alice B. Toklas* she masked the incident with the poetic license of "Poetry and Truth": she tells about "having been otherwise engrossed" during the final examination period and when she appeared for the philosophy test, writing at the top of her paper: "Dear Professor James, I am so sorry but really I do not feel a bit like an examination paper in philosophy to-day." With that, the story goes, she left. The next day she had a post card from William James saying, "Dear Miss Stein, I understand perfectly how you feel. I often feel like that myself." And underneath it he gave her work the highest mark in the course.

During all the years of her growing up she was an avid reader, and in college she learned to enjoy debating whatever issues she found interesting (". . . argument is to me as the air I breathe . . ."). William James's influence on her was tremendous. Leo was very fond of him, but Gertrude developed a hero-worship for him, something rather rare with her, even though she was given to enthusiasm all her life when she became convinced that an object or subject deserved the intensity of her feelings. In one of her college papers she paid tribute and homage to the man whose ideas furnished her with the fundamental concepts for her career as a writer. She began her paper: "Is life worth living? Yes, a thousand times yes when the world holds such spirits as Prof. James."

Together with her schoolmate Leon Solomons she worked in the Psychological Laboratory. She considered him "an intimate friend" who had "left a definite mark on her life," as she wrote in both of her autobiographies. They conducted experiments in automatic responses of human beings. In one of her American lectures she told her audience about those days in which she

became more interested in psychology, and one of the things I did was testing reactions of the average college student in a state of normal activity and in a state of fatigue induced by their examinations. I was supposed to be interested in their reactions but soon I found that I was not but instead that I was enormously interested in the types of characters. . . .

In the course of her study she came to accept the concept of characterology, the classification of all persons according to psychological types whose basic characteristics do not essentially vary. Her psychological studies decisively influenced the writer in her. She was often chided by her co-workers, by her brother and her teachers for her sloppy English. Only William Vaughn Moody, professor of English at Radcliffe, saw beyond her somewhat strange, tortured and often puzzling way of expressing herself a very personal point of view that seemed to him distinguished by a touch of humor and "considerable emotional intensity." Though he often criticized her stories and made her rewrite them, she nevertheless felt encouraged by him. In those college days her exuberance compelled her to sputter and spill her thoughts onto the pages without any restraint and form.

William James's psychological ideas found their reflection in her approach to the shaping of characters and, in consequence, to an unorthodox and willful stylistic concept. All this crystallized slowly, although it seems today that her very beginnings would have left no other way open to her. She recognized a central core in a personality, a fixed nature determined by heredity and subject to change by very specific personal experiences within the limitations set by the essential character structure. It was what she referred to as "the bottom nature" in each person.

Gertrude Stein, who grew up in the nineteenth century, carried on its psychological concepts, believing in characterology as a science in whose framework one can classify all human beings. The human being seen as a type is essentially constant and predictable in his reactions. He is there as a psychological totality at any given moment and he appears as if unencumbered by the remembrance of things past. Thus the human being existed for Gertrude Stein within the contours of his typical qualities, not within the context of his past experiences, nor projecting inner growth into the future. Without the sequence of events in time, living in a continuous present, the past-present-future must of necessity pile up into growing layers of sameness. The colors of otherness are inherent in simplified repetitions. In her *Selected Writings* she tries to explain her approach:

In beginning writing I wrote a book called *Three Lives* this was written in 1905. I wrote a Negro story called *Melanctha*. In that there was a constant recurring and beginning there was a marked direction in the direction of being in the present although naturally I had been accustomed to past present and future, and why, because the composition formation around me was a prolonged present.

The most likely parallel to the results she finally achieved can be found in cubism, and it is therefore no wonder that, early in this century, she was one of the first persons to take wholeheartedly to the new attempts of Picasso, Braque and Juan Gris, finding a kindred spirit in their daring. In her writing as much as in their paintings the power of the inner Gestalt of an individual knew no expected order to re-create the totality from parts, relived, re-experienced.

The Making of Americans, Gertrude Stein's Forsyte Saga on an American family over several generations, the history of her own family, is the most important book she wrote and the one that best exemplifies her style. It erases any logical sequence of time and place. Events happen, nevertheless, and the fate of each family member is chronicled from birth to death. No attempt is made, however, to weigh the detail and to arrive at a coherent conclusion at the end. A thousand pages and a half million words make up a huge canvas of repetitive verbosity, yet it is a remarkable achievement, an epitome of the commonplace and banal.

Through the growth of a family, it attempts to re-create an American consciousness:

Sometime there is a history of each one, of everyone who ever has living in them and repeating in them and has there being coming out from them in their repeating that is always in all being. Sometime there is a history of everyone.

"In *The Making of Americans*," she said, "I began to do that one can make diagrams and describe every individual man and woman who ever was or is or will be living." Anyone can be typecast in the two principal groups of the "independent dependent kind" and the "dependent independent kind," as she found out. The monotony in the repetitions with their infinite patterns characterizing types for which "the actual words they said or the thoughts they had" were of less importance than "the movement of their thoughts, endlessly the same and endlessly different," led to a huge canvas finally frightening the ear and tiring the eye. This was why Edmund Wilson could say in *Axel's Castle*: "I confess that I have not read the book all through and I do not know whether it is possible to do so."

Gertrude Stein was fooling neither herself nor any potential reader. She wrote for herself and the stranger and was convinced that her struggle to shape a literary happening the way she saw it was artistically valid.

While still at Radcliffe doing her experiments with Leon Solomons she "came to feel that I could come sometime to describe every kind there is of men and women and the bottom nature of them and the way it was mixed up with the other natures in them, I kept notes of each one of them and watched the difference between being active and being tired, the way it made some go faster and some go slower." All those early experiments that originally were planned to probe the automatic writing of people in different situations sidetracked her into finding out more about the "bottom nature" of people which, in turn, led to her approach and use of creative language. She envisioned language as a reflection of life-as-a-continuous-happening, and believed in the necessity of writing "to go on." At one of her American lectures she linked such a language, constantly on the move, to the technique of the motion picture:

Funnily enough the cinema has offered a solution of this thing. By a continuously moving picture of any one there is no memory of any other thing and there is that thing existing. . . .

From her college days Gertrude Stein trained herself to listen to the rhythm of people's speech patterns, and doing so with a kind of absorbed inattentiveness she heard things differently and yet more acutely. If nothing else, she knew "how everybody said the same thing over and over with infinite variations."

After four years at Radcliffe College Gertrude matriculated at Johns Hopkins University School of Medicine in 1897. At that time the general consensus was that it was not ladylike to take up the study of medicine. But Gertrude enjoyed her first two years of medical study very much, particularly because it involved a great deal of laboratory work. But "the practice and theory" courses of the last two years bored her, and out of sheer inertia she continued to go on with it, but her grades were very poor and she finally failed to take her medical degree.

Whether the professor of obstetrics was to be blamed for it or not is difficult to say. But he did not see eye to eye with her, and she had great distaste for delivering babies. That she gave up was a matter of concern to the women who, at that time, had to raise money to make female education possible and for whom her defection was a black spot on their record in the struggle for woman's emancipation. To all their reproaches Gertrude would only say that they did not know what it meant to be bored.

When she started her medical studies Gertrude had delivered a lecture for a group of Baltimore suffragettes about the need for a college education for women. A woman, she contended, should not sell herself into matrimony. Education and the ability to be man's equal in her function in society is necessary to realign and purify her sexual drives. To work beside the male "does not tend to unsex but to rightly sex women," and she must always envision herself as "an individual first and a member of a sex only when the time of functional usefulness begins." In this speech Gertrude Stein hardly said much that was new then or today in the woman's struggle to be man's equal. But these questions were much on her mind at that time and when she raised her voice in favor of a sexually independent woman, she spoke for herself and with the conviction of her own needs.

Just as Gertrude had gone to Johns Hopkins University because Leo had taken up his studies there, she also followed him on his European tours during the summers. There she became acquainted with the young art historian Bernard Berenson and the British philosopher Bertrand Russell. In Berenson's elegant home they came closer to understanding some of the painters, and it was Berenson who called their attention to Paul Cézanne, some of whose paintings

they later found and bought at a dealer's shop on rue Lafitte in Paris.
The dealer's name was Ambroise Vollard, and he was the only person
who handled Cézanne's work in those days. To understand modern
art, they would have to learn to love Cézanne, they were told. His
paintings were to exert a great influence on Gertrude. She was very
grateful to Berenson for making her seek and find this painter,
making her seek and find herself. She was then less impressed by
Bertrand Russell, although Leo was ready to admire the great mind
of the British philosopher. Gertrude was also emotionally preoccupied that summer and preferred to spend most of her time in the
British Museum where she devoured volume after volume.

Gertrude's grades during the last two years of her medical studies
were probably so poor because she was emotionally absorbed and
frustrated by a passionate romance with a Baltimore friend, May
Bookstaver. Gertrude wrote a novel about this unhappy affair which
she called *Q.E.D.*, but which, after her death, her editor and most
devoted friend, Carl Van Vechten, entitled *Things As They Are*. This
novel was almost unknown during her lifetime. In 1903 when it was
written, its subject—three young women in an insoluble love
situation—was everything but acceptable.

It was a most harassing experience for Gertrude Stein and quite
decisive for her future. When everything seemed to have been lost
and over, Gertrude traveled once more from Paris to New York in the
hope of a reconciliation between May and herself. Had she been
successful, she might not have stayed with her brother at 27 rue de
Fleurus in Paris, but would have tried to be near her love somewhere
in the United States.

May had an intimate relationship with Mabel Haynes, whose
protective hand held May ensnared. Mabel took her on trips
wherever she went and paid the bills. It seems that, in the beginning,
May was playing with Gertrude and enjoyed teasing her about her
clumsiness and ignorance while Gertrude, under May's spell, could
only think of a submissive answer: "I could undertake to be an
efficient pupil if it were possible to find an efficient teacher." But all
May did was to laugh in Gertrude's face. She, in turn, never forgot
how it felt to have been so humiliated for showing and admitting her

innocence. Gertrude was unaware of the subtle gestures in the play of love, but since her senses and passion were aroused, she plunged into knowing more and all about it.

To her great dismay Gertrude found out that May was passionate, but not emotional or tenderhearted. If May wanted to have a thing, she would go all out for it until she got it. For Gertrude the thing itself meant less than to understand it. She went through severe struggles with May and with herself. She found it difficult to reconcile the two different persons May was; one she could not help adoring, the other she watched with revulsion. Gertrude went through months of deep depressions while in London and separated from May; then, when they were together again and Gertrude had learned enough so that no difference in experience separated them, she realized that their varying "rhythms" and the differences in their "bottom natures" continuously stood in their way.

Gertrude went to Paris in 1903. Months of despair, melancholy, sluggishness and inability to work followed this unhappy experience. To make her forget May, Leo took her on a trip to Rome where, unfortunately, she ran into May and Mabel. Again Gertrude could not stay away from May, and their frequent meetings only threw both into a state of gloom. Gertrude admitted to having become "sad with longing and sick with desire." The impasse from which she could not extricate herself so easily left her a sad and cynical person for some time. When she wrote *Q.E.D.*, she not only freed herself from the painfulness of the emotional trial she had undergone, but did it without self-pity. In fact, she exposed her own self-deception in this confessional work with objectivity and a touch of irony. In the beginning she unmasked herself as "a hopeless coward" who is afraid of hurting herself or anyone else.

At that point in her life, Gertrude Stein adhered to the middle-class point of view: all normalcy and safety. She was not yet quite ready to sin and fall. "All I want to do is to meditate endlessly and think and talk." And yet when she took up the challenge and became involved in this affair, she remained an analytic observer and recorder of her own feelings. She re-created her own suffering in the novel while accepting it. The novelistic version is closely linked to the poetry of the experienced truth because Gertrude Stein based her story on the letters written by and to her. How strong Gertrude's passion was can be easily deduced from the fact that Alice B. Toklas—the only other woman of great importance in Gertrude's life—admitted, or boasted, that she destroyed these letters "in a passion" in 1932.

Leo Out, Alice In

"My brother and myself had always been together," she stated over and over in many of her writings. As the two last-born children and much younger than the other siblings (also much brighter and with far-reaching interests in the arts), Leo and Gertrude shared many points of identification. As the youngest, she had acquired the habit of looking up to him in her early childhood. She needed a series of jolts and the gradual awakening to a full realization of herself to wean herself away from him. As her older brother, Leo took it upon himself to exert his influence as a God-given power.

Undoubtedly, he was a bright young man handicapped by not enough daring in the mental grasp of his intellectual pursuits. By the same token, he was given to self-glorification that would have been less unpleasant had he been able to hide it behind a certain amount of charm. But his self-centered attitude often made him brutally articulate about what he thought. Leo strongly believed in the blessings of selective nutrition, beautiful women and lucid thinking, and on all three counts Gertrude had difficulties in coming close to his idealizations.

Even as an adult Gertrude admitted that "the tie to my brother is one of the strongest," but she had always realized that he was oblivious to his own shortcomings and that, in his opinionated attitudes, his mind remained inflexible. In the days when they had long arguments about almost anything, he always believed in what he said, and gradually she began to find it rather uninteresting. Gertrude never denied his share of brilliance, but Leo was a good example of the truism that character can easily defeat genius. His compulsive preoccupation with himself led to her remark in *The Making of Americans* that "Some love themselves so much immortality can have no meaning for them."

When they discovered Cézanne together in 1904, Leo became very articulate in his enthusiasm. He felt that Cézanne always showed "this remorseless intensity, this endless, unending, gripping of the form, the unceasing of the effort to force it to reveal its absolute self-existing quality of mass." Cézanne impressed him with his nonrepresentational visualizations and his "non-dramatic" approach. Of the painters he and his sister were interested in at that early period when they first started to buy paintings, of Renoir, Monet, Degas and especially Cézanne, he said: "When figures are composed in a group their relations are merely spatial. At most they are relations of movement concurrent or opposite."

The two books Leo authored, *Journey Into Self* and *Appreciation: Painting, Poetry and Prose*, show him as an astute connoisseur of twentieth-century art, as a theorist who recognized the daring of the new but would be frightened by extreme experiments caused by such daring. When it came to Picasso's cubist revolution, Leo recoiled and played the role of the conservative aesthete. André Gide's remark may have been correct that Leo Stein only liked an artist's work "because it can be grasped without effort."

In those early Parisian years Leo dominated the conversation during their regular Saturday-night parties at 27 rue de Fleurus. He was a brilliant *causeur*, convincing in his confident way of presenting his ideas. A touch of self-adulation was in the hardly veiled arrogance of his monologues. He spoke better than he wrote, as is often the case with splendid speakers and inspiring conversationalists. About Leo's soirees Gertrude said: "Now first he had no enemies and no one thought but he could." She played the silent listener with the many of his guests.

When Leo sat down to write, his brilliance lost its brightness. The same happened to his attempts at painting. The things he visualized never took shape as artistically valid statements. His aggressiveness grew with his frustration and neurotic symptoms. He intellectualized what he expected from somebody's creativity, insinuating what and how he would create if he only could. In his *Appreciation* he finally conceded that "the same neurosis that kept me from painting kept me from writing also."

In the years in which Leo's sense of superiority over everyone, above all Gertrude, fought a vain struggle with his thwarted creative impulses, Gertrude was continuously writing and trying to find a very personal way of expressing herself. She never received any encouragement from her brother—on the contrary, scorn and rejection for whatever she did. In the beginning her dependence on her brother was evident in all her reactions, but with the years he changed into a stern father figure from which she had to liberate herself.

In a hundred and forty-two pages entitled, *Two: Gertrude Stein and Her Brother*, we find an apotheosis of Steinian verbose eccentricity. Based on a monotonous variety of sound her relationship to and conflict with her brother is dramatically elucidated. In and between the lines she makes the reader sense her struggle to draw away from him who finally disappears in clouds of self-centeredness. Also her growing feelings for Alice can be perceived, culminating in the triumphant assertion that "There were two, she and she was there . . ." Gertrude and Leo developed into two different and contrasting worlds. Gertrude could sense her process of becoming:

She in discovering was feeling that discovering being existing and discovering having meaning, she was expressing that she was telling what was meaning.

She could also see Leo fade away with noisy gestures in his delusions of grandeur:

Sound had been coming out of him. He had been understanding anything. He had been understanding everything. Sound had been coming out of him.

Her own belief in herself began to grow, and soon her brother's overbearance was matched by her conviction that she was unique as a writer and, what is more, that real genius was in her. "It takes a lot of time to be a genius," she said, "you have to sit around so much doing nothing, really doing nothing." The idea of what a genius is had always been on her mind, and this question appears and reappears in her two autobiographies. So we read at the beginning of the third chapter in *Everybody's Autobiography*: "What is a genius. Picasso and I used to talk about that a lot." And it is very doubtful that these two geniuses—if we are willing to grant Gertrude Stein this epithet with the same conviction with which she arrogated it to herself— came to any definition. Since Gertrude thought that genius does not make you more different from yourself inside than it makes anyone else who is not a genius, "so what is it that makes you a genius" after all, she asked without a question mark. Without any question mark she was sure of her own genius, and she seemed to have been on the right track when she realized that you might be a genius even if "you have stopped writing."

She may not have told Leo that she thought she had genius; he must have recognized what she did not spell out for him. At a certain point when her work began to absorb and gratify her, she gave herself away by stopping all arguments with him, her action not caused by his growing inability to hear well. What she had to say she felt she said in her writings. Leo detested what she wrote and the way she wrote it. He said: "Gertrude was in her pre-'cubist' days a barbarian in her use of language." He was convinced that she "never could use words with precision and force," and he concluded that she was "basically stupid."

That he was hard of hearing was to her more than a physical manifestation. It was symbolic of his being hard of hearing psycho- logically. An unconscious competitive struggle between the two grew from month to month and from year to year after they had set up their studio in Paris, until their first serious break occurred in 1911 followed by their final parting in 1914. Gertrude admitted that she could no longer take his egocentric, condescending attitude, and he felt the sting of her silent superiority, of her being different and so very different from the expected that he bowed out when Alice B. Toklas finally moved into Gertrude's life as a fixture. He developed a dislike for Picasso and the experimental cubist trend the more Gertrude became friends with Picasso and involved with the movement of the young painters. In 1913 Leo took a greater interest in Nina Auzias, a woman he had befriended three years previously, and to whom he slowly moved toward marrying. These reasons helped toward his separation from his sister, whose writings, moreover, were very much in the news in that year since her name was strongly tied to the famed Armory Show in New York and cubist painting. In his *Journey Into Self* Leo wrote on February 7, 1913: "One of the greatest changes that has become decisive in recent times is the fairly definite 'disaggregations' of Gertrude and myself." He went to Italy, while she stayed in Paris at the rue de Fleurus, their salon, which by then had become known as the "museum of modern art" in Paris.

In *Everybody's Autobiography* she commented on his departure from her life in characteristically Steinian articulation: "It is funny this thing of being a genius, there is no reason for it, there is no reason that it should be you . . ." She realized that Leo could have been a genius as well, but wasn't, and that he resented the genius in her as he had resented how easily things came her way during their college days when he had had to work so hard for everything he got. She mused about why he was so different from her or she from him: ". . . that is he was that and had always been and I had not been that but I had been it enough to be following, now why should it come to be that it should be something else now just why should it." She could only think of one basic reason leading to their separation: ". . . it was I who was the genius, there was no reason for it but I was, and he was not there was a reason for it but he was not and that was the beginning of the ending and we always had been together and now we were never at all together. Little by little we never met again."

In his own recollections Leo minimized their quarrels and thought they "simply differed and went [their] own ways." But in *Two* she pictured their isolation and inability to communicate: "They were not differing as they were not hearing . . ." Many years later her brother made several conciliatory overtures which Gertrude ignored. He did not realize how serious she was about her writings; in them she had done away with him for good. Leo always thought that a small clique of friends idealized her and praised her work to please her. In *Everybody's Autobiography* she referred to it by saying: "And it did not trouble me and as it did not trouble me I knew it was not true . . ." Beyond and despite her conditioned reiterations, it did trouble her a great deal because she concluded in her illogical logic: "But it destroyed him for me and it destroyed me for him."

Leo played such a significant role in her conscious and unconscious life that she had to kill him vicariously several times. She was about to finish *The Making of Americans* in those decisive years. Besides trying to make a bid for world-wide recognition as a woman of letters—an effort in which she succeeded despite the book's length and unevenness—she managed to free herself from Leo by killing his fictional stand-in and by finally exorcising her father's image. Their menace must have been very real in an unreal way to her, and she had to do everything to liberate herself from their almost demonic influence. It was of the greatest importance that at this point Alice B. Toklas entered her life, having offered her services to copy the novel. She had first to learn typewriting. She had first to learn to understand Gertrude Stein who, at Alice's first visit, was furious that she had to wait for her. She appeared to a frightened Alice like "a vengeful goddess" as she opened the door, paced the room for some time and then stopped short in front of her visitor, who had sent an apologetic message ahead warning Gertrude she would be somewhat delayed. She said: "Now you understand. It is over. It is not too late for a walk. You can look at the pictures while I change my clothes." Gertrude had then seen Alice for the second time in her life. Was Gertrude unwittingly furious about Alice coming so late into her life?

In *The Autobiography of Alice B. Toklas* she suppressed Leo as best she could. Unable to wipe out his image or her memory of him, she did the next best thing: she did not mention him by name, referring to him as "her brother" only. Nameless, he was a shadow, something affixed to her past life that cannot be denied from an historic viewpoint, but which she felt compelled to reduce to a by-product—"existing since it existed," she might have said.

Leo and Gertrude had shared their Parisian years between 1903 and 1907; for both it was an exciting period in which they discovered modern art, educating themselves for it through their gradual appreciation of Cézanne. Through many winter months they had gone to Vollard's gallery to look at paintings, but mainly at Cézanne's works, until they had finally bought one of his bigger canvases, the portrait of a woman.

Leo was more impressed by the portrait of a man, but then had given in to his sister's wish. There can be no doubt about the relevance of the sex in her choice. She must have been strongly attached to this portrait since it played a great part in her life as a writer and helped her not only to understand herself and her ideas better, it also opened her eyes to the essential laws and needs of twentieth-century artistic expression. "In looking and looking at this picture" she gained the strength to write her book, *Three Lives.*

But to give the historical devil his due, it must be said that Leo's enthusiasm for Flaubert made her read and translate Flaubert's *Three Fables.* Mystery was hidden behind a superficial simplicity of the characters whose spatial and temporal limitations asked the reader to find their psychological intricacies. Flaubert's realism impressed Gertrude, and his attempts to establish high aesthetic principles for his craft inspired her to find her own expressiveness in the groping of her time for new aesthetic rules.

It is difficult to say how much she was influenced by Flaubert beyond being confirmed in her feeling that she was on the right track. In looking at Cézanne she learned that the traditional form of composition around a central idea had to be abandoned, that all elements were of equal importance deserving the artist's attention as much as any focal point. She was so impressed by this concept that she began to see her own ideas more clearly. She sat down to write *Three Lives.* In her portrait of Cézanne she gave us to understand that it was his example that gave her the final impetus: "I began my writing."

Her attitude toward modern art crystallized in those days. Later, during her lecture tours in America, she was very articulate about her self-education and discovery of modern art. Telling her listeners that she learned to look out of museum windows for no other reason than to make her impressions more complete, she meant to say that she had to confront and enlarge the representational world in oil with the world of reality outside. That she liked to lie down on the benches of the museums in order "to sleep and dream in front of oil paintings" insinuates that the old world of painting made her fall asleep and extend their representations into a world of more abstract or surrealistic imagery. What she felt about modern art was a very subjective response: "I like to look at it." In her eyes, a work of art was a work of art since "it has achieved an existence in and for itself"; for it to hold one's attention, what really mattered was how much vitality it had. She accepted vitality and not clarity as a decisive criterion. What was clarity to her since "nobody listens and nobody knows what you mean no matter what you mean . . ." It echoes her concept that "a rose is a rose is a rose" is able to give new meaning and vitality to a cliché-worn image.

After the Cézanne painting the Steins had acquired Matisse's *La Femme au Chapeau*, which they had seen in the first exhibition at the Salon d'Automne where the rebels and experimental painters showed their independence. This was in the fall of 1905. Gertrude had needed some time to feel at home with Cézanne, but she immediately felt that the Matisse was "perfectly natural," even though the people made fun of its strange colors and the even stranger anatomy of the depicted woman. Gertrude could not understand what infuriated the people about it, as little as she could later understand why people were indignant about her prose since it seemed so natural to her.

Matisse was then virtually an unknown painter and suffered from being the target of people's derision. The purchase of this painting rescued him from his financial miseries and pushed him into the foreground of interest. It also liberated him from deep depressions which, to a great extent, were caused by his struggle for recognition. The Steins and Matisses became friends. Matisse and his wife came to the Saturday soirees at the Stein salon, and Leo and Gertrude were often luncheon guests at the Matisse house, now that he could afford to invite people. Derain was one of the regular guests with Matisse. Gertrude had not taken to his way of painting, nor had she liked his philosophy of life, which, like his paintings, she found lacking in depth, vitality and validity. The very first time she had met Derain, she had become involved in a heated debate with him, and this was the beginning of the end. Although she saw a great deal of Matisse and learned through his work—and later even more so through Picasso's work—that ugliness is a subjective condition and inherent in everything new and original, which is one of the essential principles of twentieth-century art—her friendship with Matisse did not last or deepen at any time. Despite her initial enthusiasm she soon came to realize that, although Matisse was a part of the great innovating forces of the era, he had neither Cézanne's greatness nor Picasso's genius. The final break occurred because Matisse became "irritated by the growing friendship between Picasso and Gertrude Stein."

It was in November, 1905, a few weeks after they had bought the Matisse painting, that "her brother" visited the gallery of Clovis Sagot in the rue Lafitte by chance. There he saw the work of two Spaniards, one now forgotten, the other one celebrated as one of the unique geniuses of this century. The Steins bought a watercolor from the former and a painting from the latter for 150 francs. It was Picasso's *Young Girl With a Basket of Flowers*.

Leo Stein was strongly drawn to the painting while Gertrude, when she first saw it, was rather appalled, repelled and shocked, to use her own verbs. She did not want to have the picture in the house, but finally gave in, realizing how fond her brother was of it.

Picasso and Gertrude met, and if ever any meeting of two minds had meaning, this one seems to have had great significance. Not only did the minds of two strongly profiled personalities discover one another, it was also the meeting of two dynamic forces that moved independently of each other in the same direction within their different media about the same time. Both had gone through a decisive phase of inner reorientation, both tried to overcome a dead point. She was about to finish *Three Lives* and to continue to work on *The Making of Americans* and, as she said in *The Autobiography of Alice B. Toklas*, to struggle with her sentences, those long sentences, which had to be built exactly. Sentences, not only words, were her passion. Picasso had outgrown his blue and pink periods; the painting

Leo Stein had bought was a product of the pink or Harlequin period.

Her accounts about their meeting vary and are very feeble. In her monograph on Picasso she mentions that she met Picasso at the art dealer Sagot's; in her autobiography it was a young man, a faithful nonentity, who knew everyone who was somebody in Paris and who often saw the Steins and introduced Leo to Picasso. She consciously tries to keep the beginning of their acquaintanceship in darkness. In a most casual way she reiterates that neither she nor Picasso could later remember what had happened between his first visit at the rue de Fleurus and the day when she came to his studio at the rue de Ravignan to sit for his painting. She underlined that "in between is an empty spot."

But there is one reference to their first dinner, when Gertrude sat next to this dark, lively man who had very big eyes. She reached out for a piece of bread; he vehemently took it away from her saying that it was *his* bread. She laughed, and he seemed embarrassed. This, as she explains, was the beginning of their affection for one another, and she assures us that they understood each other from the very first moment. We are left in doubt, however, about how Picasso came to paint Gertrude's portrait and how Gertrude came to permit him to do so. She had never thought of having a portrait done, and he had never had anyone pose for him. Since she had to sit for her portrait eighty or ninety times, we understand her remark that a great many things happened in that time. The one thing that was certainly happening was the realization of a lifelong friendship between her and Picasso.

Alice B. Toklas entered Gertrude's life in 1907. By then Gertrude's friendship with Picasso was established. Alice, meeting the Steins, was at the same time meeting the community of painters who fundamentally changed modern man's understanding of art as well as himself. In the beginning Alice was a bit bewildered. When she first saw the Stein atelier, Alice exclaimed in Gertrude's *The Autobiography of Alice B. Toklas*: "Now I was confused and I looked and I looked and I was confused." And when Alice was introduced to the

Saturday-night gatherings, she could only wonder that "there could be so many kinds of men making and looking at pictures."

Alice and Gertrude, who was her senior by three years, had many things in common. Alice came from a similar background, was born and raised in San Francisco and had stayed in Europe as a child. She was no prettier, in the ordinary sense of the word, than Gertrude. Alice had much black hair framing a somewhat Mediterranean and sensuous face. She was a well-bred, intelligent woman who had enjoyed the blessings of the usual education found necessary and fitting for a young lady of her background in those days. She learned to play the piano, attended the university, even though for one year only, was well-read and knew a great deal about housekeeping, which she practiced for her widowed father and later for Gertrude Stein.

She could impress people with her aristocratic flair and grande-dame façade, but she could also behave unconventionally; at times she delighted in being mischievous. It was as if Alice had come out of the world of Henry James, for whom she had great admiration and an especially kindred feeling. Thus, she entered the European scene like one of Henry James's American heroines, wide-eyed and strong-willed, ready to walk with disarming innocence through a depraved and corrupt society. What Alice really found was a life that had the touch of a day-by-day *vernissage:* men and women looking at pictures and people who have painted them, nibbling at food and thoughts that seem to have been food for thought for some and for others morsels they did not care to pick up, while chatting amusingly and amused, imbibing an intellectual and semi-intellectual atmosphere they all helped to create.

Alice soon noticed that Gertrude was not used to, and therefore unable to cope with, matters of daily routine or the necessary accessories to life. And Alice knew how to make them her concern. It began with proofreading the galleys of *Three Lives* and learning to type in order to prepare the one-thousand-page manuscript of *The Making of Americans*. Did she know how to make herself indispensable? When, in 1909, Alice's American companion Harriet Levy, with whom Alice had traveled in Europe and stayed in Paris, decided to return to the States, Gertrude asked Alice to join her in case she did not prefer to stay alone. She did not "want to go back to the apartment alone," and so she stayed with Gertrude at 27 rue de Fleurus, moving into Gertrude's life for good, for better and for worse.

Alice was very diplomatic and always remained in the background. But it was she who had the greatest influence on Gertrude. Alice thought she was *only* assisting her friend in planning this and that, in making decisions about travels and cooking, in keeping up Gertrude's correspondence. She was soon *the* person who could block one's way to Gertrude Stein or facilitate it. Consequently, people feared her influence on and power over Gertrude, and in many cases they openly or covertly expressed their resentment. This went so far that voices rebuked her for having achieved the position of a factotum in the Stein household as well as in Gertrude's life, and even blamed Alice for having dislodged Leo.

No one who knew of Alice's iron will and determination to succeed ever doubted that this reproach had a great deal of truth. But she could not have so easily accomplished Leo's dethronement or the crowning of herself as Gertrude's chief counselor, manager of all earthly affairs, adviser in spiritual matters, recipient and bestower of love, had Gertrude not achieved fame and, to some extent, notoriety, in the years between 1909 and 1914, to the great displeasure of "her brother."

First, *Three Lives* was well received, and publishers became interested in this strange writer whose English was faulty or distorted and yet compelling, however shocking. Bennett Cerf at Random House decided to publish whatever she wrote. The photographer Alfred Stieglitz printed her long essay on Matisse and Picasso in his *Camera Work*. *Tender Buttons* was written in 1912 and published two years later, a rarefied description of rooms and objects, of attitudes and impressions. In 1913, the New York Armory Show exposed the American public to modern art for the first time (or vice versa) and Gertrude's name was closely associated with the latest cry and outcry of artistic expression, with abstract and cubist trends. Gertrude's

"Portrait of Mabel Dodge," "directly inspired by Picasso's latest form," as Leo derisively stated, appeared in a special issue of *Arts and Decorations* that year, together with an essay by Mabel Dodge, a famous art patron, on Gertrude Stein.

Leo was also very much disillusioned with Picasso's progressively willful distortions of reality in his excursion into cubism. Gertrude's friendship with and belief in Picasso accelerated Leo's spiritual and emotional estrangement from his sister. In his eyes, the two were one, a single insult to his aesthetic feelings. There can be no better proof of it than his own biting words in *Appreciation*: "When once you know that a nose is not a nose is not a nose you can go on to discover what all the other things are not . . ." or when he said in *Journey Into Self*: "I can't abide her stuff and think it abominable."

Brother and sister were no longer attuned to the same spiritual and emotional vibrations. From her early dependence on Leo she had become an inattentive listener to his monologues and finally one who remained stubbornly silent. The king was dead, long live the queen!

At this point in her life Gertrude had found herself. More and more she insisted on being wholly dedicated to the rational operation of the mind and on her objectivity in what she said and the way she had to say it. In a letter to her friend Kate Buss in 1922 she stressed that there was no threshold between her conscious and unconscious mind. Time and again she reiterated that the "human mind is the mind that writes." In a similar instance, Shakespeare wrote, "The lady doth protest too much, methinks"; and Freud cast his doubts on her assertion when he wrote, "It is really not easy to form an idea of the wealth of trains of unconscious thought striving for expression in our minds . . ."

Gertrude Stein was always hostile to the concept of the unconscious, and in her *Autobiography of Alice B. Toklas* she went so far as to say: "Gertrude Stein never had subconscious reactions . . ." She rejected Freud all her life. And this, undoubtedly, had deeply imbedded unconscious reasons.

She enjoyed wearing many masks and appearing in disguises. In his study of Gertrude Stein, Richard Bridgman points out that she often used a private vocabulary to render her meaning ambiguous. Her most obvious play-acting feat was changing roles with Alice B. Toklas, as she did while writing *The Autobiography of Alice B. Toklas*. She affirmed their common identity when she said: "Trembling was all living, living was all loving, someone was then the other one."

Alice took care of transcribing all of Gertrude's writings; it has never been clearly ascertained how much of this famous book shows Alice's mental fingerprints or how great her influence on Gertrude's works was in general, directly or indirectly. We know from conversations with Gertrude that she found it difficult to maintain a single topic for long and that Alice often had to steer her back to a lost train of thought. But to give the Stein phenomenon its due, I must say that this weakness of hers in no way diminished her influence on the many people who came to her in admiration, wonder and search of counsel. She appeared very strong and sure of herself, even though her balance was often threatened by her tempestuous emotions. Nevertheless, her philosophic message came across; in the main, it said that something must always happen, that chance is the challenge of our "being existing," that, for all of us, there is always a possibility that we can create and turn into something new. Her vision of chance and the possibility of the new was always conveyed with such convincing intensity and with such personal wit that many who came to talk to her left as enriched listeners. But even then she may have worn one of her many masks.

Alice must have had a difficult time deciphering Gertrude's handwriting, which was notoriously bad. Her illegible hand was a habit she assumed rather early during her schooldays. Sometimes even she found it difficult to read her writing. Was she trying to escape into visual obscurity through this expressive gesture, hoping not to be recognized as the person she was? Was she simply impatient with herself when she wrote "x" for "ex" at the beginning of words (a habit she also acquired early in youth and never even tried to get rid of)? In all this her unconscious played its tricky games, above all making her reject what she did not like to be true.

She referred to her girlhood in California and her years in college as "the dark and dreadful days of adolescence" and, in retrospect, she was not too happy about her "rather desperate inner life." At an early age she acutely felt she was at a disadvantage because of her "unfeminine beauty," a phrase with which some writers euphemistically described the plumpness and plainness of her appearance. She reached the awesome weight of more than two hundred pounds, and in her book, *Wars I Have Seen*, she admits that in her childhood there was ". . . a great deal of eating as an excitement and as an orgy," a statement carrying quite some unconscious weight—whether she liked it or not.

As we have seen, Gertrude consciously rejected—to the point of loathing—her father's image and the role he played in her life. She would only gratefully acknowledge that he left her in a financially independent situation. Later, she rejected Leo, too, killing him in her writings repeatedly. As the temperamental child she was, Gertrude may unconsciously have tried to pay Leo back for criticizing her.

In 1912, after she had severed all ties with her past and, in particular, with Leo, she worked on *Tender Buttons*; in it, her experimental style reached its most eccentric cubist form of nonconformity. True, she found encouragement for her linguistic experiments through her relationship with Picasso and cubism. This support, however, did not precede, but followed, her inner process of self-estrangement. The style for which she became notoriously famous must be seen as a successful, although symbolic, attempt at total alienation from her past. She treated language the way a child plays with its toys; she depaternalized and deculturalized it in her attempt to give a new life and new meaning to threadbare words.

Her definition of language "as a real thing" that is "not imitation either of sounds or colors or emotions," but "is an intellectual recreation . . ." tries to support her notion that it is the mind only that writes. In fact, language is a subtle system of symbols whose meanings are decided by the sociocultural background from which it emerges and in which it lives like any other living thing. Its cerebration and coding are accompanied by emotion and intuition in form of valuation. The development and mainstay of any oral· or written communication depends on man's ability to communicate in grammatically significant sequences.

Linguistically, grammar stands for law and order, for the accept-
ance of the past experiences of those who teach us this system of
symbols. Gertrude Stein loathed the house built by her father, its
conveniences and conventions and tools. In order to destroy it she
had to destroy the grammar, the sentence structure. "The question
is," she said, "if you have a vocabulary have you any need of
grammar." Of course not, was her reaction. As far as she was
concerned, traditional verbal order impeded the organic immediacy
resulting from the interior life of mind. It is the grammar that, with
authoritative gestures, tells each word how to function.

She came to the conclusion that "sentences are not natural," "a
sentence is not emotional." There she caught herself in her logical
noose. From defining language as a cerebral activity, she then jumped
to the statement that a sentence is not emotional, not intuitive
enough, but a paragraph is, "paragraphs are natural and I am
desperately trying to find out why." We could have told her. A
sentence obliges the writer to adhere to rules set by the past, to a
traditional system. A paragraph can be envisioned as a new unity of a
group of words falling together by chance or premeditated chance. It
is a new house built in defiance of old rules. In *Painted Lace*, written
in 1914, Gertrude Stein wrote: "She is my wife. That is what a
paragraph is. Always at home. A paragraph hopes for houses. We
have a house two houses. My wife and I are at home." Still eight
years later, in *As Fine As Melanctha*, she echoed herself: "A sentence
is a hope of a paragraph."

After Leo had moved out, Gertrude was finally at home in 27 rue
de Fleurus, and she was not alone. She had all the vocabularies at her
disposal and used grammar only when and how it pleased her.

"Anything Is an Autobiography"

Gertrude was never interested in traveling on known routes. She
made her artistic experiences and their expression difficult for herself

by asking, "If it can be done, why do it?" She liked to explore and did not mind accepting journeys in the wrong direction or through the thicket of linguistic meanings and emphases. Obscurity was the price she paid for such efforts. One may accept or reject the possibility that her peculiar style was her *persona*, a mask in which she wished to appear to the world, ambiguous and in an exaggerated vagueness while protecting herself from being confronted with her ego.

When she wrote *Many Many Women* in 1910, a year after Alice joined the Stein household to share Gertrude's intimacy, she seemed to have reached a climactic point of opaque writing. In those seventy-nine pages we are introduced to several suffering, studying and marrying women, but one can hardly decipher who is referred to (if reference is made) since our eyes have to wander through a wilderness in which the signposts of "she" and "they" and "some" lead nowhere. But this opus is nevertheless revealing. It is a triumph of coded writing. Speaking of "one," she begins her description: "Any one is one having been that one. Any one is such a one." But this "one" is undoubtedly loving and loved. Despite all ambiguity she is shown kissing, and despite a most desperate attempt not to let us know the real aspects of reality, we are made to feel that a life without love is a sterile life; that from a feeling of lonesomeness she was moving toward "feeding something" and that this something was "being one" who knew something. The one who knew could not have been anyone else but Gertrude, who described the "one"—who could only have been Alice—as the one who soon "was loving some one and some one was loving her then."

Gertrude had a serious problem in her affections for women. After her disastrous experience with May, it seems to have taken her some time to become reconciled to her lesbian leanings. Living with her problem, she gradually understood that most people only tolerate "one way of loving" but that someone may say yes to "another way of loving." And finally she came to the conclusion that "I like loving." But liking loving in a heterosexual world compelled her to make a generous gesture toward this world by saying that she liked "mostly all the ways any one can have of having loving feeling in them." And insinuating that she expects the same understanding and tolerance from other people as she feels and practices, she stated: "Slowly it has come to be in me that any way of being a loving one is interesting and not unpleasant to me."

It is doubtful that Gertrude Stein ever tried to pretend not to be the "one" and the way she was. But it is just as certain that, however unconsciously, she felt the pressures of the "normal" world and their imputation of her inadequacy on a certain emotional and physical level. These circumstances must have teased her—if not forced her—into seeking cover in her writings and into finding a way to be the being of not being she.

Edmund Wilson first thought of this problem in her writing and description of sexual relationships, but later weakened his viewpoint. As Richard Bridgman rightly pointed out in his work *Gertrude Stein in Pieces*, she seemed to have been conscious of this problem herself. In *The Making of Americans* we come across a passage in which she promises to tell the full story of a rather ugly woman, and "this one will not know then it is this one. That is the very nice thing in this writing." Thus she admitted she knew the advantages of vagueness, obfuscation and deception. What she may not have admitted to herself was the degree of intensity with which she tried to shield herself.

That she practiced deception in her writings she never denied. In a piece called *All Sunday*, written in 1916, she said verbatim: "I am sadly tormented with flies, I do not mean flies." Alice, no doubt, also exerted great influence on her by criticizing Gertrude, and it seems she often did it in a harsh tone, as reflected in a passage of *Bonne Année*, penned in the same year:

This must not be put in a book.
Why not.
Because it mustn't.
Yes sir.

Frictions may have arisen in their "marriage" in the year of 1916 because Gertrude concedes that she was ashamed of having knuckled under Alice's will:

I have been so careful.
I will not say what I feel.

This also appears in *All Sunday*, written during their stay in Mallorca. It is full of intimate allusions to daily-life happenings in their ménage. In bits and pieces, veiled and blatantly frank, we find Alice turning up as a shrewd woman, making herself indispensable with criticism, as a source of information and a wife with instinct and advice.

No one could mistake the roles these two women played: Alice being the wife and wifely all the time, Gertrude the man. In writing a long piece called *Lifting Belly*, a Steinian love poem, she must have decided to drop all masks. (But this, as were similar pieces, was kept in her drawers and published posthumously.) *Lifting Belly* is a name and a sensual act and both interchange at a whim's notice. On fifty pages of *Lifting Belly* the bliss of all banality triumphs in erotic rapture. She—or it may be he—could go on with lifting the belly forever, and it almost sounds as if the writer had been in a trance of orgastic ecstasy when we read: "*Lifting Belly* is so strong. I love cherish idolise adore and worship you." There are such unmistakable exclamations as "Darling wifie is so good" and "Little hubbie is good." Spending some of the war months of 1915/16 on the Mediterranean island of Mallorca, Gertrude was cut off from her Parisian environment, all alone, as it were, with Alice, living a pastoral idyll. Another such honeymoon period occurred in 1922, as it is reflected in a piece whose title is more than suggestive: *Didn't Nelly and Lilly Love You*. Here, Gertrude and Alice as husband and wife exult in the most dizzying commonplace tirades of love loving love.

No love could be more completely demonstrated than by re-creating artistically one's own existence through the existence of the person one loves, by speaking and sharing one's own voice with the voice of one's beloved. That was exactly what Gertrude did when she wrote the history of her friends and time in *The Autobiography of Alice B. Toklas*. (As I've observed, no one knows how much of Alice's voice we actually hear emerging from those sentences so atypical of Gertrude's experimental work with words and sounds.) This autobiography is written in an entertaining style with no linguistic hurdles whatsoever, in an easy flow of lightly amusing portraits and vignettes always given an ironic touch.

How much the intimate closeness of mind and body, the sharing of daily routines and daily excitement created a collaborative effort is difficult to say. Alice typed all of Gertrude's manuscripts; she often corrected inaccuracies and sometimes changed a few words. *Ada*, the very first portrait of Alice, has a great many touches that seem to show Alice's mental handwriting. The much longer and more important *The Autobiography of Alice B. Toklas* comes closest to Alice's own memoirs, *What Is Remembered*. In style and conception, it is far closer than Gertrude's sequel, *Everybody's Autobiography*, in which she reverts to her own type of verbal complexities. Who influenced whom and when and where can never be ascertained in such a close give-and-take situation, all the more since two of their closest friends, William Rogers and Virgil Thomson, added new fuel to suspicion, doubt and uncertainty by their remarks.

Rogers met Gertrude and Alice as an American soldier serving in France during World War I. They had named him Kiddie or William the Kiddie and "took him everywhere. We always had taken him everywhere." They both liked him very much and also saw a great deal of him during Gertrude's American lecture tours. She thought about the difference between good speaking and writing and spoke with American students about William Rogers being a part of American literature or not, as Gertrude mentioned in *Everybody's Autobiography*. However this may be, Rogers knew them well, and we have it from the horse's biting mouth that "one way to rile Miss Toklas, and one out of many, is to tell her you suspect her touch in the Stein genius . . ." Her vehement reaction could have had opposing reasons, the honest denunciation of a false insinuation or the evasion from the truth.

Virgil Thomson had a weakness for Gertrude Stein. He had already composed some shorter pieces of her writings when, in 1927, he asked her to write the libretto for an opera for him. He knew of her interest in operas and, with her love for saints, they decided that the libretto should be about them instead of a historic figure such as George Washington whose name Gertrude submitted. Gertrude had had a flair for Saint Therese since her early youth, perhaps because of the strong erotic implications in her writings. The other saint close to her heart was Ignatius of Loyola, the mystic and advocate of discipline. It is a curious selection and juxtaposition of saints, but it mattered little since she was not interested in plot and dramatic lucidity. She did not have the imaginative grasp for, nor the technical know-how of, the needs of stagecraft and, making a virtue of her shortcomings, her lyric inventions dwelt on sound and senseless imagery, a beautiful refrain of staying power in its lilting echo: "When this you see remember me." She also introduced some sensuous lyric touches, for example about water, rain and a river.

She added two saints of her own invention, Saint Plan and Saint Settlement, in-jokes at best. *Four Saints* did not emerge as a religious opera and, if interpretation and a measure of meaning can be applied at all, there is something positive about it: an affirmation of life and a plea to accept our earthly existence. This was underlined by Virgil Thomson's idea of choosing a black cast when a production finally was mounted in 1934. Marc Connelly's *The Green Pastures*, premiered on Broadway in 1930, inspired Thomson to use blacks. He even thought—only for a fleeting moment, fortunately—of having the blacks painted white.

There can be no doubt that Virgil Thomson belonged to the intimate circle of Gertrude and Alice's friends and was more than equipped to overlook the scene and to judge the relationship of the two women. Gertrude was certainly very articulate, but she had the bad habit of losing her way to the point of a story, then repeating herself and escaping into obscure phrases. Thomson tells us that Alice would then save her, usually by saying: " 'I'm sorry, Lovey; it wasn't like that at all.' 'All right, Pussy,' Gertrude would say. 'You tell it.' Alice's way was the definite version." But still there is a difference between storytelling and writing. Carefully, so that he may not step on anyone's vain toe, Thomson added that "In every way except actual authorship," *The Autobiography of Alice B. Toklas* was "Alice Toklas' book." The meaning of this statement can only be that, in his opinion, Gertrude wrote the way Alice would have written about herself, her thoughts and experiences. Lovey might have often wondered and asked: Pussy, how was it at that time and what would you say about . . . ?

There was only one other great friendship in Gertrude's life and one other person of great influence on her, but Alice was clever enough not to oppose it or to show any jealousy. It was Gertrude's friendship with Picasso which grew gradually—though, as we have seen, an animal instinct seemed to have made them recognize one another immediately at their very first meeting. Gertrude may have felt the vitality, the magnificent and even brutal strength in him when she sat next to him at the dinner table for the first time. There was a kind of gentleness about their relationship that made them tremble when they embraced. Although she did not like the way he painted when she first saw what he did, she became one of the most vociferous voices fighting for his genius. And later, whenever they had important ideas to discuss and their discussions grew more and more intense, they would sit close, quite close together, so that her knee touched his.

Once, for a two-year period, they did not see one another. It was caused by a stupid incident in Gertrude's studio. She was reading aloud passages from her *Autobiography of Alice B. Toklas*. Picasso had a way of looking and listening, as if he wanted to devour what he looked at or listened to. And, as she tells the story in *Everybody's Autobiography*:

. . . he was listening and his eyes were wide open and then suddenly his wife Olga Picasso got up and said she would not listen she would go away she said. What's the matter, we said, I do not know that woman she said and left. Pablo said go on reading, I said no you must go after your wife, he said oh I said oh, and he left and until this year and that was two years in between we did not see each other again but now he has left his wife and we have seen each other again.

While Picasso was painting her portrait in 1905, they faced one another for many hours. These hours and then the painting itself had the power of cementing their thoughts and feelings, which already ran on similar tracks. Whether she sat for the portrait eighty or ninety times is irrelevant. Many months passed during which they saw a great deal of one another, and we must imagine that out of silence emerged sympathy that struck roots; and perhaps from some trivialities arose an understanding that went beyond the obvious. Although Picasso worked quite some time on the painting, he was dissatisfied with the head. Finally, he just painted over it in a fit of fury and said he could no longer look at her. Then he left for Spain and Gertrude for Italy. When she returned, she found Picasso back in Paris. Meanwhile, he had painted her face without the benefit of having her as a model.

Gertrude loved the painting and said it would be the only portrait of her in which she would always recognize herself. When people wondered about her likeness, Picasso used to reply: "If she does not look like it now, it does not really matter since she will look like it one day." He gave Gertrude the painting as a present. In 1909 she wrote a brief portrait about him, a two-page paean in which she said in her verbal ecstasy:

This one always had something being coming out of this one. This one was working. This one always had been working. This one was always having something that was coming out of this one that was a solid thing, a charming thing, a lovely thing, a perplexing thing, a disconcerting thing, a simple thing, a clear thing, a complicated thing, an interesting thing, a disturbing thing, a repellent thing, a very pretty thing. . . .

He did have some following. They were always following him. Some were certainly following him. He was one who was working. He was one having something coming out of him something having meaning. He was not ever completely working.

Thirty years later she wrote about Picasso again, a little book in the traditional style. She recalled the year 1909 when Picasso had returned from a trip to Spain and brought a few strange paintings with him. Shortly before cubism came into being, Matisse was the first artist to become enthusiastic about African sculpture. That was at the time when Picasso had finished Gertrude's portrait. Matisse's sculpture changed from then on; not his paintings, however. The discovery of African art was far more decisive for Picasso. Gertrude said in her monograph on him that in the beginning it affected his vision and form rather than his imagination. This new influence began to get a hold on his fantasy when Jean Cocteau convinced him to try his hand at a stage design. The atmosphere of Serge Diaghilev's

Ballet Russe, the Eastern touch superimposed on the Russian art gave Picasso's cubist work wings of imagination.

Gertrude tells us how excited Picasso was to have been invited to meet in Rome with Eric Satie, Jean Cocteau and Leonide Massine where these artists prepared the ballet *Parade*, a work opening the gates to new and endless experimentation. It was the first time that Picasso had the opportunity to see Italy—and how delighted he was! It was the first time that he had created a scenic design which, as Gertrude indicated, put cubism on the artistic map:

That was really the beginning of the general recognition of Picasso's work, when a work is put on stage of course everyone has to look at it and in a sense if it is put on the stage everyone is forced to look and since they are forced to look at it, of course, they must accept it, there is nothing else to do.

Guillaume Apollinaire wrote the text for the program bill for *Parade*. He who had coined sometime previously the term "cubism," now for the first time used the term "surrealism." *Parade* was a sensational scandal. It not only made balletic history but helped establish the reputation of Picasso as a daring pioneer in the twentieth-century art movements. *Parade* had been Cocteau's idea, and Picasso ought to have been grateful to him for having given him this chance. But Picasso could not abide Cocteau the busybody, and even less Cocteau the draftsman. Gertrude described her own attitude toward Cocteau with tongue in cheek. He was the first French writer who had taken notice of her and discussed her work publicly. Thus they met a few times, and their friendship was a strange one. They often wrote each other and liked one another well. They had many mutual friends, young and old friends, but he was never invited to come to 27 rue de Fleurus, nor was she seen in his house, which indicates that they never were really close since all her best friends came to see her and were invited for her Saturday soirees.

Picasso was very close to her heart, and he was utterly devoted to Gertrude. We also know this from Françoise Gilot's *Life With Picasso*. One day he gave her *The Autobiography of Alice B. Toklas* to read and said, "this week we are going to visit Gertrude Stein.

You'll have fun. Moreover, I believe in her judgment. If she likes you, it will confirm my good opinion about you." Gilot had a miserable time; she felt as though she were at a police station, subjected to a cultural cross-examination. In between cakes and petit fours baked by Alice (who seemed to have disliked Françoise at first sight and sat next to her on the divan wearing a huge hat, and watching her like a gendarme), Françoise was asked what she thought of cubism, the influence of blacks on the arts and, of course, of Cézanne. Gertrude also wanted to know which of her works she knew and whether she had read any other American authors. In her book Mme. Picasso-Gilot—who once was one of those who were Picasso's wives, as Gertrude might have expressed it—retaliated for this cross-examination. She tells us how Gertrude made it unmistakably clear to her that she was the spiritual mother of all of them, of Sherwood Anderson, Ernest Hemingway and Scott Fitzgerald, and particularly of John Dos Passos, who was very much influenced by her. Moreover, Gertrude asked Françoise whether she was aware of her influence on even those who never sat at her feet, writers like Faulkner and Steinbeck, and did she realize that, without her, modern American literature, as we know it, would be unthinkable?

Gertrude gave Françoise three of her books and wrote something in each of them. One was *Wars I Have Seen*, and her dedication read: "A rose is a rose is a rose is a rose—once more for Françoise Gilot." Then she told Françoise she might come and see her again, alone if Françoise wanted, an invitation that was one of the high distinctions she rarely bestowed on newly introduced visitors. At that moment Françoise was sure she had passed the examination, but, at the same time, she decided never to go and see Gertrude. All this time Picasso had not said a word and was watching his wife trying desperately to get through her ordeal. Picasso loved Gertrude. It seems he was more attached to her than to any of his wives: there was a spiritual bridge between them that no flesh-inspired emotion could destroy.

When Picasso read her monograph on him, he realized the truth of what she said, the truth about his early struggle with new forms and ideas, about his being misunderstood and miserable. Yes, if it had not been for her! Gertrude had written: "I was alone at this time in understanding him, perhaps because I was expressing the same thing in literature."

By then realism was dead, and so was post-impressionism and fauvism. The artists in those days before World War I were testing themselves, and, in their dazzling daring, challenged the public's senses with such "isms" as orphism, futurism, purism, and expressionism. The doors were then flung wide open for cubism, dadaism, constructivism and surrealism. A world falling apart challenged the artists, who challenged what was still left of the world. It all telescoped the basic need to envision the reality of a nonreality. Gertrude expressed her and Picasso's concepts best when she said that it was essential to both of them to express things as they are when one sees them without remembering having looked at them. In what one could call her early Picasso period, Gertrude wrote a great many "portraits," as she called some of her writings. She explained she was trying to do abstract portraits with words, "the same as Picasso was doing in his paintings." The concept of painting with words was the result of her preoccupation and fascination with the rebellious painters in Paris at that time.

The still-life paintings in *Tender Buttons*, written while on a trip in Spain in 1912, combine a simplistic imagination à la Klee with Picasso's powerful brush stroke and create the impression of playful and unrestrained verbal rapture. Gertrude said in her *Lectures* about it that then she "was very much taken with the beauty of the sounds as they came from me as I made them." As an example I quote:

A Box

Out of kindness comes redness and out of rudeness comes rapid same question, out of an eye comes research, out of selection comes painful cattle. So then the order is that a white way of being round is something suggesting a pin and is it disappointing, it is not, it is so rudimentary to be analyzed and see a fine substance strangely, it is so earnest to have a green point not to red but to point again.

It was at that time that Gertrude fully realized and asserted the need for shock and incoherence. She anticipated the first attack on the sequential order of the traditional aesthetic laws, crowned by the

dada movement after World War I and with even greater vehe-
mence administered in the sixties. W. B. Yeats's prophetic words in
"The Second Coming," if "Things fall apart, the center cannot hold,"
were translated into terms of a full comprehension of her time when
she said: "Act so that there is no use in a centre." To her, the center
was rest and quiet and custom. Since everything moved and changed,
it was illogical to believe in a constant center, and the very
visualization of a center as a possible point of stabilization creates the
image of a false reality. Gertrude stood in the forefront of those who
believed in unseating the customary, since "the custom is in the
centre."

Wisdom and nonsense are superimposed on one another in her
writings before 1914. In those years she also began to write what she
called "plays" which, of course, were not plays but speech fragments
in the vein of her still lifes. About 1912 she had met Apollinaire, for
whom she had reserved several epithets, "he is wonderful . . . he
was very beautiful and very interesting." When she looked at him,
she had to think of a Roman emperor. He was always three steps
ahead of his time. His artistic war cry was "Surprise! surprise!" This
slogan was in the air, but it was Apollinaire who started it. In the
same year, 1912, Diaghilev also challenged Cocteau with the same
words: "Surprise me!" which fully materialized five years later with
the Cocteau-Picasso-Satie balletic work *Parade*. When Diaghilev
puzzled Cocteau with his challenge, Cocteau admitted: "The idea of
surprise, so entrancing in Apollinaire, had never occurred to me."

Wilhelm Albert Wladimir Alexandre Apollinaire de Kostrowitzky,
known as Guillaume Apollinaire, was born in Rome, the illegitimate
child of Polish parents. The artistic world in Paris before and during
World War I is unthinkable without this leading spokesman for all
radical new movements. He was a poet, short-story writer, essayist,
draftsman, painter, art critic, impresario, editor, journalist and
professional bohemian. He was articulate and convincing in whatever
he did. When he wrote his drama, *The Breasts of Tiresias*, in 1917, he
called it *Drame sur-réaliste*, then using for the first time this new term
for a "New Spirit that . . . shall not fail to captivate the elite and
promises to transform arts and manners into universal joy," as he

stated. He invented the *calligrammes*, the typographical derange-
ment of poems.

Small wonder that Gertrude felt a close kinship to him when she
discovered that they both experimented with cubist prose. His
poèmes-conversations with their nonsequitur passages, with their
superimposed disconnected snatches of everyday speech and the
omission of any punctuation impressed Gertrude. The feeling that
she was not alone gave her courage to continue on similar paths.

Apollinaire was part of that blessed circle of Parisian artists who
gave the entire world a twentieth-century face. Through his physical
height and commanding presence, Apollinaire could not be over-
looked. Gertrude said of him that he was extraordinarily clever and
witty, that he immediately caught the essential point of any
conversation and, without having any particular knowledge of the
matter in question, his imaginative mind made it possible for him to
penetrate and illuminate the subject better than anyone else.

For many years he was the lover of Marie Laurencin, whom
Apollinaire brought with him to Gertrude's studio. The very first time
Gertrude saw her, Marie took a seat next to her on the divan and told
her the story of her life. She had angular features and looked like
French medieval primitives, Gertrude thought, like a wooden
madonna face. She was delicate and moved with inimitable grace. It
was also the way she painted. When she was still associated with
Apollinaire—during the early cubist period—she created a "strange
painting," portraits of Apollinaire, Picasso and his wife, Fernande,
and herself. Gertrude bought it as soon as she saw it. It was the first
picture Marie Laurencin sold. When Apollinaire had left her shortly
before the outbreak of World War I she married a German. Feeling
so very much French and being married to a German and receiving
patriotic letters from Apollinaire, she naturally felt very unhappy
during the war. After the war was over she divorced her husband and
returned to her beloved France. On Saturday nights she returned to
27 rue de Fleurus with Eric Satie.

She had been a part of Apollinaire and the crowd around him and
Gertrude. Also, Georges Braque was always with them. Laurencin

had studied with Braque on how not to paint and, as long as they were at the Academy together, they painted each other's portraits. Then Braque began to paint what Gertrude called "geographic landscapes," in his color scheme influenced by Matisse. All this took place before he met Picasso. Six months later Braque and Derain became Picasso's followers. It was inevitable that Braque and Picasso should become intimate friends and co-workers, and it was just as inevitable that each of them thought he had invented cubism. Rivalry finally ended their friendship. Picasso, echoing Gertrude, once characterized Braque by saying that he and James Joyce were two incomprehensibles whom the entire world could understand.

Gertrude was not too fond of Braque since he occasionally made people believe "that he was the one that had all the ideas that made cubism and modern painting." Braque had a way of seducing everyone. Juan Gris, who also belonged to this circle, felt the same, having been somewhat afraid of Braque and awed by Picasso, whom he called *cher maître* and who detested being addressed like this by his young, gauche and effusive compatriot. Gris became a master at using printed and painted letters in juxtaposition to the painted surface that had to measure up to something rigid. His work was considered too cerebral. It was very difficult to sell his paintings, although the famed dealer of the cubists, D.-H. Kahnweiler, was a master of his trade. Elliot Paul, who then edited the avant-garde magazine *transition,* became interested in Juan Gris; he published Gris's essay, *Défense de la Peinture,* after the painter's death.

Next to Picasso, Gertrude loved Gris best. When he suddenly died in 1927, only forty years old, she deeply mourned his death. She had purchased some of his work as early as 1914 and, after a short period of estrangement, they remained very good friends during the last seven years of his life. He respected her judgment, and not only because she always was a potential buyer. He hoped she would once write about him: "No one will write better about my painting than yourself." Gertrude wrote a very moving elegy on him, *The Life of Juan Gris. The Life and Death of Juan Gris.* Since this was a time in which Gertrude did not see too much of Picasso, Braque or Matisse and she felt like Juan Gris's first and last patron, the ending of the elegy jarred a bit in its need for self-adulation: "And he smiled so gently and said I was everything."

Death always seemed to move Gertrude. In *The Autobiography of Alice B. Toklas* she takes great pains to describe Apollinaire's tragic end. There was no need for him to enlist voluntarily in the French army. He suffered a serious head wound at the front. For a long time afterwards people remembered this tall, impressive man as he—the famous wounded war veteran, with his head bandaged—shielded the perpetrators of *Parade* against an irate audience ready to lynch Cocteau and company. Apollinaire never recovered from his wound. There was an ironic touch to his fate. The night after armistice was proclaimed in 1918, he was lying in bed fighting death. The Picassos were with him that evening. It was a mild night. The windows stood wide open when a crowd passed by shouting, *"à bas Guillaume!"* They meant "Down with Wilhelm!" the German emperor, but in his delirium Apollinaire could probably only perceive that the mob was shouting him down. That night he died.

"I Am the Most Important Writer Writing Today"

Probably no one can become a great writer—or any kind of artist, for that matter—if he or she has not learned to listen with ears as well as to see with eyes, for listening is observing. Gertrude went through a hard school of self-discipline for one who loved to talk much. But she taught herself to listen. Her spiritual separation from her brother Leo was already far advanced before Alice Toklas and Pablo Picasso became the most important people in her life. She admits in *Everybody's Autobiography,* "We both loved to talk a great deal although I do believe that I listened more or at least if I did not listen more I was silent more."

Photographer and editor Alfred Stieglitz liked to speak of the Steins as he found them in their early Parisian years, of Leo who was painting and Gertrude who was writing. She remembered "his being there he was there for several hours and my brother was talking and he went away with the greatest admiration and said he had never known any woman well perhaps anybody to sit still so long without talking." Stieglitz traveled with this story and could not tell it often enough, so wondrous did it seem to him. At that time, absorbed by her writing, Gertrude no longer felt the need to argue. Thinking and listening, observing and thinking were of importance to her. Listening, looking and thinking, she thought, gave her the right to talk.

It was a fascinating adventure to enter the Stein studio and to sit there facing those many strange paintings, new and bewildering to the eye, and Gertrude sitting in front of Picasso's portrait of her; to be seen by her eyes, which did not seem to perceive any person as the logical sequential image of head being straight on top of the trunk, with its heart somewhere to the left of center, or with the eyes being clearly separated by a nose leading to the mouth. Did she not see the image of the personality, his "bottom nature," as it were, as a totality of the inner Gestalt made of parts that she could fit together as she saw them? When listening did she hear the meaning of the words spoken, or the repetitive fall of sounds forming sentences that painted verbal images, structured with the fury of the geometric logic of distortion?

Thornton Wilder, who saw Gertrude on his frequent European trips and who was with her in the days of her American lecture tours, tells us in his introduction to her book, *What Are Masterpieces and Why Are There So Few of Them?* about one of his conversations with Gertrude Stein when she spoke about the art of listening. Wilder emphasizes that she was known to at least two generations of American war veterans who, when coming to Paris, wanted to see the Eiffel tower and Gertrude Stein.

Only the one who was such an eager listener had also the right to demand that he be listened to, she thought. Everyone had some genius when young, since then he can really listen, simultaneously listen and speak. When growing older, many people become tired and listen less and less. Some may still listen, but one day they too become too old to listen. Gertrude never stopped listening, and whoever spoke to her was expected to unpack his "knowledge," that is, his "genius." Probably she was so closely attuned to the concept of listening, since her way of writing asked for good listeners. Her readers had to shut out the outside world and its annoying noise in order to hear what they read.

When listening, Gertrude Stein could also read in a person what he said or rather what he wanted to say and did not, or ought to have said. Her quality of listening had a great deal to do with her ability to lose herself in another person, a habit perhaps from her college days when analysis of personality was more than an exciting pastime. Had it become routine to show interest in people, or did she simply play-act, was it a part she thought she was cast for? She jumped to certain contestable conclusions. For instance, she maintained that the writer's fantasy emerges from observation and organization of what he wants to say, provided that some imagination is there to begin with. This was the advice she had for many young writers who came to listen to her.

One of those better known was the young Ernest Hemingway, who once wrote in one of his stories that Gertrude Stein always knew what was good about a Cézanne painting. She looked at him as only Gertrude Stein could look at someone, with penetrating and frightening kindness, saying: "Hemingway, remarks are not yet literature." This advice and phrase must have impressed Gertrude Stein, and she certainly must often have recalled it, since in her autobiography she returned to the very same sentence on another occasion. Hemingway showed her a manuscript of stories to which he had added as an afterthought a short meditative piece on e. e. cummings's *The Enormous Room*, praising it as the most wonderful book he had ever read. Referring to this phrase Gertrude told him: "Hemingway, remarks are not yet literature."

It was in 1922 that the twenty-three-year old Ernest Hemingway came to her with a letter of recommendation from Sherwood Anderson. There was something strange about Hemingway's expression, with passionately interested, rather than interesting, eyes. Gertrude soon enjoyed watching how he sat opposite her, listening and looking. He wanted her to read some of what he had written. She liked some of his poetry, but she found little to praise about a novel he showed her. Start it once more, she suggested, and give it more depth.

She once told Dashiell Hammett that she was puzzled about contemporary male writers. In the nineteenth century they could create different male characters. In our time, she contended, "The men all write about themselves." The reason seemed to lie in the psyche of modern man. He seems to feel inferior in many ways and must, to overcompensate, glorify his ego. Undoubtedly, she thought of Ernest Hemingway as a prime example. Obsessed with sex, violence and death, Hemingway was one of those male authors who had to prove themselves time and again. In her attitude was the hidden belief that it was now the woman writer's turn to replace the male. There was something cowardly in Hemingway, she thought, as in all men who have to prove themselves. Was then the virility, courage and toughness of his characters a reflection only of his own need to overcompensate?

It was Gertrude who led Hemingway onto the track of his favorite themes. She was fascinated by Spain, its people and customs, and probably her friendship with Picasso, her love for Juan Gris and her ambivalent feelings for the artist Francis Picabia helped deepen her liking of everything Spanish. Gertrude was very fond of Spanish dancing and bullfights, and she showed Hemingway photographs of famous toreros and exciting bullfights. She spoke of them with glowing enthusiasm. And these became some of Hemingway's major topics, which later made him famous.

Gertrude had a weakness for Hemingway; she even promised him she would never feel differently, since he was instrumental in getting sections of *The Making of Americans* published in Ford Madox Ford's *Transatlantic Review*. She also had a weakness for Hemingway because she felt he was one of her best pupils; he listened and acted according to her advice. At the beginning of his career as a writer she told him to stop putting out journalistic trash and turn to serious fiction. And so he did. She taught him a great deal about a writer's vision and how to put it on paper. He sat down and wrote stories that were soon published under the title, *In Our Time*. He talked with her for hours on end, and many of their conversations she found again in Hemingway's book, *The Sun Also Rises*. He made some of her peculiarities his own, imitating ironic repetitions in several of his early stories, particularly in "Mr. and Mrs. Elliot." He borrowed from her the technique of phrasing elliptic sentences that gave his writing the virile character that became his trademark. But Hemingway showed his gratitude in hailing Gertrude's *The Making of Americans* as the beginning of all modern literature. Whether he meant it or not is a moot question. Gertrude, who so often felt isolated from the mainstream of literature, needed to be told that she was not only great but the greatest.

On the other hand, Hemingway was less kind and grateful to Sherwood Anderson, who had done much for him and of whom Gertrude Stein was very fond. Anderson was never the forceful writer Hemingway turned out to be. He was very much concerned with what happened inside a person or an event, and this was why naturalism was not his forte. In looking into other characters deeply, he lost himself in his own ego, a fact that gave most of his figures a sheen of sameness. One may also easily claim that his village mysticism had a false ring and his "folksiness" soon tired the reader. But he was a master of painting mood pictures, and some of his very short pieces were quite impressive.

In spite of Hemingway's super-realism, he learned discipline and characterization from Sherwood Anderson. Nevertheless, Hemingway slighted him and blamed him for a lack of taste. Gertrude, however, thought that Anderson had genius in the way he could shape a sentence to convey a feeling. She knew no one in contemporary American literature who could write such lucid and passionate phrases as he did. Of course, Anderson was not the only writer of whom she was fond. Scott Fitzgerald may have come close to being idealized by Gertrude. She was convinced that his novels, *This Side of Paradise* and *The Great Gatsby*, re-created better than any other novels of the roaring twenties the new desperate generation. Fitzgerald always thought she was making fun of him, knowing her sharp critical eye. He went so far as to make no secret of the fact that her good opinion of his work could have been nothing else but a cruel act of hers. But whenever they met, Gertrude stressed in her autobiography, they had a wonderful time together and found it very amusing to take themselves apart and especially to do the same to Hemingway.

One can never know how serious Gertrude was in telling Françoise Gilot that even John Dos Passos and William Faulkner would be unthinkable without her. The narratives of both writers show, in form and style, distinct traces of Steinian concepts of writing from inside out and of not making the narrative a superficial and necessarily coherent and sequential experience. What they achieved was the ultimate in painting a thing beyond its reality, in moving in every direction, in creating something that happens with unmistakable immediacy.

The problem of narrative bothered and occupied her mind all her life. She tried to re-create whatever was happening and not really what happened. It bothered and occupied her so much that she failed quite often. "No one in our time," she said, "had really been able to tell anything without anything but just telling that thing." She often spoke about these problems to Thornton Wilder, who had such great understanding for her accomplishments and failures. He was one of the few people who touched a responsive chord in her. He tells us of Gertrude's habit of meditating every day, simply by being with herself and "pursuing a certain train of thought for an hour or two at a time." It seemed to have been a mental process, an exercise in concentration. He wrote in his preface to Gertrude's *Four in America*:

It has often seemed to me that Miss Stein was engaged in a series of spiritual exercises whose aim was to eliminate during the hours of writing all those whispers into the ear from the outside and inside world where the audience dwells.

She liked Thornton Wilder, who, as a conversationalist, was a match for her own abilities. He also helped to make life easy for her while she lectured in Chicago. She trusted him and had originally made him her literary executor. Then, probably believing that in his enthusiasm and despite his admiration for her he might let other people get their hands on her material, she finally appointed Carl Van Vechten to watch over her words beyond her death. Alice made copies of all the as yet unpublished writings of Gertrude Stein and sent them to Carl for safe keeping. He turned out to be a conscientious and understanding editor. We can certainly wonder if Carl Van Vechten shared Gertrude's opinion that she was the most important writer writing at that time. But he definitely thought it worthwhile to preserve and edit whatever she wrote.

"The Mother of Us All"

The two women survived World War II and the Nazi occupation of France. They were undoubtedly in danger, if for no other reason than that they were Jews. They were advised to cross the frontier into Switzerland to avoid being put into a concentration camp, but they never left France. Nothing ever happened to them, either because they had friends in high positions and high society, or they were known to some German officers, literary-oriented, as those two crazy literary American ladies. It seems to be very characteristic of Gertrude Stein that she wondered about "the unreality" of "the whole affair" while the world was bleeding and burning.

A kind of diary kept between early 1943 and the end of August, 1944, led to her book, *Wars I Have Seen*, as a record of her experiences during the last fifteen months of the war. It was a long monologue written in a most Steinian way, but it can be read by readers willing to work their way from one oasis—a memorable sentence—to another. Yet there is too little one can hold on to; the material was too loosely thrown onto the paper.

In 1945 she began to work on a book called *Brewsie and Willie*, a work in which she recorded snatches of conversations between American soldiers and nurses. They are ordinary soldiers trying to pick up the pieces of a shattered world and wondering how to put them together again to prepare a better world for themselves and the coming generations.

Brewsie and Willie are two different types who in many ways complemented one another. Dialogue seems to have become her favorite means of conveying ideas. Brewsie, it seems, is a stand-in for Gertrude Stein. She saw many army bases in Germany and held long talks with the soldiers, to the chagrin of some officers who feared she confused their men with her crazy notions about life, money, and industrialism. She was shocked to hear most of the men expressing a liking for the Germans. Yes, Gertrude said, these Americans were flattered by the way the Germans obeyed them. She found the American men immature, "spoiled babies" who believed that life was just another movie, only more real, and who found relief by looking at pin-up girls. Industrialism was at the root of all evil, making automatons of men who stop thinking and feeling; it "Makes 'em all feel alike." This book is a pessimistic account of the soldiers after the war and the male in particular.

She was even less pleasant about the male sex in her very last work, a libretto, the second collaboration with Virgil Thomson. *The Mother of Us All* no longer shows the disdain she felt for the American male as dramatized in *Brewsie and Willie*. What was a scornful laugh before was now revealed as real anger emerging from purely hostile feeling. The anger waxed hot when she flaunted her contempt for the heterosexual world: "If there are men and women, it is rather horrible, and if it is rather horrible, then there are children . . ." It was as if she had surmised that this was her swan song, and no longer cared about dropping all pretenses to get her message across.

The leading figure in the opera was Susan B. Anthony, the nineteenth-century fighter for women's right to vote, a struggle that was to end victoriously fourteen years after her death with the ratification of the 19th Amendment in 1920. Through Susan B. Anthony's person Gertrude could prove the woman's superiority over the male, her vision and courage to fight for fairness and justice for her sex. With Daniel Webster as her counterpart, Gertrude characterized male tyranny, which tries to keep women and the black minority from their rightful share of the money there is and the happiness this money can buy. As a wonderful throwback we can see how Gertrude, now on the threshold of death, still fighting her father, saw in Daniel Webster the features of that tyrannical man whose name was Daniel too.

Susan B. Anthony took a grim view of mankind and believed that at the moment when women could vote like men the women would be in danger of becoming like men in their outlook. The strong man and persecutor, Daniel Webster, is also juxtaposed to a wifey woman, a "mouse" named Angel More, who can only see her part as one of servitude in behalf of man.

A fighting mood ends on a pessimistic note because the mother of us all has remained helpless and sterile through all times. One thing, however, must be said for Susan B. Anthony. She never compromises herself, and therefore her ideas have to be victorious one day, whereas the other characters remain unchanged by time and events. Will the world ever change, we are asked, or will everything remain "the bleak sum of mother's wisdom"?

When Gertrude Stein finished *The Mother of Us All* it was late in her life. She did not live long enough to witness the first production of this opera at Columbia University in New York on May 7, 1947. Shortly before her death she complained of abdominal troubles. Alice Toklas describes the end of Gertrude's life in her memoirs, *What Is Remembered*:

By this time Gertrude Stein was in a sad state of indecision and worry. I sat next to her and she said to me early in the afternoon, What is the answer? I was silent. In that case, she said, what is the question? Then the whole afternoon was troubled, confused and very uncertain, and later in the afternoon they took her away on a wheeled stretcher to the operating room and I never saw her again.

She had fallen ill on July 19th in 1946. On July 27th she died after an unsuccessful operation for cancer. Buried at the Père Lachaise Cemetery, her tombstone misspells the place of her birth: "Allfghany" and prolongs her life by two days, naming the date of her death as July 29, 1946.

Words, letters, dates, sounds. . . . The laugh of dislocation and disconnection, a final triumph of nonsequitur, followed her into her nonbeing. A word is a word is a . . .

In 1912.

An early photograph.

Lou Andreas-Salomé
Mind and Body

The Nietzsche Affair

F ROM what stars have we fallen to meet here?" Friedrich
Nietzsche asked Lou Salomé, when they met for the first time. He
and the striking young woman stood beneath the vast dome of St.
Peter's Cathedral in Rome. Those first words and the grandeur of the
place set the tone for what was to become an articulate, ambivalent
and highly romantic love affair.

Only Nietzsche could have thought of such a phrase and dared to
approach her with it. But Lou was more intrigued by this strange
man than by his surprising salutation. The first impression he made
on her was mesmerizing; it gave her an odd feeling. His laughter was
gentle and so was his way of talking. With his bent shoulders and his
careful, wistful gait, he generated an aura of hidden solitude.

Lou was also impressed by his hands, which she found "incompara-
bly beautifully and nobly shaped." Nietzsche himself believed that
his hands revealed his spirit. His eyes betrayed him too, she thought.
Half-blind, these eyes seemed to her "like the custodians and
preservers of personal treasures, of silent secrets meant for no
intruding glance." His defective eyesight lent his features a certain
special magic, not reflecting varying outer impressions but only
"what was passing through him inwardly." In these first few minutes,
as she wrote long afterward, she was perplexed and deceived by his
attempt to capture an Apollonian mood. She was struck by what

could have been a studied gesture, an all-too-conscious false pathos. From then on many ironic and, above all, tragicomic elements marred their intense and short-lived relationship.

Nietzsche knew little about this twenty-one-year-old girl, even though he had received a detailed description of her from his friend, the young philosopher Paul Reé, who was in love with Lou. Reé's report was a blending of idealization and surprise, describing a Russian girl who then appeared to his eyes as almost too good for this world, a martyr to knowledge since infancy, renouncing all the joys and comforts of life for the sake of truth. In a later letter Reé said of her that "she is a forceful, incredibly clever being with the most girlish, even childlike qualities."

What more did Nietzsche need in a quixotic mood to conjure up the image of the female disciple for whom he longed? His speculative mind envisioned the unfolding of a Dionysian quality in this girl to which he was ready to contribute his Apollonian spirit. He had come to St. Peter's with the premonition that something unusual would happen to him. He wrote to his friend, Franz Overbeck, before going to Rome: "I need a young person in my proximity who is intelligent and sufficiently learned to be able to work with me. I would not mind concluding a two-year-marriage pact for this purpose." Without yet having seen her, he had the notion of having found a disciple in this young Russian girl: She would help him, inspire him, carry on his ideas.

Reé had arranged this appointment, and Nietzsche was in a euphoric state when he arrived at St. Peter's. In the dim light of the cathedral and with his poor eyesight he could hardly see what Lou looked like. She was stunning. Lou had a tall body, boyish and slender in build, with the height to draw attention wherever she went and to enable her to look straight into the face of her dreams. She had bright blue eyes, big and deep-set under a high arched forehead. She wore her long auburn hair with bangs that she removed later in life. Nietzsche's composer friend, Peter Gast, praised her "ancient Roman facial expression." Her lips were nicely drawn and full, hungry in their demands, ready in their desires, revealing some of her emotional intensity. Lou had a very supple gait and impressed with a guileless, no doubt deceptively simple, manner. There was something disarming and bewitching about her that captivated men the moment they entered her aura. And yet she betrayed a shyness that was as easily recognizable as the challenging mind hidden behind it.

Nietzsche was only one of the many brilliant men, certainly one of the more fulminant figures, whom Lou attracted and by whom she was fascinated. Before she met Nietzsche, other men had already acted out their parts in her life in order to make it the life she envisioned for herself. This life was a vast country full of hidden secrets and wonders that she set out to find and explore, to experience to the full and to delight in. Wherever she went and whatever she did, it was always the heart of the matter that interested her and that she turned into the matter of her heart.

Among the men preceding Nietzsche, one must mention her father, since her relationship with him went beyond any father-fixation. (He died at the age of seventy when Lou was seventeen.) He was a father-God figure whose imprint marked her all her life. Gustav von Salomé, of Huguenot descent, general of the Russian army, was a handsome, imposing man with a strong character; he believed in decency and decorum, otherwise he would have been a ladies' man. We know little of his private life before he married at the late age of forty, except that he was a brilliant man who loved the company of other brilliant men, an inclination that became most pronounced in his daughter. Lou recounted that the poets Pushkin and Lermontov belonged to the circle of his friends.

After five sons, Lou was born, and she resembled her father in many ways. She was the great joy of General Salomé, and she saw in her father an all-powerful and omnipresent image. He was her first great love: "In my earliest childhood my father and I were tied to one another by a little secret tenderness," she carefully worded it in her autobiography *Lebensrückblick* (Reflections on My Life). It was blissful excitement to her to be kissed, cuddled and lifted close to his manly face.

He provided her with an enchanting environment, sheltered from the realities of life, thus enabling her to build her own private world whose special fairy-tale quality could be projected into her everyday existence. In these early years the foundation was laid for a life in which the line between her inner adventures and outer experience often became blurred, in which poetry and truth were unnoticeably interchanged.

In this intense dream life there was one central figure of unchallenged greatness. It was a God figure that had emerged from the exalted image of her father, transcending his own reality. Her relationship to God became a very personal one. She talked to him in the dark each night before going to sleep and told him all her real and imagined experiences. She began her one-sided conversation with him with the words: "As you know." But she felt the need to tell him "stories of real happenings or encounters with men, animals or objects." The fairy-tale atmosphere was fully realized through "the silent God-listener."

The first serious trauma of her childhood was her loss of faith in the imagined reality of God; the story sounds like a Russian fairy tale written by a minor Tolstoi. The caretaker of their summer house told her one day about an older couple standing in front of the house in the snow. The couple, he said, had asked to be let in since they were very cold, but he could not permit them to enter the house. When the servant came the next time, Lou inquired about Mr. and Mrs. Snow, whom her fantasy had endowed with the corporeality of living persons. She was afraid that they might have frozen to death in the meanwhile. Where had they gone? Nowhere, he reported. Then they are still standing there? No, not really. They had become thinner and thinner until one morning nothing was left of them "except the black buttons of the woman's white coat and the old man's battered hat." But the spot where all this had happened was still covered with the frozen tears of both people.

No longer was she occupied merely by compassion for this unfortunate couple, but by "the riddle of their mortality." The ever-listening God was forced to answer that night. Lou knew how busy he was, but she wanted him to say, "Mr. and Mrs. Snow," to acknowledge what had happened. That his invisible lips did not open became a "personal catastrophe" for her. Suddenly the curtain behind which had lived something of inexpressible strangeness tore apart. God, who had been painted on the curtain, not only disappeared for her, she said, but for the entire universe.

Although her faith in God as a living presence disappeared, her ability to believe did not. She continued to tell her stories at bedtime, even though the great listener was absent. The phenomenon of God and religion occupied her mind for the rest of her life. Her first book was *A Struggle for God*, written in 1885, when she was twenty-four years old, and published under the pseudonym of Henri Lou. In it the hero Kuno asks the vital and perplexing question of whether man can live without God in a godless universe. Can faith in reason be a substitute for faith in God? His younger brother's reply is an existentialist thought: No, we must face the truth that life is meaningless and futile, that our only salvation and hope lie in the belief in nothingness. But Kuno, speaking for Lou, is against man's resignation and, despite his doubts, sees man's sacred duty in believing and extolling life as the highest means to the highest goal. Lou's almost militant affirmation of life—a quality she shared with Alma Mahler as much as with Gertrude Stein—had taken root at an early stage of her development; it became the propelling power of her existence.

Lou remembered another incident which she recounted in her memoirs and which is symbolically significant beyond her own interpretation. She thought that a cracker bonbon that her father had brought home for her from a court festivity contained golden dresses. When she was told that the dresses were only made of tissue paper, she decided not to open the package. "Thus," she concluded, "they remained golden dresses for me nevertheless." Was it true that this method enabled her to keep any doubt away from herself, as she surmised? More than that, this incident anticipated her ability to enjoy fully, however vicariously, a sensory experience that only took place in her mind. Her imagination triumphed over her curiosity to lay bare what might conceal little more than disappointment. This inner strength was a major component in her sensual relationship to men in the early part of her mature life, during which she preserved her virginity while having the most intense love affairs with men.

A third traumatic experience had a decisive impact on her life. Without realizing it, she transferred the worship and adoration of God that had once enfolded her young soul to Hendrik Gillot, minister of the Dutch Reformed Church in St. Petersburg, and her mentor during her crucial adolescent period. Gillot, as impressive as her father, was a well-educated person and a brilliant orator with progressive notions.

Annoyed by the dogmatic conservatism of the Lutheran pastor who was to enlighten her in preparation for confirmation, she decided to listen to one of Gillot's sermons. With an actor's skill and a prophet's vision, Gillot could cast a spell upon his listeners. He, more than his sermons, captivated Lou, who was determined to meet him. Just at that time her father died, and Lou needed another father-God image. (She felt very lonesome in her growing years and confided her thoughts and feelings to notebooks that she kept all her life, some of whose entries turned later into stories and books.) She said in her memoirs that she recognized how her childish fantasy and dreams had moved a step into reality: "A living being took their place: he did not enter my life next to them but embraced these dreams in their totality while being the epitome of all reality. There is no more precise word for the shock he caused than the one circumscribing the most surprising, never expected event united with the most familiar and always hoped-for: 'Man'!"

Gillot was elated in her presence, and Lou adored him more and more. He was then in his forties, and she seventeen. He was married and had two daughters who were Lou's age. He began to tutor her, giving her an all-embracing frame of reference, although certain subjects went far beyond the conception of a seventeen-year-old girl. Gillot recognized that she moved in and out of dream and reality as if they were one and the same. Relentlessly, he strove to make her divorce her fictionalized thoughts from reality.

Lou was delighted to study with him. For her it was a major step toward freedom, toward becoming. Gillot felt he was about to create his masterpiece of a student. He went so far as to permit her to write some of his sermons and, once, when he was reprimanded by the Dutch ambassador and told to stick to the Bible, he delivered Lou's sermon based on Goethe's line in *Faust*: "Name is sound and fury" without changing a line. Lou enjoyed observing the reaction of her own words on the congregation.

Gillot became more and more enamored of the personal creation he called Lou, since he could not pronounce—or refused to—the Russian version of her name: Lolja. One day he surprised her by taking her into his arms and asking her to marry him. He had already made the preparations for it without letting her know. He was so sure of himself, he did not consider making sure of her. He deceived himself, as many after him were to do.

All the while she had looked at him as a saint in man's clothing. He had stood behind a veil of deification. Now, the veil—like the curtain before it—tore: there was the man Gillot. She may not have been fully aware of what she had been doing. She had not been without fault in building a relationship that could neither negate nor escape a good deal of eroticism. When suddenly she had to face the consequences, she did not know what was happening to her: the first god *she* chose dethroned himself.

Several years later she fictionalized this experience in her novel, *Ruth*, in which a young girl falls in love with her teacher. The story is an unadorned copy of her experiences with Gillot. The teacher wants to direct the channels of the girl's dream world into creative and constructive realism while becoming enamored of the genius of her mind and the charm of her womanly beauty. That this romantic tale of a young girl's love for her teacher became a best-seller in 1895 and established Lou's reputation as a writer is less surprising than her psychological insight into the complexities of love: the innocent adoration, the desire to surrender and the fear of it, the various shades of male aggressiveness. Most significant is that almost fifteen years after this incident, Lou pictured herself as half-innocent, half-knowing. She could experience the passion of a mature woman who, caught in the dream world of a child, was afraid of yielding to her own feelings.

After *l'affaire Gillot*, Lou wanted to escape. She decided to leave Russia for Zürich, a cosmopolitan city playing host to the greatest minds of Europe, to kings and those revolutionaries preparing to overthrow them. There was also a colony of young Russians studying for missionary work. Zürich was famous for its University at that time, and it was the opportunity to live in Zürich that attracted Lou to continue her studies there. Had not Gillot prepared her for such an advanced step into life? Her decision to leave came as a surprise to Gillot as much as her rejection of his love. It made things final for him.

Was it her "persistent childlikeness," as she claimed, that stood between them, or was it that she loved an image and not a man? He did not awaken the woman in her and only shocked her into the realization that the most tender feelings cannot endure and, at a point, are crushed by the crudeness of reality. Apparently, he never quite fathomed what went wrong. She, on the other hand, felt overwhelmed by the events, and escape was the only way out for her. Perhaps at that point she still thought she could thus save the innocence of her love.

But how innocent could her love have been when she insisted on being confirmed by Gillot, who, acquiescing at that point to any of her demands, suggested a small place in Holland for that purpose? And how innocent could it have been, considering the text she chose for this ceremony, taken from the Lord's words to Israel: "Fear not, for I have chosen you; I have called you by name, you are mine." And Lou answered: "You bless me, for I do not leave you." It was undoubtedly an unorthodox and unusual ceremony officiated over by a man who had fallen in love with a young girl, and it foreshadowed the nature of the rest of life: hers was a destiny of the unorthodox and unusual. The ceremony took place in May, 1880, when Lou had passed her nineteenth birthday. Eight years later, on October 31st, she recalled this incident in her diary and how in her mind Gillot's role changed from that of a god to that of a priest "who consecrated me unto everything high and beautiful toward which I was striving."

This ceremony was a symbol for her, but one with far-reaching consequences. She felt newly born. Gillot had instilled in her a vision of life that she was resolved to model in the image of what she then felt was "her whole person," a life that had to lead to "heightened productivity so that it can create God and law beyond itself." At the moment of the ceremony she was enthralled by her own childlike rapture in receiving and accepting a challenge, in separating her idealization of a man from an ideal to live for, fully "aware that I wished, and ought, to live for it alone, without him."

All her life she needed a god to enthrone, to dominate, and to dethrone when he had served her needs. She always pushed her dreams to the edge of reality. She always lived in a state of ecstasy, believing that a miracle waited for her around the corner. Because she so strongly believed in it and because she was the kind of person who could transform any occurrence into a miracle, the miracles, no doubt, were always waiting for her around the next corner.

Lou had been sickly ever since her work and final break with Gillot. In spite of her poor health, this period was the beginning of her total affirmation of life ("I fell ill in full joy and life-affirmation," her diary says). While studying in Zürich she wrote a great deal of poetry, also the poem "Hymn to Life," which Nietzsche later put to music in a slightly changed version. Lou became a member of the literary circle around the minor but at that time much revered Swiss poet Gottfried Kinkel, who must have sent some of her poems to Malwida von Meysenbug, because she wrote Lou on March 14, 1882, shortly before Lou went to Rome: "Your poems touched me deeply. . . . They disclose what I behold with ever purer delight: your inner life, which is meant for blossoms so noble that you must keep it most holy. . . . Yours is a great task . . ."

Malwida was one of those fascinating figures of an era whose contradictions became manifest in her personality. At that time Victorian prudery went hand in hand with the militant spirit of a new social conscience. Incriminated by the rebellions of 1848, she was forced to flee from Berlin and take up residence in London, where many of the freedom fighters found asylum. She never stood on barricades, but was soon known in Europe as the patroness of the revolutionaries. Her *Memoirs of an Idealist* became a best-seller in 1876, and Malwida was celebrated as *the* idealist of her day, helping to prepare the way for the emancipation of women.

It was a matter of course that such a person as Lou would deeply impress Malwida. The notion of what an idealist is can be easily stretched, but Lou fitted Malwida's formulae superficially, at least. She had done with religion in its patriarchal and orthodox sense without giving up deep, inner belief. She was a drawing-room revolutionary like Malwida, aware of the world's need for social change, while desperately holding on to the pension she received from the Czar's government after her father's death. Lou was a self-styled exile at a time when a great number of the intellectual elite were exiled from their home countries. She had lofty notions about the sexes living together in spiritual closeness and personal freedom, while being wary of sexual passion. Her shock experience with Gillot excluded sex from her associations with men for some time to come. All this found Malwida's approval.

1882 was the year and Rome was the place where Lou's life began to unfold and her great task started, the task of exploring life and gaining fame as an ambassadress extraordinary in the world of the intelligentsia. Simultaneously she acquired the reputation of a *femme fatale* by default. She could be certain that in whatever salon she happened to visit, at least one man would fall in love with her.

One night that spring Paul Reé encountered Lou in Malwida's villa, and she was impressed by his "sharply cut profile and clever eyes." They quickly took to one another, talking with great ease and joy about philosophy, life and themselves. From that night on they met daily at Malwida's and walked from her villa in the Via della Polveriera through the streets of Rome on their way home. They walked for hours, long after midnight, enjoying detours and short-cuts, walking "arm in arm," a gesture that Lou considered totally innocent.

Paul Reé, a disciple of Schopenhauer and a positivist, was a philosopher-friend of Friedrich Nietzsche. Referring to one of his books, *Psychological Observations*, Nietzsche said that Reé was "a moralist with the keenest vision—quite a rarity among Germans." These two philosophers often spent time together, Reé occasionally reading to Nietzsche to spare his weak eyes—only to develop similar symptoms. But their friendship soon turned to a love-hate relationship that Lou's presence only complicated more. What the two philosophers had in common was their love for the epigram, polished language. But Nietzsche was a man of far greater vision; he was more original and Dionysian in his power of expression. The best Nietzsche had to say about his friend was that he recognized him as "one of the boldest but coldest thinkers." In their hours of hatred, Reé wrote about Nietzsche: "I have never been able to read him. He is brilliant but has few thoughts." Nietzsche, on the other hand, once wrote to Malwida about his friend: " 'He's a poor fellow, one must push him along'—how often have I told myself this when his miserable, dishonest way of thinking and living revolted me."

Paul Reé was one of those intellectuals who possess a passport to greatness, but never quite muster the strength to make the journey. He was of Jewish descent and eaten up with self-hatred. His was an exemplary case of character defeating genius. Lou recognized the innermost tortures he suffered in denying himself his past, but she also noted "his supernatural kindness growing out of his incredibly painful self-hatred. Nobody knew that better than I . . ." Reé was a brilliant conversationalist, witty and at times sharp-tongued, his ironic humor often turned against himself. He was a slow and painstaking worker who brooded over problems for months and years. But in spite of his personal difficulties, he was a warm and lovable human being. Malwida despised his philosophical writings since they ran counter to her idealistic notions, but she recognized his personable qualities and always made him feel welcome and protected. Lou immediately sensed his reliability and kindness, two ready-made features for her unorthodox plans. Meeting Lou seemed to complicate Reé's private life as much as his friendship with Nietzsche complicated his career as a philosopher. He was not a match for either of them.

When Lou met Reé she visualized a plan, fascinating to her and more than daring for the *fin de siècle*: to live with Reé and a third person like good comrades in the same living quarters and in a spiritual exchange while studying. Vienna was first mentioned as a likely place, then Paris. While this plan was discussed, Reé did a foolish thing, probably the most foolish thing he could have done. Infatuated with the beauty of her mind and appearance but not understanding either, he did what almost all men meeting Lou after him did: he proposed marriage. He went first to her mother, asking for the hand of her daughter in the good old-fashioned manner. That was the worst thing he could have done, since Lou was about to break with all taboos. His argument that a marriage would be more advantageous to their plan than having a third person around was quickly refuted by Lou. Learning to submit to Lou's will, Reé suggested Nietzsche as the third person. He was his best friend, a mature man and pensioned professor of thirty-eight years. He would be an excellent chaperon of their newly established sister-brother relationship.

A rendezvous was arranged by Reé. They were to meet at St. Peter's in front of Michelangelo's *Pietà*. What more fitting place could there be for Nietzsche to face Lou for the first time? And what more fitting salutation could he have thought of in this hallowed spot than: "From what stars have we fallen to meet here?" A few days after he met her, he did a very unphilosophic thing. He who had written "A married philosopher belongs to comedy" asked Reé to propose to her for him. It was undoubtedly the absurd idea of an utterly unrealistic man afraid of himself.

Reé and Lou were upset about the turn of events. They both did not want to see their "holy trinity" and their plan to study together destroyed, even though for different reasons. Lou was afraid her mother would force her to return with her to Russia. All she wanted was to spend the coming winter in the company of great men. Reé had not yet quite given up his hope of living with Lou. Thus, no definite decision at that moment was the only solution. In the most gentle way possible, Reé tried to explain to Nietzsche that through her marriage to him Lou would lose her Russian stipend, and Nietzsche's salary would not suffice for two.

The three, with Lou's mother, planned to travel to the northern part of Italy and from there to Switzerland together. But Nietzsche had to stay back for a few days because he had fallen ill, and Reé kept him company. In Orta they got together again. Nietzsche felt fit. He and Lou climbed to the top of the nearby Monte Sacro, while Reé kept Madame von Salomé company in the valley. No one will ever know what happened to the two on Monte Sacro. They stayed up there much longer than they—or Reé and her mother—anticipated. Nietzsche came down a changed man. He was unusually elated. Much later he referred to this walk with the words: "I owe you the most beautiful dream of my life." "The Lou of Monte Sacro" was a recurring phrase in his life's vocabulary that had a very definite meaning for him. And Lou spoke excitedly about his being truly of "a religious nature."

There can be no doubt that the two were magnetized by one another, although meaning and intentions may have differed a great deal. When in her old age she was asked about that excursion, Lou remarked, "Whether I kissed Nietzsche on the Monte Sacro—I no longer know;" the remark does not clarify matters. On the contrary, it leaves us with the impression that both were carried away by this experience. In fact, they had several things in common: their belief in the power of life, their search for a life in which man can assert and outdistance himself, where he can grow out and beyond any average existence. He probably spoke like a prophet with winged words. When later on he mentioned time and again Lou's extraordinary capacity for understanding, saying that she was an inspiring listener who could ignite new thoughts and ideas, all this must have begun on Monte Sacro. Even if the events up there remained restricted to a spiritual plane, the elation on both sides must have been brushed by sensual excitement. There could be no doubt about one thing: they both needed and were ready to use one another.

Nietzsche left for Basel to discuss his future with Franz and Ida Overbeck. The latter clearly defined Nietzsche's mood when she explained that he "had given himself to the hope of having found his alter ego in Miss Salomé—of working with her and, through her help, toward his goals." But everything that happened after Monte Sacro was an unfortunate anticlimax, full of intrigues, bickering and malicious slander.

In Basel Nietzsche was hopeful. He wrote Reé about their coming rendezvous in Lucerne where he wanted Lou to see Tribschen, the home of his former friend Richard Wagner: "I absolutely must speak with Miss Salomé once again, perhaps in the Löwengraben" (a historic site in Lucerne). It was there that Lou made it clear to Nietzsche that a marriage between them was out of the question. He showed neither surprise nor pain. Lou was under the impression that he felt relieved and spoke positively of their joint studies that coming winter. All three stayed together in Lucerne where Nietzsche insisted on being photographed with her and Reé. Nietzsche apparently staged the scene in a self-mortifying mood: Lou on top of a cart pulled by the two men. He intended to show how the two philosophers would put their strength into the service of the young lady driving them on with inspiration. This scene may have been on his mind when he had the old woman tell Zarathustra that man should not forget his whip when going to woman. In fact, he requested a whip for Lou which she might crack over his and Reé's heads. (The photograph has since become one of the best known of that period.)

The next significant station in their relationship was Tautenburg, a Thuringian resort, where Lou spent one summer month with Nietzsche, who was there for a longer period. Nietzsche's sister, Elisabeth, was also there. He was overjoyed, as his letters prove. To Lou: ". . . my health has come back, I don't know from where, and everybody tells me that I look younger than ever . . . from now on, when you will advise me, I shall be well advised . . . I do not want to be lonely anymore, I want to learn to be human again . . ." To Malwida: "This year . . . has been made very beautiful, thanks to the charm and graciousness of this young, truly heroic soul. I hope to have in her a pupil and, if my life should not last much longer, an heir and disciple."

Elisabeth Nietzsche had met Lou in Bayreuth, and the difference between the two had made itself felt in mutual distrust. These two women—the one, unorthodox, carefree, with a wild dream of life; the other petty, malicious, vengeful—were destined to be enemies. Whatever Lou did in Bayreuth, whether it was to chat with Richard Wagner, now Nietzsche's adversary, or to become friendly with her compatriot, the Russian set designer, Count Jukovsky, Elisabeth thought they were things done only to discredit her brother. Also

Malwida von Meysenbug, who had introduced Lou to Wagner's inner circle, seemed no longer so fond of Lou as she had been. This idealist and freedom fighter was suspicious of Lou's idea to set up a household together with two philosophers. Malwida would rather have seen Lou go it alone, as she had advised her from the outset, if only to prove that women also can accomplish the greatest things. Lou may have been indiscreet and bragged about her daring plan in the presence of Wagner and may even have shown the funny photograph taken in Lucerne.

Lou sensed how much Nietzsche's sister disliked and disapproved of her. Like a child she reacted by grossly exaggerating her uninhibited behavior whenever she knew she was being observed. The night when the two women stayed in the house of friends at Jena on their way to Tautenburg, Elisabeth used the opportunity to reprimand Lou about everything she could think of. It may have started with the older woman admonishing the young girl, but it led from misgivings to outbreaks of hatred: that Lou misbehaved, that she made light of Friedrich before the entire Wagner clique, that she tried to blacken his name by dragging him into that "trinity plan" of hers. Lou supposedly burst into a flood of insults, shouting that Nietzsche was soiling their study plan with his dirty designs of a concubinage. She assured Elisabeth she was not interested in her brother as a man and could sleep in the same room with him without ever getting any amorous notions.

Elisabeth might not have reported this incident had she not seen her brother in an affectionate mood waiting for them at the station and kissing Lou's hand with a meaningful gesture. She felt she had to interfere and save her brother from further foolish acts. A series of reproaches followed. Lou defended her right to associate with whomever she wished, and declared, moreover, that Nietzsche's quarrels with Wagner were not hers. It is not certain whether Lou threatened to leave and Nietzsche kept her back; or, as Elisabeth wrote her friends, that Lou was asked to leave the next day, but that she, Elisabeth, took pity on the girl who had begged Nietzsche to let her stay, particularly since Lou pretended to be ill. Given Elisabeth's reputation, especially her possessiveness of her brother, and Lou's proud and often ruthless reactions, choosing between these two versions may not be too difficult.

The month Lou spent with Nietzsche passed quickly. She promised to keep Reé informed about what went on: ". . . Nietzsche . . . is a man of powerful needs. . . . After a day of being together with me . . . our old intimacy was re-established. He came up to my room again and again; and in the evening he took my hand, kissed it twice. . . . During the following days I had to stay in bed; he sent letters to my room and spoke to me through the door . . . today we spent a beautiful day in the dark quiet pine woods . . ."

She found talking to Nietzsche very exciting and wondered how well they understood each other. "I had intended to take notes of our conversations but that is almost impossible because they range from the nearest to the most distant thoughts and do not lend themselves to precise formulations." She learned a great deal and thought highly of him as a teacher. He found her prose still wanting and corrected an essay she had written about womanhood.

Nietzsche neglected his own work during this month to be able to work with her. When she expressed guilt about keeping him from his own manuscripts, he supposedly said: "I have had so rarely an opportunity for doing it that I enjoy it like a child." They often talked about religion, heaven and hell. What they had in common was a basically religious trait; they were "freethinkers in the most extreme sense of the word. . . . We shall yet witness his becoming the prophet of a new religion, and it will be one that seeks heroes for disciples," she jotted down in her diary. Much of what was discussed in Tautenburg found its way into her book, *A Struggle for God.* Nietzsche acknowledged its brilliance and found that she had made good use of her month under his tutelage. It is noteworthy that his kudos was written at a time when he had lost her through his sister's intrigues as much as his own moments of madness and had finally given up hope of being rescued from his loneliness by any woman.

The only thing that disturbed Lou during her Tautenburg idyll with Nietzsche was his attempt to undermine her feelings of friendship for Reé. Nietzsche skillfully built derogatory remarks about him into their talks. Lou merely wrote Reé that Nietzsche "had within him many dark dungeons and hidden passages which one does not see at first sight and which may contain his true character. Strange, the other day the thought suddenly struck me that one day we might even be enemies."

And enemies they became. Elisabeth made up her mind that her brother's infatuation with that Russian girl had to be ended. Lou was "a poisonous reptile to be destroyed at all costs," she said to Malwida. He had to be saved from this evil woman, this adventuress, whom she even suspected of being a Jewess—which was the worst that could happen to one who harbored deep-seated anti-Semitic feelings. She knew how to stir up a family quarrel so that Nietzsche was driven to Italy again.

At this time Elisabeth became engaged to Bernhard Förster, a militant anti-Semite and precursor of Nazism. Strangely enough, Nietzsche used his sister's antagonistic attitude toward Lou and Reé, but only to turn around later to denounce and deny Elisabeth. ("Souls such as yours, my dear sister, I do not like: and I like them least when they are morally bloated.")

While still in Germany he saw Lou and Reé quite often, but mistrust and unnerving friction were felt by all of them. During his wintery loneliness in Santa Margherita he brooded over his loss of Lou and felt as though he had been thrown overboard by her and Reé. His letters to them had a nasty tone and became more and more hostile. Some of them showed the despair of a man who felt deceived by life more than by a woman.

The exchange of letters and the use of invectives often went beyond the human, the all-too-human. Lou would charge him with "delusions of grandeur" and refer to his "wounded vanity." Nietzsche would try to solicit Reé's help to make Lou apologize for treating him "like a twenty-year-old student . . . who had fallen in love with her." And to Reé: "How can you stand being near such a creature?"

It would have come almost to a duel between Nietzsche and Paul Reé, whose brother Georg, moreover, threatened Nietzsche with a libel suit. In one of Nietzsche's letters to Georg Reé, written from Sils

Maria in the summer of 1883, he said among other niceties: ". . . Now I know he [Paul Reé] acted behind my back like a slimy, lying fellow. . . . It is he who reproached me that I pursued dirty intentions behind the mask of ideal aims in regard to Fräulein Salomé: It is he who dares speak contemptuously of my mind as if I were a lunatic who does not know what he wants. . . . And whenever I presented your brother with my stern judgment about this girl's character, do you think he had ever had for her a word of excuse? He always said nothing but: 'You are perfectly right about Lou! But this does not change my relationship to her!' In one of his letters he once called her his fate: *Quel goût*, this lean, dirty, evil-smelling she-monkey with her false breasts—his fate! Pardon me! How she talks about your brother, this shall remain a matter of my discretion . . ."

Nietzsche wore many masks, but each mask was a genuine Nietzsche. He wrote to Ida Overbeck: ". . . I miss her, for all her bad qualities . . . I have found no one so unprejudiced, so clever, so well prepared for my sort of problems . . ." And to his mother: "Whatever may be said against this girl—and surely much more than my sister says—the fact remains that I have found no more gifted, more reflective creature."

His relations with Lou were in "their last, most painful throes" when he wrote: ". . . Today I blame you only for not having been truthful at the right moment . . . I want you to condemn yourself and determine your own punishment. . . . My dear Lou, take care! If now I reject you, it will mean a frightful indictment of your whole being! . . . note well that I need no further argument against all little self-seekers and pleasure-seekers than disgust. . . . Adieu, my dear Lou, I shall not see you again. Preserve your soul from such doings, and make good with others, particularly with my friend Reé, what you can no longer make good with me. . . . Adieu, dear Lou, I did not finish your letter, but I read too much already."

And then these outcries to other friends: "Heavens! how lonely I am!" His agony about having said his final adieu: "I am a hermit once again, and more than ever; and am—consequently—thinking about something new. It seems to me that only the condition of pregnancy binds us to life ever anew."

In all this struggle, in his desperate attempt to find a way to his better self from an insufferable loneliness, madly attaching himself to an idealized ideal, being insanely in love with the hope of being able to love, a prophet calling his disciples, a god looking for his apostles, Nietzsche wrote, in the fever of a few weeks, *Thus Spake Zarathustra.*

Lou had challenged his mind, she had made his enthusiasm soar. The idea of *Zarathustra* was the result of his encounter with her. It was his reaction to his suffering through Lou, it was his revenge upon her. Does not the old woman admonish Zarathustra that, when going to women, he should not forget the whip? Does not Zarathustra apostrophize Paul Reé when saying, "One should honor in his friend even the enemy." In Lou's essay on women, which she discussed with Nietzsche in Tautenburg and which he corrected, she had written: "Pregnancy is the cardinal state which has gradually, in the course of time, determined the nature of woman." Zarathustra says: "Everything about women is a riddle. And everything about women has one solution—its name is pregnancy."

Ida Overbeck noted that, "in spite of various contributory impulses leading to *Zarathustra,* Lou had a direct share in it by inspiring Nietzsche to make his philosophic-religious and moralistic-prophetic statement as a substitute for religion and morality." And Peter Gast, another of Nietzsche's close friends, said Lou's intelligence and femininity carried Nietzsche to the heights of ecstasy. Those heights undoubtedly began on Monte Sacro.

In her fury and disgust Elisabeth wrote to her friend Clara Gelzer about a conversation between Nietzsche and Lou overheard in Tautenburg: "What horrid talk the two carried on together! What was a lie? Nothing! What was a breach of confidence? Nothing! What was doing one's duty? Silliness. What was the most derisive talk about true friends? Right judgment. What was compassion? Contemptible. Never have I seen my brother together with his philosophy so mean, so paltry."

Poor Elisabeth! She did not know that these were the first pangs of labor. The child was Superman. "Man is something that is to be surpassed."

A Circle That Never Closed

After the "trinity" fell apart and Lou's study plan with her two philosophers failed to materialize, she and Paul Reé decided to settle down in Berlin. Her mother had meanwhile returned to Russia. In 1883 they moved into a three-room apartment, with two bedrooms separated by a large living room that Lou visualized as a "salon" where the great ones of her time should meet, a salon like the one Malwida von Meysenbug had in Rome.

Her idea of living with Reé as brother and sister was, whatever else, unusual at the end of the Victorian era with its double standard of morality. Lou enjoyed being different at any price and was amused by people's reactions, by their suspicions and cagey questions. Reé's position was not an enviable one, though he was an ideal partner for Lou. He could not have felt honored for having been chosen by her for this strange partnership, which lasted five years. Nor should he have wondered if he was manipulated by her—he undoubtedly was; being weak, tortured by self-doubts as well as by his love for Lou, he became a toy in her playful hands. He often wanted to leave her because he realized how unpleasant a role she made him play; how little she cared about his personal feelings when she made him watch her flirting with other, mostly older, men. Only his strongly masochistic feelings, his deep-seated self-hatred made it possible for him to live by her side with the unmanly epithet of being Lou's "maid-of-honor."

He was there to protect Lou and to let her have her will in whatever came to her mind. When the vicious and vituperative attacks of Nietzsche's sister upon Lou's character made her fear that her mother would insist that she return to St. Petersburg, she wanted to prove that she was not an eternal student or an idle society lady, but a lady of letters, recognized by her fellow writers. She told Reé that they each had to write and publish a book. They went into seclusion in Meran, then a well-known spa in the Austrian mountains. Reé finished his philosophic treatise, *The Emergence of Conscience*, and Lou wrote her book, *A Struggle for God*. Unfortunately for Reé, Lou's work was a resounding success, while his was found wanting in spirit and substance. Nietzsche's reactions to both works were indicative of the public's consensus. He wrote to Overbeck: "I ought to like it heartily. She has finally fulfilled the hopes placed in her by me in Tautenburg. For the rest, the devil take her." And in another letter referring to Reé's book: "How empty, how dull, how false! . . . Pity there is no more 'contents' in such a garment." But Lou's work "struck me quite the other way round. What a contrast between the girlish, tame manner and the matter strong in will and wisdom! There is loftiness in it, and even though it is not the eternal feminine that draws this pseudogirl upwards, then it is perhaps the eternal masculine. A hundred times was I also reminded of our Tautenburg talks!"

Reé had hoped that this work would help him to a position at a university. When he was turned down by the philosophical faculty of Strasbourg, he decided to study medicine. Financially independent, he determinedly devoted his medical knowledge to helping the sick who were poor. Lou, on the other hand, fully accomplished with her book what she had hoped for. It became a best-seller, and she was talked about as one of the upcoming writers of her time. Her salon flourished whenever she was in Berlin. Among her visitors were writers, philosophers and scientists. One could easily mention two dozen of some of the best minds in Bismarck's Germany frequenting her salon and being enchanted by the young Russian girl's brilliance. Of course, she had more suitors than Reé could keep count of.

Ludwig Hüter, a student of philosophy, gave Malwida a lively account of what was happening in Lou's salon: ". . . Reé—somewhat jealous (understandably, for Louise Salomé is beautiful and emotionally bewitching); she—well, if she can flirt, she does so almost unconsciously, but there she is after all playing a little with serious older men and—does not say what she thinks (unreservedly) without danger. With such remarks (perhaps primarily meant as aesthetic, but grazing naïve sensuality) she can pit two rivals against each other . . . too odd a girl to be easily made out . . . a likable, winning, truly feminine being who renounces all womanly resources in the struggle for existence and instead takes up men's weapons with a certain harsh exclusiveness. Sharp judging and, as it turns out, condemning everything; no trace of mercy, so dear to woman; clear resoluteness in every word, yet her character only appears the more one-sided for being so resolute in its one direction; music, art, poetry are discussed, to be sure, but gauged by a strange standard: not pure joy over their beauty, pleasure in their form, comprehension of their substance, poetic enjoyment with heart and soul, no—only a cold, too often negative, corrosive philosophizing about them. . . . Behind her stands Dr. Reé . . ."

Reé, who only seemed to wait for a fitting opportunity to make an end to his partly ludicrous, partly torturous existence as his queen's consort, was finally able to do so when Friedrich Carl Andreas entered her life. Reé literally disappeared overnight. She was surprised about his sudden decision, because her clever self-deception kept her from comprehending what must have gone on in the man for all those years. Had she conveniently forgotten that he desired to marry her?

There must have been something fatal in her physical and intellectual charms. Suicide or attempted suicide occurred rather frequently to those who loved her. One such case, and the first one, was Friedrich Carl Andreas. The only reason why she suddenly married him was that he attempted suicide. Andreas was a fascinating and frightening figure. His partly scholarly, partly monkish appearance, his black-bearded face and short, stocky-built body did not impress her. But when he told her the story of his life (he was in his early forties when he met Lou, who was fifteen years younger), she felt a curious interest in this man whose character and abilities were composed of contrasting features. There was something demonic about the intensity that he could manifest as well as hide. Gerhart Hauptmann, who as a dramatist instinctively sensed dra-

matic conflicts, once characterized Andreas's ability to love with the
words: "how wild and how gentle."

He was born in Batavia. His mother was half-German, half-
Malayan, his father an Armenian. Andreas studied in Swiss and
German schools, but he felt drawn to the East and became an
outstanding philologist. A linguistic genius, he mastered German,
French, English and Dutch, and was thoroughly at ease with Greek,
Latin, Hebrew and Sanskrit, but he also was fluent in Javanese,
Aramaic, Pahlavi, Hindi, Turkish, Arabic, Armenian. To top all these
accomplishments, he knew every Persian dialect and was familiar
with the history and religions, the folklore, geography and archaeol-
ogy of each country. As about all other things in life, he had a wild
passion for scholarly research and the painstaking patience needed to
relate one thing to another. For many years he tried to get a
university appointment, until finally he became a faculty member at
the University at Göttingen. One day he would finish the crowning
work of his life, he always said, a book in which his creative thoughts
would triumph, his intuition would be wedded to the analysis of the
researched knowledge that was his. But this book remained unfinished. The few essays he published had touches of greatness, but,
as a whole, his work was unfulfilled.

He was probably the most passionate suitor Lou ever had. To win
her, he ran a knife into his chest. ("It was lying on the table at which
he sat. With a calm movement he grasped and thrust it into his
breast.") His physical life was saved, but not his spiritual being.
Pushed forcibly into this situation, Lou tried to master it as best she
could. In his helplessness and her own despair she consented to
marry him, but in name only. She would never be his. Moreover, he
had to grant her complete independence. He was willing, secretly
hoping that time would be on his side. Their first years of marriage
were hellish: the more he pleaded and raged, the stronger became
her resistance.

She traveled a great deal. In the beginning he rarely accompanied
her and later stayed home altogether. Lou often said she wished her
husband would find a companion ("Who could have thought with
what ardor I at all times of my life would have wished my husband

. . . the nicest, best, most beautiful mistress?"). They engaged a housekeeper. Her name was Marie. She took care of Andreas and became a part of their household life. Andreas was no longer quite alone. Marie had two illegitimate children; one died and the other stayed in their Göttingen house with Lou even after Marie and Andreas were dead.

Only when Andreas was in his eighties, visiting Lou after an operation she had had to undergo, did they discover each other. She wrote Sigmund Freud about it on May 3, 1930:

And now I have something wonderful, but at the same time almost comical, to tell: as my husband sat and talked to me day after day at my bedside in the nursing home at the appointed visiting hours, we noticed, we two old people, how much we had to say to each other—for which we had never really had the time. Busy as we had always been, we had never had much taste for "chatting together round the fireside." Later my husband rubbed me with the embrocations he told Anne about and which he strongly recommended for you. He enjoyed doing it. . . .

A few weeks later Friedrich Carl Andreas was dead.

Lou's rebellious spirit and her compulsive search for the new and exciting in life reflected her time. The ten years from 1895 to 1905 that shook the world out of its Renaissance dream laid the foundation of a new era. White men had divided the colonial world, the exploitation of which had come to a point of saturation fore-shadowing the resurgent upheavals of colored men everywhere. The turn of the century brought about significant changes in the arts. The directional and conceptual ideas of Renaissance man, who was gradually dethroned, had run their course. In areas remote from the arts, man's accomplishments were most stunning and, of course, destined to exert great influence on the arts as time passed.

From our vantage point now, some of the changes have the stamp of inevitability. They prepared the cataclysmic events of the twentieth century, clearing the way for the realization of man's oldest dreams and undreamt-of discoveries: the advent of mechanis-tic science with the discoveries of the Curies and Roentgen looking through man with X-ray eyes, while Freud began to probe man's psyche. Edison developed the kinetoscope and Marconi sent long-wave signals over a distance of more than a mile. Horseless carriages started to rattle along rutted roads. In 1903 the Wright brothers made Leonardo da Vinci's Renaissance dream of the flying machine come true. Einstein repudiated Newton and began to rebuild the world of Galileo and Copernicus.

The arts kept pace with science, also trying to recondition the senses of the people, to reconstruct the visual and aural world of imagination and make-believe. Architects began to build the first unornamented cubic houses, preparing the way for the great monolithic block, the huge single concrete steel or glass cube. Adolf Loos, today overshadowed by the master builders of the Bauhaus and such giants as Le Corbusier, was the first to build, in 1910, an unornamented façade into a baroque environment; it scandalized the feudal taste of the bourgeois Viennese who loved his Kaiser as much as his *Gemütlichkeit*. Arnold Schönberg turned away from Wagner and went to the early Greeks for inspiration and the atonal mode of musical expression, while Pablo Picasso learned to paint cubistically from Congo masks, and Isadora Duncan threw off the artificiality of the nineteenth-century classical ballet. Gustav Klimt, supported by a group of Austrian painters, broke away from tradition and founded the Vienna *Sezession*. He became the leading spirit of Art Nouveau. In short, tradition per se reached the point of no return. It was anathema, a condition that a few decades later, of necessity, had to create an artistic climate in which non-art and the cliché of the anti-cliché triumphed.

At the turn of the century the artist desperately began to search for his identity and, in the chaotic pursuit of himself, ran from "ism" to "ism." Everything archaic and medieval, primitive and Oriental became a source of inspiration. When Paul Klee wrote, "I want to be as though new-born . . . knowing no pictures, entirely without impulses, almost in an original state," he was voicing Lou's sentiments.

By natural instinct, feeling the clashing conflicts within it, she was drawn to the drama and theater. In those years Adolphe Appia rejected naturalism in the theater. He and his disciple, Gordon Craig,

advanced the concept of suggestiveness. Maurice Maeterlinck created a surrealistic, puppet- and dreamlike theatrical experience, a
drama of interior awareness, of the mystery of existence. Constantine
Stanislavsky's "theatre of inner feeling" was trying to do away with
the hollow pathos of the classical method of acting and its
counterpart of superficial realism. This was preceded by theatrical
iconoclasts like André Antoine and his *Théâtre Libre*, which was
supported by Zola, Daudet and other naturalists; in 1887, they
rebelled against the meretricious well-made plays of Scribe and
Sardou. The naturalistic movement tried to stop the romantic trend
and, with the help of such giants as Henrik Ibsen, succeeded. Lou
became first acquainted with Ibsen in Berlin where *Die Freie Bühne*
followed the same aims as Antoine's *Théâtre Libre* in Paris. Otto
Brahm was the directorial genius in Berlin, producing Strindberg,
Tolstoi and Hauptmann as well as Ibsen. Gerhart Hauptmann, who
started as a naturalist with such powerful plays as *Before Sunrise* and
The Weavers, then mingled naturalism and neo-romanticism in his
Hannele and, like Strindberg, moved from the real to the surreal.

It was an altogether exciting era in which the spirit of freedom and
experimentation prevailed, old bastions were stormed and new ways
forged into an artistic wilderness in which no one knew exactly how
to discover his artistic Rome, nor whether Rome was still the place he
wanted to reach. But there was a determined will in the creative
minds of that time to move on to a new world. Being her
unconventional self, Lou was very much the child of this era.

It was obvious that she would be moving in those circles in which
the revolutionary will prophetically point to the new. In her role as a
writer and a woman she was soon in the midst of love and creativity
whose interrelation she was soon to stress and to experience. She
never wrote a play until late in her life, but she began to review plays
and be a part of the forces around *Die Freie Bühne* in Berlin.

Deeply impressed by Ibsen and his struggle for social justice and
equality of the sexes, she wrote about six *Women Characters in
Henrik Ibsen* in which she interpreted the dramatist's treatment of
women in captivity. " 'I felt as if I were a man!' Nora says. It is her
strength and independence which slowly awakes, begins to unfold,

clandestinely groping in the dark for liberation. . . . Even though the unattainable and uncertainty are included in what we can call the 'wonderful,' nevertheless, unlimited possibilities, endless perspectives open up. Although Nora faces struggle, she accepts it, strong and young . . . it may be pain in which she leaves, however it is not only a sad and martyrlike pain about a lost ideal, but, at the same time, it shows the dauntless fighter and wrestler for a new ideal . . ." This is the tone and tenor of the book that placed her in the forefront of those women struggling against outworn taboos and for the recognition of a woman's rights.

In the early years of her marriage, using it as a convenient protection for her virginity and unassailability, she moved freely in the theatrical circles of Berlin. Among her friends were the famous publicist Maximilian Harden, to whose magazine she contributed; Max Halbe; and somewhat later Max Reinhardt and the actor Alexander Moissi; the poets Arno Holz and Richard Dehmel; and, above all, Germany's greatest dramatist of her day, Gerhart Hauptmann.

That Hauptmann—who about twenty years later fell in love with Alma Mahler—was one of the many who could not resist Lou seems to be borne out by his note written to her soon after their first meeting: "You must let me come and see you, dear and cherished woman," the note said. It is very likely that the leading character, an intellectually strong, emancipated woman in his play *Lonely People*, was fashioned after Lou, who, however, criticized Hauptmann for not being able to dramatize the importance and scope of the modern woman. But she particularly praised his *Hannele*, a poetic fusion of realism and fantasy. Lou felt akin to the figure of Hannele and found the simplicity of the drama and the glorified naïve religiosity of her dream world utterly moving, with the village teacher appearing as Jesus in the purity of the girl's dying moments. Later, Hauptmann said about this "history of a child's soul" and Lou that "the first reviews to show full understanding came from her."

We do not know too much about Hauptmann's feeling for Lou, who at best saw in him another father figure. But one line from a letter to Lou, very likely written in December, 1900, says: "I despair

of ever being able to tell you what you have meant to me these days."
Hauptmann was an intuitive writer of great abilities, but he often
spoke haltingly and never presented himself as an intellectual. This
may explain his alleged remark that he was too stupid for Lou.

At the turn of the century, as well as a few years preceding and
following it, Lou urgently felt the need to write: emotionally in order
to prove herself and establish a sound reputation as a writer,
economically to add to her Russian stipend. A greater amount of
money gave her the freedom to travel and live where she pleased.
Writing and traveling satisfied her restlessness and eagerness to
explore and experience life. Thus, one book followed the other in
quick succession. After her book on Ibsen's woman characters she
wrote her study on Nietzsche, then came *Ruth, From a Troubled
Soul, Fenitschka, Children of Man, Ma*, and *In the Twilight Zone* in
1902. With the exception of writing a few short essays or reviews, she
then stopped for a few years. The pace of her life was too hectic and
she had doubts about being more than a minor writer albeit of a
fascinating format.

In 1892 when her book on Ibsen appeared, Georg Ledebour, a
Marxist-oriented journalist, orator and socialist politician, fell in love
with Lou, then thirty-one years old and still a virgin, although
married for five years. In strength of will he was a match for her
husband-in-name, but Ledebour was far more balanced a personality
than Andreas, who wanted to stab his rival but refused to talk to him.
Ledebour saw through the whole masquerade of her marriage and
demanded to talk to her husband. From her diary we learn: "He did
not know how impossible it would be and that Fred spoke only with
knives and tears." She too was in love with Ledebour, but apparently
still afraid to give up her freedom and virginity.

In 1893 Ledebour was sentenced to a year in jail for political
reasons. Determined never to see him again, Lou nonetheless found
herself at the workers' clubs where he spoke and lectured. He
demanded that she divorce Andreas. She did so neither then nor at
any time later. Lou saw Ledebour until later in February, 1894, when
she left for Paris and new adventures.

The Wedekind Incident

In Paris in 1894, Lou "was together with Frank Wedekind most of the time," as she said in her autobiography, visiting the Louvre or friends, meeting him for a stroll, sitting in cafés for a friendly and often heated exchange of ideas. She was introduced to him in the house of the Hungarian Countess Emmy de Nemeth who, at that time, had translated some of Strindberg's plays into French. That evening Wedekind was captivated by Lou. After they had spent hours together, when night was almost morning in an onion-soup bistro opposite Les Halles, he asked her to come up to his room in the rue Monsieur le Prince. She went.

Lou kindly referred to this incident as a "misunderstanding on Wedekind's part." In their talks about love and sex, a topic that occupied both with an explorer's passion, he found in her a most enlightened woman. When she accepted his invitation without hesitating for a moment, he could not help assuming that she would spend the night with him. He was surprised when his entire scale of seductive playfulness failed. He finally let her go. The next day he appeared at her hotel formally dressed, with a bouquet of flowers in his hands to apologize for his behavior.

Lou tells us that one could easily find Wedekind at the cafés of the Quartier Latin where he would sit scribbling poems and waiting for the closing hour and one of the streetwalkers to take him home with her to give him shelter, breakfast and some love. Though he may have done this from time to time to play-act the real bohemian, it was really a literary flourish. She also tells us that he often took her to one of the poorest furnished rooms in the poorest sections of Paris to visit the widow of Georg Herwegh; he had been one of Germany's great freedom fighters and his revolutionary poems had appeared in the underground press. Wedekind would always bring with him a ready-made dinner of food the old lady liked.

In 1891, three years before Wedekind met Lou, his play, *Spring's Awakening*, had shocked and scandalized the philistine bourgeois world, which had, of course, a Victorian attitude toward sex. Long before D. H. Lawrence hailed sex as a sacred mystery extolling the power of the dark gods, of the virginal spirit, and laid bare the primitive powers within sophisticated man, Wedekind set out to present uncompromisingly the physical and psychological phenomena of the animal in man and to celebrate the liberating spirit of sex.

His *Spring's Awakening* exploded in the frightened faces of the burghers at the very beginning of the "Gay Nineties" when women with wasplike waists swept the streets with their frou-frou ruffles; when on the public beaches people basked in the sun and swam with bodies fully covered; when men sported monocles and both men and women rode bicycles for fun and transportation; when one met in overstuffed rooms and recited poetry in cozy Turkish corners with the divan half-hidden behind a bead portiere. Behind all this sham glitter and laughter of the *fin de siècle* was an anguish and weariness which no frantic and meaningless "after us the deluge" attitude could cure. Wedekind was not the only spiritual Frankenstein of the era. Ibsen's Nora had just slammed the door of her doll's house behind her. The growing number of factories and machines created unrest and strikes. One was frightened by Gerhart Hauptmann's *Weavers* and shocked by Zola's *Nana* and *Germinal*. People were deeply impressed by the works of Dostoevski and Tolstoi. Even though one tried to cushion one's fear with plush, the uneasiness remained.

Undoubtedly, Lou was very much aware of the social contrasts then in existence, but, being financially independent and totally immersed in the cultural-artistic aspects of the time, she viewed the actual problems of poverty more or less with literary eyes. In writing her memoirs about four decades later, she still felt "urged to tell of a fleeting, insignificant acquaintanceship" she made ·on the street in front of the Louvre. The event she was compelled to tell about is indicative of the flamboyant gesture that was more important than the deed itself, for it was the gesture that lingered in her mind.

Lou had become acquainted with an Alsacian flower vendor who had to take care of her tubercular son. One evening the woman fainted in the street and had to be taken home. Chancing to pass by, Lou quickly decided to get into the woman's Alsacian costume and, together with her friend Sophie von Bülow, she walked the vendor's route in the Quartier Latin, not overlooking a single restaurant, café, or nightclub. At half past three in the morning "we had sold the last flower and with excess profit." Since neither of them looked their part, they were questioned with compassion by the flower-buying gentlemen. Lou does not tell us what her answers were, but considering her lively fantasy we may be sure that she lived up to her role. It was a noble gesture (she gave the proceeds to the real flower vendor), and a somewhat "literary" adventure.

Her disguise and play-acting as a flower seller into the late hours of the night must have been full of vicarious erotic excitement for Lou. This summer of 1894 was a most important period in her life, with the Wedekind incident symbolizing a last curtain falling on her virginal existence. Eroticism and sex had always played a decisive part in her life, to which many of her writings testify. As early as 1900 she wrote a long essay, "Thoughts on the Problems of Love," for the periodical *Neue Deutsche Rundschau*, and ten years later, at the suggestion of her friend Martin Buber, she put down her ideas on this topic in her book, *Eroticism*. She returned to it time and again, as her *Freud Journal* indicates.

Her questions about sex and love must have been written all over her when she discussed them with Wedekind into the wee hours of the night. Even if she had not yet fully formalized her notions by then, they probably were all there, in their fragmentary and embryonic shape, inspiring the dramatist. To understand her future reactions, her then revolutionary and today often banal-sounding thoughts about morals and immorality, to know what prompted her to live the way she did, we first have to capsule what Lou revealed of herself in her writings.

Lou felt intuitively and in a rather literary manner what, at the same time, Sigmund Freud had begun to explore as a psychic phenomenon: man's sexual urge as one of his most formidable life forces. Sexual urge was equated by her with hunger and thirst, but because of its spiritual ramifications it played the most important part of man's animalistic needs. Rooted in his subliminal existence, man finds sex associated with such subconscious processes as nightly dreams, as well as daydreams in which imagination romanticizes and idealizes sex, elevating it to what we loosely call love.

Because she knew that the secret of love lies far from the purely physical act, Lou was able to write about and to discuss the primary sources of being, the very nature of sexual love with disarming detachment. She knew all about the mind in relationship to its body; she had fully intellectualized passion at a time when she was still a virgin. This made it very easy for her to reject Wedekind, who, while trying to undress her, was not aware of having wrapped her in an impenetrable verbal fabric. For a long time she had the genius of a classic hetaera without having to expose her body in the intriguing game of love she played.

This changed a few weeks or months after she met Wedekind. Later, after various experiences of total surrender, she could say with an authoritative voice that not to have loved means not to have lived. Are we entitled to read into this statement a hidden self-reproach for having denied herself for so long? Perhaps to some extent. She must have felt that she was always loved and wanted. She may also have waited for something, not quite sure what it was. Describing the last phase of her virginal life in her memoirs, she speaks of "new people and impressions" she would never have liked to miss. But whenever she was on the point of yielding to the sexual demands, something suddenly seemed to beckon her away. It could hardly have been fear of commitment or of losing control. That would contradict the very essence of her makeup. But it could easily have been a remembrance of the past, the not-yet-overcome feeling for the father-Gillot-God figure whose shadow—however seemingly uninvited—pushed itself in between. In her thirty-third year someone must finally have been able to keep this from happening at a crucial, unwary moment and to force her surrender. But no one will ever be able to say with certainty why Lou, who held love in such high esteem, remained a virgin for so long.

Without doubt, we do know that she liked to philosophize about sex and love and was fully aware of their complications. She thought that both equally demand total union which, however, has different connotations for man and woman. She was convinced that feminine sexuality was closest to the original union since the realities in a woman's life are far more total and self-contained than in man's. Woman per se is not pursuing any dream images, neither the unattainable nor the infinite as man seems compelled to. She is the symbol of the unattainable, the *Ewig Weibliche*, Goethe's Eternal Feminine that draws man upward, which, in his simile, meant toward fulfillment. Total union is always synonymous with total surrender, for which the male partner is little equipped, she thought. The union is coincidental to him and the actuality of it heightens the sense of his own existence. This is where the meaningfulness of his biological need comes in, kindling the flame of self-assurance as well as releasing potentially creative forces in him.

She envisioned a wonderful interrelation between the exaltation of the spirit and that of the body. Then she came to the truistic conclusion: the stronger the spiritual love, the more meaningful the physical union. She believed that sexual love, the creative urge and religious zeal are parts of one and the same life force. They are the realizations of primary needs and the loftiest dreams of the human species. In the woman's existence these three aspects find their expression and fulfillment in her different functions as mistress, mother and madonna.

She also reminds us that the animal instinct quickly reaches satiation and accepts change as something self-evident. Even if we desire permanent union with one person, we cannot expect it to last or to continue on the same level of intensity. We should recognize sexual love as the transitory state it is, and two people should enjoy each other's happiness as long as it lasts. Lou argued passionately and, in some way, persuasively, that we all need a haven in life, a partner as an understanding friend who respects the need of the other to find rejuvenation of the spirit through the physical union with someone else. However, Lou would have rejected any kind of indiscriminate promiscuity. For her "to surrender" had to be a solemn and sacred act of meaningfulness. But this did not contradict her notion that "the natural love life in all its manifestations, and perhaps most of all in its highest forms, is based on the principle of infidelity."

"People who are not faithful do not necessarily desert one person for another, but are simply driven *home to themselves* and only then may make their way back to mankind again, as though from a free universe," she wrote. Their infidelity—as all infidelity prompted by a higher purpose—was no betrayal in her eyes. Another statement: "A woman has no other choice than to be unfaithful or to be only half herself." If she does not want to remain struck and shattered by one lightning bolt all the time, then she must renew herself again and again.

What puzzled Lou (though she fully accepted it as a way of life) was that the very quality in a man that delighted her yesterday would alienate her from him tomorrow. She admitted that, at the height of passion, she might unconsciously look for tiny treacherous weaknesses which, at one point of the relationship, would permit her to find the emergency exit. Of course, one was tolerant of unsympathetic traits for quite some time; she learned to accept them, like the realization of death, with a smile of resignation.

Lou was much too involved in her own self in a literary and philosophical way and too preoccupied with her own importance ever to be a guiding spirit to the feminist movement, let alone a follower. And yet she was the emancipated woman par excellence and a *femme fatale* rolled into one. She was never a one-sided person. Because she saw in fidelity the image of a sick fixation, she resisted all the temptations of a one-track existence. Because and in spite of her intriguing, inspiring and seductive complexity, she aspired to a fully integrated totality of being.

Many years later when she died, Freud described Lou as a person beyond human frailty. This was euphemistically true since she was strong because of her weaknesses, she was total because of the manifoldness of her character. She was all mind and body. She could fully give herself and yet be so strangely aloof and determinedly hard as to drive men to suicide.

She who devoured men and needed them to prove herself had an ambivalent attitude toward maleness. Masculine greatness was for her the creation of the woman, as all creativity was closely related to femininity. It is the feminine element in man which causes him to be an artist and creator. Thus, femininity was a positive manifestation of life, and Lou's idealization of womanhood was, indeed, beyond human frailty and showed touches of the ancient image of a mother-goddess. She attributed to woman an intuitive knowledge of life and mind that man, the weaker sex, cannot claim. Also, she thought that "male and female are basic constituents of *all* life, they both enter at some point into the formation of the man as well as the woman." But she believed that woman, whose sex is spirit and whose spirit is sex, unites opposites more completely "in her own more integrated being" than man. Physical union was to her an absolute symbol of spiritual union, a crowning act of final fulfillment and, above all, of self-fulfillment. She thought so even while she was a virgin and when she faced Wedekind that night, denying him what she proclaimed to be self-evident and sacred.

If we accept Otto Weininger's concept that a woman is either dominated by the feelings of a mother or a hetaera, then the latter were the propelling forces in Lou. She rejected the notion of the woman as a domestic animal, destined to bear children and take care of the household, of her husband and children and the boring chores necessitated by daily living.

Lou's complexities of mind and body were unique and colorful. She may have had an exaggerated image of herself, but in her desire to live up to it—she once told Anna Freud that the only sin one can perpetrate is to be untrue to oneself—she may at times have overextended her fascination without always being able to account for the consequences. Possessing the undefined and undefinable power of a *femme fatale*, she never consciously used it for her personal advantage—except to prove herself and to grow while her longing for her own self was displaced and related to the partner.

She desired to face her lover, brother and father images like a man facing a man with the hidden power of *the* woman. Apparently, the reassurance of being loved and the mere presence of the lover gave her the sensation of gratification followed by ennui, a feeling usually ascribed to man as a copulating creature. Perhaps it can be best explained by the very physicality of her heightened spiritual experience. She could be so intensely immersed in her partner that the excitement of his very being whipped up her feelings to a point where her emotional capacity needed a respite.

Her innate fear of being caught in some kind of spiritual slavery was a factor she could rationalize on an emotional level. It was the fear of the loss of freedom. The thought of a life-long tie with a single person was repugnant to her. The rejection of monogamy was also caused by her excessive fantasy and the excitement she demanded and expected from life. In her essay, "Thoughts on the Problems of Love," she refers to the excitement and stimulation coming from the strangeness and novelty of the loving pair as basic to lovers as sexual beings. It can be claimed that such a neurotic need is the result of a deeply imbedded anxiety. On the other hand, she could afford to demand such ever-changing stimulation because her sexual being was so rich she could not help *taking* when she felt so sure of how much she had to *give*.

With all her physical and mental abundance she may have had a desperate need to be reassured of being loved time and again, to know that the intellectual in her was loved in spite of her womanly beauty and the woman in her adored regardless of her brilliant mind. She was constantly in competition with herself, which made her all the more fascinating.

It was this fascination that also trapped Frank Wedekind during his first encounter with Lou. Having been engrossed for some time in the creation of a dramatic figure he called Lulu, perhaps fashioned after the demonic Lilith, he was mystified and gladdened to have found a female echo. Although they had the same road and direction in common, neither their point of departure nor their destination was identical. With the figure of Lulu, Wedekind wanted to express his doubts about the trend of feminine emancipation that became so strongly manifest in the second half of the last century, a trend in which he saw only the danger of woman's masculinization. All he wanted was to save the femininity in the woman. In underlining the animalistic forces in her, he intended to lead her back to nature and herself. In many ways, he was close to Nietzsche's concept of the enmity of the sexes and hearkened back to the resilience and vitality of the *Übermensch*.

There are many elements in Lulu's philosophy that Lou Salomé shared: above all, to see her goal in life as self-fulfillment, no matter how much suffering it might cause. There was the obvious need to attract men, to be adored and wanted desperately—with one great difference: Wedekind's Lulu functioned on one level only, the body. Lou, in all naïveté, may not have attributed sin to the body, but she was the master of her mind and the intellectual woman, that emancipated type that Wedekind loathed and rejected.

When Wedekind invited her to come with him to his room, he miscalculated her calculated naïveté and the power of her intellect. In wooing and trying to seduce her, Wedekind could not realize that Lou was undoubtedly ready to give herself at that point of her life, but that she expected something one could only define as male strength and tenderness, applied in the right dose at the right time. He was unaware that, in her eyes, he had satisfied her vicariously by intellectualizing the very thing he aimed for. After having spoken about sex so many hours, he had talked to death what ought to have happened all by itself as a miracle of the moment. And this miracle did happen to her very soon after this incident.

Lou's biographers erred in thinking that Wedekind took his revenge on Lou when, a year later, his play *Erdgeist* (Earth Spirit), whose leading character was Lulu, was published. When Lou later in her life jokingly referred to herself as Lulu, she honored Wedekind's creation and the memory of the night of their meeting facetiously. The dates speak for themselves: he ran into Lou on the eve of Bastille Day in 1894. Wedekind's letters and Parisian diary notes make it clear that he had already begun to work on his Lulu tragedy on June 12, 1892.

Of the two it was Lou who, four years later, returned to this incident to exploit it in her book of two novellas, *Fenitschka* and *A Dissipation*. In the first novella she accurately depicts her adventure with Wedekind when describing how a young Russian girl runs into a young German who utterly dislikes intellectual women, but is impressed by Fenitschka's disarming frankness about the most intimate problems of life. This scene is followed by his failure to seduce her and, in consequence, by his apology. This story is a photographic replica of life done with little imagination, trusting reality with its inventiveness.

The second novella, *A Dissipation*, a sequel to the first, is of greater interest. The young German meets the Russian girl again sometime later in St. Petersburg and discovers that she has a lover. Lou makes it clear that there is no intellectual bond between her and her lover; he made her discover the woman in her, teaching her that love is "the good blessed bread with which we still our hunger."

This is no longer a mere memory piece of a real incident. *A Dissipation* is psychologically explanatory, unraveling the complexities of her own doubts and desires, laying bare her mysterious and uncontrollable motivations. Her heroine did not know that she was longing for a man who would make her surrender on his terms. She discovered that she wanted the excitement of the brutal hand of a dominating male. Unconsciously she felt the menace and thrill of sex with the almost physical recall of a childhood scene: she remembered her nurse being beaten "over the head by her husband, while her eyes hung on him with amorous humility."

In writing this story several years later and looking back on her experience, Lou may have wondered how to express what had happened to her at that crucial point of her life without spelling it out. It did not turn out to be a greater story than it was. But it is significant for being a perfect case history in anticipation of psychoanalysis, which was not yet born. This quality makes *A Dissipation* the work of an imaginative and perceptive writer.

Lou may have heard of Sigmund Freud as an experimental neurologist because a certain Dr. Friederich Pineles, called Zemek by his friends, was one of a handful of students who matriculated at the Vienna University for Freud's seminar on neuroses in the winter semester of 1895-96. And Zemek was one of Lou's first lovers. Perhaps he was the male she had waited for. Or perhaps it was a Russian emigré, a certain Dr. Ssawely, a Russian anarchist, of whom Lou wrote that he was as tall as a tree and that he "could tear the strongest nails from the wall with his shining white teeth." This simile, which she chose so many years later when she wrote her autobiography, may have symbolic meaning. The fact is that together with Dr. Ssawely she escaped the scorching heat in Paris during the summer of 1894, a few weeks after meeting Wedekind, and spent some time with the Russian in an isolated mountain hut in Switzerland. There they lived on milk, cheese, bread and berries, as she tells us. But she does not tell us more. She pictured it as a brief idyll. Considering that almost all of her writings were autobiographical, she was extremely discreet.

Whoever her first lover may have been is a moot question. She was in her thirty-third year when she could finally break out of her self-willed physical confinement and realize herself as the sexual being she was. From then on she played with the perfection of a virtuoso on her mind and body, on her body and mind, at her own choice, wilfully sometimes, but always with the full knowledge of what she was doing.

Vienna, 1895

For a short while Lou returned to her husband and home in Berlin. She began to work on one of her more important essays, "Jesus the Jew," which was published in the *Neue Deutsche Rundschau* in 1896. This essay played a very distinct role in her life and in the scope of her literary output.

She thought that man's need to believe in a sacred being was rooted in his fear of death and the unknown. Therefore, it is man who makes his gods, and she saw in Christ a man-made God whose mystery and agony transcended all reality. Jesus's belief in God was so strong he thought he could challenge God to keep faith with his people. Since the Jews did not doubt their God, "but suffered and lived and felt him," Christ remained within the tradition of Judaism.

Jesus the Jew was "an individual religious genius" who "gave life to a new universal religion" because he was able to experience "its true bliss and full tragedy," which led to a "wonderful and mysterious" rebirth. Lou envisioned this "poor solitary genius" who could rise to "the ultimate word of religion" as a man grown up in the Judaic tradition and grown beyond it through his belief in divine truth. She did not doubt the historical reality of Jesus the Jew. As a matter of fact, she thought that a man-made god who could give a solid and useful faith to the many must be very real.

She became strongly attached to this essay, the only manuscript she preserved and often talked about in later years. She may have thought highly of it as a literary accomplishment, but it seems more likely that she associated it with a few people who entered and enriched her life at that point. She took the first draft with her to Vienna, arriving at the end of April, 1895. In August of the same year she decided to revise the essay before getting it into print.

In Vienna—Alma Mahler's native city, though Alma was then sixteen years old—Lou became friends with some of the most articulate and characteristic representatives of the Vienna of the *fin de siècle*, mainly Jewish literati who dominated the scene and made the city the cosmopolitan center it was: Arthur Schnitzler, Richard Beer-Hofmann, Felix Salten, Peter Altenberg and Hugo von Hofmannsthal, a descendant of Spanish Jews. Lou also made the acquaintance of the novelist Marie von Ebner-Eschenbach, a gracious and witty lady, who was one of the most outstanding woman writers of her time. Lou was very much impressed by her and wrote of the unforgettable hours she spent with Marie who could look "with endlessly knowing eyes" and from whom "one could take away secret and revelation." She made it clear to Lou that a woman could combine a rich life and a great literary career.

At that time Lou had also met Zemek, the young physician with whom she had a passionate love affair. She was then a still young, but mature, woman. Having suddenly opened up like a flower, late-blooming, she had become even surer of herself and more beautiful. Zemek was an Eastern European Jew whose family had settled in Vienna, then the capital of a vast empire. He was a protean personality, cultured and learned, a strong-willed and urbane man who, like most other men, was fascinated by Lou, who, like many other women, fell in love with him. It became an affair of many years with certain interruptions. Zemek wanted to marry Lou who, fortunately for him, assured him that her husband would never give her a divorce, nor could she remain faithful to him. Zemek accepted the role of being Lou's unofficial husband in Vienna, and whenever she went there they lived together in that kind of rejuvenating bliss that was Lou's badly needed bread and caviar.

One can readily see that Lou's experiences in the Vienna of 1895 changed her life. Her contact with some of the greatest minds and the inescapable emotional involvements conditioned by the entire atmosphere of the city made her love it. She found Vienna's cultural climate very different from that of any other city. Its mood foreshadowed the various stages of cataclysmic events into which Europe was soon to plunge. The conflicting contrasts were still submerged, but the sensibilities of Vienna's great writers reacted to the impending changes like seismographs.

In her memoirs Lou remembered some of Vienna's ambience at that time. She characterized it by "an easy interplay of intellectual and erotic life. The man of the world was not distinctly a man apart from the intellectual and professional person, as was the case everywhere else. This was the charm of the Viennese whose 'sweet girls' lifted the playfulness of life onto a level of heightened eroticism which, in turn, cut the edges and removed the sharpness from the purposefulness of intellectual ambition. The competition between love and ambition left much space for male friendships which, as I observed, took quite a distinguished form."

Lou alluded to the circle of writers around Arthur Schnitzler, Richard Beer-Hofmann and Hugo von Hofmannsthal who were bound together by the intellectual and artistic atmosphere which, as Lou rightly noticed, was intrinsically interwoven with the playfulness of existence, the easygoing lightheartedness of a people who drowned their proverbially golden hearts in wine and a questionable *Gemüt-lichkeit*, whose minds suffocated in sentimentality and songs.

She felt this heightened eroticism which one could almost touch with one's hands, which one sensed in the streets, salons, coffee-houses and *chambres séparées*. It was a specific atmosphere in which the officers' striking uniforms became a fixture of every girl's dreams and in which one expected the Count to deceive his mistress, usually a famous singer or dancer, with the Countess's chambermaid. It was the time in which duels were fought over virtually nothing because it was part of the pattern of life. Music was everywhere. The Viennese had a saying that the heavens are full of violins. Everything was fun and food, almost everything glitter of gaiety. There was the beauty of the gothic and baroque buildings, there were gardens and fountains, uniforms in dashing colors and pretty women.

But in Vienna's unique cultural atmosphere only a relatively minor portion of the population actually participated in the richness of spiritual splendor that belonged to the centuries-old culture. Most of the people who often gathered in the salons had their headquarters in coffeehouses where one went not only for coffee and pastry. There one read all the magazines and newspapers over a cup of coffee and a glass of water; or one brought one's own book to read; or there one sat for hours with friends, talking about God and the world, literature and sweet nothings; or withdrew to be with one's own thoughts, to write a poem at a corner table, cut off from the world by the mist of cigarette smoke.

Schnitzler noted in his diary on May 24, 1895: "Lou leaves today. She told Richard she is 'grateful' to us. It is gratifying that, evidently quite apart from our doings, we signify something positive or even beautiful to her. Richard: she seems to ascribe to us much that is Vienna and vice versa."

The coffeehouse in which Lou often met Schnitzler and his circle was the Griensteidl where they gathered before and after going to the theater and on other occasions. All the famous literati with whom she surrounded herself were still very young and not yet too well known, with the exception of Hugo von Hofmannsthal who had stunned the world with his poems, written at the age of sixteen. Richard Beer-Hofmann, about twenty-nine, sparingly wrote some poetry and prose and yet had a great reputation. The oldest of them was the thirty-three-year-old physician Arthur Schnitzler who, at that time, had his first successful play produced, *Liebelei* (The Game of Love).

To be able to visualize the enchantment that can be found in a tired gaiety and mellow levity, so inimitably characteristic of this city then, one has to turn to its writers. Schnitzler established himself in quick succession with plays and novels penetrating the subliminal existence of man at a time when Freud was still wondering about the mechanics of the human soul. One day Freud sent a letter to Schnitzler, who lived around the block from him and whom, strangely enough, he never met. Freud expressed his surprise that "in many a psychological and erotic problem" he could find a "far-reaching agreement" between his and Schnitzler's conceptions. "I have often wondered and asked myself from where you could have taken this or that insight which I have acquired through such laborious explorations of the subject, and I finally came to the point of envying the poet whom otherwise I admired."

Schnitzler—who, some time later, became a great friend of the much younger Alma Mahler—looked at his characters as if they were his patients, realizing that they were all frightened of the angel of death and that they had little more than love to prove and find themselves. He encouraged them to go on exploring life—as long as they explored themselves at the same time. This philosophical attitude of his seemed to have impressed and attracted Lou; she had found a kindred soul. Schnitzler said in his diary, May 19th: "Lou recently said we three—Hugo, Richard, and I—are really the happiest people she ever met: first, we are not ambitious; second, we lived in Vienna, a city we like; third, we had found one another.— Today she said: Richard the happiest, sleek, nothing quite touches him—I the unhappiest, pensive, yet would best like to be 'me.' "

It was Schnitzler whom Lou had met first in Vienna, since she had known of him through a couple of one-act plays that had not yet been published and that, by chance, fell into her hands. She was impressed by the "light and tender touch" with which he treated weighty problems, but she felt that his male characters were treated with a far more critical eye than his women, and she, as a woman, objected to it. When Lou came to Vienna she was eager to meet him, and through Schnitzler she was able to enter the circle of the Viennese literati.

As Schnitzler's diary suggests, Lou seems to have been most impressed by Richard Beer-Hofmann, by the lightness with which he walked through life and the graceful ease with which he bore his vast knowledge. There was something captivating about him that she sensed. This attraction to Richard may have started at their very first meeting when he recited some poems by Hofmannsthal and others. Schnitzler's psychological instinct recognized her feelings when he made this note in his diary on May 21st: "Peculiarly vexed mood of Lou's toward Richard, out of the need to be desired." Something must have gone wrong, but they remained friends "as of old," as she put it in one of her letters.

If we wish to accept the thesis of Lou's psychoanalytic biographer, Rudolph Binion, a most enchanting comedy of errors or a comedy of *un*mistaken identities, then took place. Richard fell in love with another girl that summer whose outward similarity to Lou was striking. She was a simple edition of sophisticated Lou. Her name was Paula, and she became Mrs. Richard Beer-Hofmann. Shortly thereafter, Lou found her way to Zemek, whose features were supposedly almost identical with those of Beer-Hofmann. But Zemek had nothing of Richard's buoyancy and spiritual magic. At best, his was the magic determination of an earthbound man who did not recite verses before he took the woman he desired. Beyond the little irony of life, there could have been no doubt that Lou got what she really waited for and Richard what he needed.

Schnitzler could have written one of his wistful, bittersweet stories, full of compassion, illusion and resignation, about these incidents—but he did not. Lou, however, did. And in some of her stories her heroines struggle with the feeling that they are misunderstood and loved for what they are not. But, in whatever disguise she tried to present the reality of past events, her heroines experienced what may be a woman's greatest sensation: the feeling that she is a woman in the eyes—and arms—of a man. Schnitzler had noted one day (diary, May 11th): "Lou is turning a bit female." It is very likely that, first, Lou wanted to be accepted as a sexless, literary person in this circle of writers as their peer, so to speak, but that she could not help reverting to type—not weakening into femininity, but being forced to open up.

It is not the tangible things that necessarily weigh most heavily in life. Lou felt the magic of the unspoken and the lure of the mystery behind the poetic word. Even though she saw very little of Hofmannsthal because of his military duties that summer, she realized it was his spirit that dominated this literary circle. Whenever these friends met, Hugo von Hofmannsthal's absence was never quite real. These men were all a part of their Vienna; certainly Peter Altenberg was; his lyrical vignettes and romantic sketches reflected the exalted realism of the unreal dreams tiptoeing through the city's streets and gardens. Altenberg was Lou's neighbor, and she said about him in her memoirs that his little stories sounded new and attractive because they were based on something mysterious he expressed poetically. Also, there could not have been anything more Viennese than the sarcastic and somewhat melancholy wit of such a great writer and historian as Egon Friedell, who was closer to Altenberg than to the circle around Schnitzler; or of such a monumental figure as Karl Kraus, one of the great satirists of any time, whose prophetic cries of doom could not have come from anywhere else but the feuilletonistic spirit of Vienna.

However, no one represented more intensely the *fin de siècle* mood of this city than the young Hofmannsthal. This atmosphere anticipated so much that became crucial as a World War II manifestation: the existentialist feeling, the realization of life's futility and its incongruencies. Already in the 1890s Hofmannsthal had become acutely aware that with him an epoch was coming to an end. He was one of the first writers to call language, and consequently all human utterances, into question.

In his *Letter of Lord Chandos* he chose an Elizabethan disguise to express his inability any longer to match words to his experiences, his feeling that everything seems to change in a dizzying way and that these changes demand a new attitude toward life. Lord Chandos becomes aware of the multiplicity of existence; he suddenly feels that he does not live but is lived, that everything eludes him that he wants to express. Hofmannsthal began to realize that man, and with him the arts, stood at the crossroads, and the artist in man would be cursed and compelled to search for his identity so that he could find salvation. I bring Hofmannsthal and his awareness of twentieth-century man's dilemma so strongly into focus because it was Lou's dilemma all her life: to find herself and her identity with the compulsion of someone in fear of herself.

Hofmannsthal moved away from the rational language of everyday communication to symbolism, with which, he felt, he came closer to unraveling the mystery of life and to re-creating the beauty of being. This typified the creative and intellectual will predominant in Vienna at a time when the city carried its heavy burden of an established culture to the cultural slaughterhouse of the twentieth century. There was something prophetic and, at the same time, baroque about these writers whose wistful glance at the past and fearful look into the future found a reflection in the literary output of that era. Hofmannsthal set the tone, his poems and thoughts pointed the way—even if, for that moment perhaps, only to the Café Griensteidl.

In retrospect this coffeehouse literature and a life of lost dreams may appear to us today questionable. But living through this period in Vienna seemed the glorification of existence. People who were a part of it were of course never aware of the very specific nature of the city's air and cultural climate. Emotionally, Lou was completely absorbed by what she experienced there. Her levelheaded, observant mind was puzzled and enchanted. A letter written on May 22nd of that year by Beer-Hofmann to Hugo von Hofmannsthal about Lou tells some of the story and invites us to read between the lines:

Frau Lou is still in Vienna and with us several hours a day. It looks as if she were quite fond of us (that is, Arthur and you, me); I believe we signify something private to her or are symbols for something or other we cannot know. She is getting to like much in Vienna just because of us—and then again sees much in us that is really only Vienna. She calls us "happy people" because, among other reasons, we love the city we live in, it is the city we were born in, and we have one another. Her eyes and smile are so young that we only recently discovered how much younger we now find her than at first. . . . She likes and respects Gerhart Hauptmann and his *Hannele*—but finds us "richer."

The Making of a Poet

The sweeping power of Rainer Maria Rilke's poetic imagery, its evocative, symbolic intensity, was already surprising and puzzling at the very outset of his career. "Transfigured joy, this is the purpose of all art," he wrote Lou on November 23, 1905. His later works, the *Duino Elegies* and *Sonnets to Orpheus*, with their mysterious philosophical undertone, proved him to be a magician of visionary power who made the visible world re-emerge in images of transcending beauty and often veiled meaning. If his poetic creations were the expression of transfigured joy, then it arose from a frightful struggle between his body and soul, between his spiritual visualization of life and his death-oriented thinking.

"When one peruses what René Maria Rilke had written by the mid-1890s," Lou said in her biography of the poet (whose first name she later changed to Rainer, feeling, perhaps, that he needed the support of a name that was unmistakably masculine), "then one cannot quite escape the impression as if from the very beginning an innate relationship existed between the poet and death." Is there a discrepancy between Rilke's transfigured joy and his spiritual intimacy with death? This question has often created a misunderstanding of his poetry, which was seen in a false romantic light, Lou maintained. From his early beginnings Rilke's allusion to all that is mortal did not mean death but life. For him, she said, "poetry was that kind of reality wherein both were one . . . the poor inadequate words of 'death' and 'life' could be exchanged."

Rilke was one of the few poets for whom the creative process was a vision-turned-reality and whose intoxication and ecstasy were almost physical experiences. He worked all his life to find the ultimate in painting his imagery with verbal colors and melodies, simple in their truths and profound in their complexity. Lou thought that "his inclination was directed at mastering lyrically the almost 'inexpressible.' "

In a letter to Freud later in her life Lou wrote: "Human life, indeed all life, is poetry. We live it unconsciously—day by day like one piece after another—but in its untouchable totality it lives us, it writes our story." No one else could have better proved her notion than Rilke, whose entire life was poetized existence, determined and lived by invisible dark forces. No one else ever understood Rilke better than Lou and no one ever seems to have been closer to him, a man who was always in great need of love and human sympathy. But his daimon drove him into paroxysms of solitude. In 1903 he wrote Lou: "What else was my house to me but an alien place . . . and what more are the people close to me than visitors who do not want to leave. How I lose myself time and again when I wish to be meaningful to them; how I leave myself and yet cannot reach them, and so I am on the road between them and myself . . ." But in all his tortured "within-ness" he never left Lou and would have remained with her, had she not felt the need one day—and this day came after many years of their relationship—to expel Rilke from her custody, forcing him to accept himself and the world.

When she felt that they had to stop being lovers, Lou explained their relationship to the world and herself: "The power of your problematic nature drew me close to you"—was there really nothing else that attracted her? Her intimate liaison with Rilke was the only one she admitted publicly. Did she take some pride in the role she played in his life, or were they both too much exposed to make admission unavoidable? In her life story she treated this incident as if Rilke had been her first lover, which certainly was not the case. But from her standpoint she may have been right, because this diffident and oversensitive young man unfolded a passion that was overwhelming and surprising to her. "To me," she said, "it was like an ascension of the poetry over the poet." But it had taken her several years before she realized his poetic promise; it was to fulfill itself in later years.

At first, she was frightened by the intensity of his courtship, but then she felt pleased and flattered by the summer sun of his passion: "If I was your wife for years, that was because to me you were something unprecedentedly real, body and person inseparably one, incontestable evidence of life itself. . . . I could have admitted literally what you said when you confessed your love: 'You alone are real.' We became husband and wife even before we became friends, which we became hardly by choice but likewise from this unfathomable marriage. . . . We were brother and sister as in olden times before sibling marriages became sacrilegious."

Long before she began to study with Freud, Lou seemed fascinated by man's psychic mechanism. Her gift of observation and her keen sense of recognizing a person in relation to his *persona*, his mental somersaults, subterfuges and pretensions prepared her for her future interest in psychoanalysis. What probably bewildered her about herself became a marvel to observe in other people, particularly in a man to whom she happened to be close. This would explain her statement that the scope of Rilke's problematic nature drew her close to him and that "this effect has never ceased to exist."

There were several phases in their relationship, and they were on Rilke's part far more constant than on hers. She met the young René Maria Rilke through Jakob Wassermann, a successful novelist, in whose apartment the literati of Munich often met. Rilke, then twenty-one years old and thirteen years younger than Lou, fell in love with her. The next day he wrote her a letter in which he assured her that she was no stranger to him. He had read her essay, "Jesus the Jew." It had been a revelation to him because he had tried to express similar thoughts in his poems, *Visions of Christ*, and he hoped to be able to read some of his poems to her.

By then Rilke had published a few verses and book reviews and was very eager to establish himself as a writer to prove to his family that he could make his way with the pen. He was also anxious to be among writers and call them his friends. Lou Salomé was a well-known name, and Rilke may have needed her acquaintanceship and encouragement as much as her love. He pursued her passionately, tried to be wherever she was, carried roses in his hand looking for her all over town, and, after each of their meetings, he would write a poem with her in mind.

In the beginning she was far more ready to give her love than her encouragement. First, of course, she frowned on the strangely ecstatic and lyric assaults with which this young boy tried to conquer her, a mature woman, whose emotional spontaneity always needed a passport to freedom issued by her well-organized mind. But Rilke's concentrated efforts had the desired result, and they became lovers. She recognized the vulnerability of this young poet, his emotional insecurity. Curiosity and compassion made her yield. A knowing lover was her reward for his victory. "Our belonging to one another, ready and willing—to use your expression—for all bright and dark seasons had to prove itself despite unalterable circumstances of life [meaning her marriage to Andreas]." And it proved itself in the important formative years of his becoming a poet.

In the beginning of their relationship her lucid and logical mind could not help but reject the romantically extravagant and overecstatic outpouring of his poetry. She questioned whether she had the right to be so negative in her judgment. "It was a strange experience for me," she admitted, "that I had so little understanding of your early poems, even though they were very musical." She reiterated that she could not sufficiently sympathize with the excessive enthusiasm of most of his poetry, nor did she appreciate his effusive love letters which, in the beginning of their union, he wrote daily as if it had been part of a poetic and emotional routine. He wrote to the woman who "smiled down into his soul," as he said on June 6, 1897, and two days later: "My clear fount, through you I will see the world: for then I see, not the world, but always only you, you, you! You're my feast day, and when I go to you in dreams I always wear flowers in my hair . . ." Whenever he saw her, he said, he felt like praying to her. His feelings for her ran so deep that he could write: "I want to know nothing of the time that came before you in my days or of the people who lived in those days. . . . I now want to be you. And my heart burns before your grace like the eternal lamp before the image of the Virgin Mary. . . . What makes me be—is you. I shall often, often tell you so, ever more plainly and simply. And when I will tell it to you altogether simply one day, you will understand it simply. That will be our summer. . . . Are you coming today!?"

By doubting and criticizing his early poetry, she helped him find his inner greatness. Lou was a strict taskmaster who demanded from his work greater simplicity and purity. In 1905 at Whitsun, when she recognized how close he was coming to the realization of his own self, she became totally absorbed by his work: "From our Whitsun on I read what you created not only with you, I received and confirmed it like a message about your future which nothing could have stopped. And in this I became once more all yours for a second time—in a second maidenhood."

Her relationship with Rilke was far more complex than any of her other liaisons and functioned on several levels simultaneously. Not that Nietzsche or Reé would not have needed her as badly as Rilke did! But then she was young and lacked the compelling feeling of any responsibility. Now she was so much older than her lover and responded to his cry for motherliness ("In Wolfratshausen I came to you as a mother."). He came to her almost as a child, and she took him into her arms and gently rocked his soul, as he wrote in his Tuscan diary.

This Tuscan diary, the result of his journey to Italy in the spring of 1898, was written for Lou rather than for himself or posterity. It gives us great insight into his feelings at that time and the various influences that his ideas reflect. The first year of their great love affair had hardly passed when he returned to her from his short Italian journey, with his diary and great hopes of convincing her of his genius as a writer. He was certain that he had learned a great deal and grown considerably. He thought he would dazzle, or at least strongly impress, Lou with many new and daring notions about art and nature. The ideas he had developed in Italy ought to have reminded her of her experiences with Nietzsche, since Rilke created his own concept of superman in the shape of the artist who would create a super-race, with the rest of mankind falling by the wayside.

An arrogant and condescending tone condemned everyone who was not involved in creative work. There was no doubt in his aristocratic mind that he belonged to the select few.

Lou's cool reaction was a severe blow to him. Her unenthusiastic response to his journal was even more difficult to bear than her bland attitude toward his poetry. The reason for Lou's unfriendly, or at best indifferent, reception to his Italian notes may have been twofold. Having been the inspiration for Nietzsche's *Zarathustra*, she must have painfully recognized the derivative thoughts that went into Rilke's artist as superman. Moreover, in his enthusiasm Rilke waxed hot about the creative role of the woman as a mother ("woman fulfills herself in the child"), adding to it a glorified image of the madonna and the woman as prophetess of the artist (no doubt, meaning the male artist). Rilke made the mistake of leaving too little individual power for the creative woman in Lou. Also, his overemphasis on the woman's fulfillment through her biological function came at the worst moment, for Lou was pregnant by Rilke at that time (about which he apparently knew nothing) and later had an abortion.

The rejection of his Tuscan journal threw him into fits of despair and dismay. He felt, as he noted in his diary, that he saw in her "something too big" and would have loved to disappear "into a deep nowhere." He wanted to dazzle the woman he loved and felt punished by the mother substitute on whom he depended. In the ensuing struggle with himself he first sulked like a difficult child—Lou referred to Rilke's tantrums as the "other" Rainer—but then realized that he could not free himself from her superior intellect, that he would always be emotionally dependent on her.

This feeling runs like a thread through his whole life. Lou was the only person he never tired of as long as she permitted him to be by her side. She remained for him the constant in a sea of changes, the one person for whom he kept the strongest affections. That Lou was a center of experience for him can be proved by many remarks we find in letters written over the years. On December 17, 1906, he told his wife, Clara Westhoff, that "Lou was the first person to help me to . . . my work." On July 29, 1913, we read in a letter addressed to Maria Thurn und Taxis that Lou had "no end of significance" and on

the 24th of May, 1926, shortly before his death, he reiterated in a
letter that "my whole development could not have taken the course
it did . . . but for the influence of this extraordinary woman."

With an almost religious belief in Lou he made her privy to his
pains and panics, often telling her of the frightful misuse the body
made of the soul and referring to his own physical being as a trap or a
snare. When leukemia, his final illness, struck him, she was the one
friend to whom he sent detailed accounts of it through his nurse. To
the very last moment he held on to the belief that she would be able
to help him. Delirious, in his last hours, he still begged his physicians
to "ask Lou what is wrong with me. She is the only one who knows."
In his fading mind he envisaged her as a glorified mother image with
the eyes and smile of a madonna.

To better understand the fabric of their relationship, one must
know that Rilke was born within the confines of a shipwrecked
marriage. His mother raised and dressed him like a girl and he had to
play with dolls because he had to take the place of his sister Sophia
who had died within a year of her birth. After these early unhealthy
circumstances he was forced into a military academy by his father
who wanted him to take up the career of an officer. That Rilke would
run away from the academy after five years of a Spartan life could
have been foreseen. An uncle made it possible for the youth to
continue his studies, but these later school years were also unhappy
for him, living with a sick aunt as he had to, and left only with
tortured memories. After several wretched experiences, he eloped
with an instructress many years his senior.

Rilke had nothing but contempt and hatred for his mother, who
was eccentric, living an unreal existence full of self-dramatizations
punctuated by cheap poetic inclinations. He felt neglected and
misunderstood by her, and lived through his youth lonely and
self-centered, thrown back and forth between hardships and meretricious love. His mother's total rejection tortured him all his life. To
gratify his ego he liked to visualize his destiny as something
"prenatal."

Lou tells us that she had once met his mother and that Rilke could not understand how little Lou was disgusted by her. But his mother appeared to her only "immensely sentimental." Lou recognized how Rilke fought the distorted mirror reflection he saw of himself in his mother: "His devotional belief in superstition and affected piety, his productive bliss in mere sentimentality; all his protest against his mother's character was a faint image only of what Rainer fought against within himself with deadly horror when his truest, most blessed self . . . so acted as if she would be himself—the eternal womb of nothingness."

When, after the fiasco of his Tuscan journal, he had made peace with himself and Lou, he wrote her a letter as a postscript to his own defeat: "Be always ahead of me, dear one, only one, holy one. Let us ascend together to a great star . . . you are not one goal for me, you are a thousand goals, you are everything."

It was not to a star that they ascended. Of the many "goals," he wanted to reach Russia, the country from which Lou came and which Rilke unconsciously associated with her. He traveled there twice despite his loathing for long journeys by train. First, he traveled with Lou and her husband, the second time with Lou alone, pretending to be cousins for the sake of convenience. Altogether Rilke spent six months there, in which time he could hardly have penetrated the spirit of the people or acquainted himself with the vastness of the country.

When, years later, he still spoke of returning to Russia as if to his home, it was only one of his dreams and only one of the imaginary spiritual ties without which he could not live. He, of course, expressed it differently: "That Russia is my home belongs to one of those great and concealed certainties on which I live." Only if we substitute Lou for Russia does his statement make any sense because he never even attempted to return to Russia after Lou left him at the end of their second Russian trip.

He idealized and romanticized this country as he was apt to do anyway. They went to Yasnaya Polyana to see the great, wise, old man Leo Tolstoi. On their first visit Lou conversed with him in Russian. The two seemed to have spoken a great deal about the

Russians' predilection for piety, and Tolstoi warned her not to accept surface experiences and superstition for piety. But it was the one thing that had strongly impressed Rilke. Easter, at the Moscow churches, the chiming of the bells and the ecclesiastic gestures all pointed the way to God. Russia, God and Lou—and probably not in this sequence—inspired him to write one of his great books of poetry, *The Book of Hours*. Neither Lou's husband nor Rilke could follow Tolstoi's arguments and they had to depend on Lou's interpretation later on. As a token of his somewhat bewildered awe, Rilke left a copy of his latest book, *Two Tales of Prague*, with Count Tolstoi.

All the more puzzling, then, was their second visit a few months later: Tolstoi did not recognize them He treated Lou and Rilke as intruders rather than as visitors. Asked what he was doing, Rilke said he was a poet, whereupon Tolstoi belittled poetry as a useless pastime and advised Rilke to do something positive in life. Tolstoi made them accompany him on a walk. They then gained insight into the tortured mind and life of this seventy-one-year-old man who was at odds with his family, church and government. Only the people loved him. On their walk they saw him talk to a few peasants who revered the Count as a living saint.

Perhaps this was reason enough for Rilke to dramatize this experience. A peasant woman kissing him and telling him that he was one of them did not help him understand the Russian peasantry, but it may have considerably aided his excitable mind to attach itself to the country, to its vast plains and virgin forests, its rivers and churches. He felt there was something impenetrable about this landscape and its simple people. He was intrigued by such contrasts as their passion and servility, their melancholy and strength. He would not have been Rilke had he not been exalted by their inner strength; in it he saw the greatest well of creativity.

Rilke was the man with whom Lou had the longest physical relationship. But she would not have been true to her own nature had she not felt compelled to put an end to it. This happened on their second journey to Russia. Rilke sensed the change going on in her, and his desperate reaction only hastened her decision. When she had left for Finland to be with her family, Rilke remained in St.

Petersburg, writing her yearning letters with the refrain: "I long for you." Or: "Come back to me, come back to me soon." And in one of his letters he recalled the young squirrels that he kept on chains when in Italy: "Perhaps it was wrong to impose my will on their nimble lives (when they were already grown up and did not need me anymore), but it was also a little their intention to count on me in the future, for they often came running after me so that it seemed to me as if they wished for a chain."

This story was too obvious in its symbolism for Lou. She needed her freedom and did not want him to feel that, like a child, he could depend on her. In her memoirs she explained: "No haste was needed that you would find the way to freedom, space and distance and, above all, to growth which still waited for you. . . . Who can fathom the dark of ultimate proximity and remoteness from one another! In that anxious, ardent state of being close to you, I nevertheless stood outside of what unites man and woman, and this has never changed again for me." Searching in herself for the answer to her feelings and reactions, Lou could only cite a sentence she found in her diary: "I remain faithful to my memories: never shall I be faithful to a human being." Rilke was not the only man who had to reconcile the ecstasy of his feelings to the will of her mind.

Lou realized that his Russian experience liberated Rilke from his innate excessiveness, that it was like "the cry for God (to give it the briefest of all names)—the cry for the place, the imagined space in which the immeasurable becomes visible in the smallest of things and the inner distress of the poet finds its expression in a hymn, a prayer."

Feeling at this point that Rilke had found himself, Lou was adamant about her own freedom. Her journeys to Russia made her feel as if she had found home again after so many years of absence. She was overcome by a longing for her youth, a feeling that cried out for freedom again. "I have had to go on growing," she wrote, "growing into my youth. For only now I am young, only now can I be what others are when they are eighteen: entirely myself." Her mind was made up: she made Rilke walk alone into life after four years of custody. Beside the selfish reason of gaining her personal freedom was the selfless decision that it was time to make him "grow beyond himself." And he did.

But at first Rilke felt motherless and despondent. In the artists' colony Wrepswede near Bremen he met two young artists, the painter Paula Becker and the sculptor Clara Westhoff. They all met quite often, discussed art, life and God until late into the night. The two girls invited him to their studios and listened to his poetry with far more willingness and enthusiasm than Lou could ever muster. He sensed love and motherly warmth, took a great interest in Paula, but finally married Clara when it turned out that Paula was engaged to someone else. Lou warned Rilke not to do it. Were her feelings hurt that he turned so quickly to another woman? Since she was not willing to take him back and he needed someone by his side now more than ever, he went through with the marriage. Lou was right. It did not last long.

Clara was Auguste Rodin's pupil, and Rilke became Rodin's secretary. Rodin had made a "superhuman impression" on him, as he wrote Lou, who from then on received his letters at different intervals depending on the moods and needs of his troubled mind. And trouble was soon to approach him. Lou foresaw that Rodin's influence would be a hard thing for Rilke to take. Rodin was too much of a rocklike giant for him. Even though the twenty-eight-year-old Rilke felt dwarfed by the impressive figure of the master, he also sensed a strong kinship with him who, like him, was "seeking: the grace of the great things."

In writing about Rodin he started with statements that were self-reflective: "Rodin was solitary before fame came to him, and afterward he became perhaps still more solitary. For fame is ultimately but the summary of all misunderstandings that crystallize about a new name." The master's secret was no longer a secret: *travailler toujours*. Would he ever be able to translate it into the language of his life? Never to feel desperate and stymied by despair, by the "other one" in him, but to work day after day? He learned one more thing: to give a sculptural feeling to his words. First, however, he had to wrestle with the monumental figure of this sculptor before he could hope to find the key to a more distinctly unique sculptural expression of his imagery. While groping along the way toward this goal he wrote his greatest prose work: *The Notebooks of Malte Laurids Brigge.*

He regularly wrote Lou about the struggle he had to wage with himself in Paris, and some of the letters addressed to her found their way into his book. Lou was afraid that "the heroic compulsion" to work and work would crush Rilke and turn against him as a destructive specter. But finally Lou could say that "out of your fear you gave birth to creation of things frightening."

Rilke's poetry was in Lou's eyes "a release into himself and not a form of human communication." Rilke's emphasis on and escape into the unconventional—under whatever pretense of simplicity—were also an escape from reality, a denial of the very essence of society and his environment. He belongs with such poets as Blake and Hölderlin whose visionary power was also very much a part of their private lives. It is difficult to separate Rilke the man from the work of the poet.

In the beginning of their love affair Lou tried to embrace the man while neglecting the poet. She soon realized that doing this would slight both. Today we may mainly be interested in the meaning and importance of his work. However, his entire life, as much as his *oeuvre,* was symbolic of the ambivalence of a period that was gradually disintegrating, while desperately trying to build a new world.

It is difficult to measure the significance of one person for another in an intimate relationship lasting many years, since one cannot weigh joys and sighs nor fathom how a word or glance or the pressure of a hand can reach farther than sound, sight and touch. We should remember an incident that occurred during their Russian sojourn. While traveling on the Volga upstream, they had almost found themselves on two different steamers. Rilke's remark to Lou was most characteristic for him: "Even if we had to go upstream on quite different ships, it would still be for us the same way—because it is one and the same source waiting for us." He could hardly have better expressed his conviction that he was as much a part of her life as she was of his. He was propelled by the same ruthless intensity of inwardness and was as determined to live the totality of his existence as Lou Salomé was to live hers.

The Road from Rilke to Freud

In the autumn of 1911 Lou participated in the Weimar Congress of the International Psychoanalytical Association. At that point Freud laughed at her ardent desire to take up the study of psychoanalysis as if it were a mere toy. Rilke was at the Castle of Duino then and wrote a poem in which he once more conjured up and somehow summed up the years he had lived with Lou:

> I ripened rarely
> in every impulse of omitted youth,
> and you yourself, above my heart, beloved,
> entered upon a kind of wildest childhood.

Ten years had then passed. When in 1901 she had left Rilke, she had celebrated her fortieth birthday with the radiance of a young woman still looking forward to the hidden wonders of life. She no longer had the naïveté of the inexperienced, but a mature woman's challenge to life to yield its secrets. She was ready for new adventures.

It would be wrong to assume that Lou gained little more from her affair with Rilke than a youthful vibrance that she wore extremely well in spite of her age. She was at that time more inspired to write than ever before or afterwards. And to have lived with Rilke was for her an experience that made her write stories in which her psychological insight reached far beyond anything that was scientifically established at the turn of the century. Moreover, it also made her realize that she was far more interested in the living experience of man's psyche than in writing about it.

Her stories were also praised for their psychological interest far more than for their literary value. *Im Zwischenland* (In the Years In Between) pictured those perilous years of transition to maturity, stories that dealt with the often painful experiences of growing up of which Lou explained, "even the most exceptional well-meaning 'grownups' know nothing . . . understand nothing." While the literary critics were not too friendly, *Im Zwischenland* became a source book for child psychologists. Elevated to its highest point ethically, her novel *Ma* is a paean on the childbearing woman who "bears the child as a part of herself and later tenderly identifies herself with it." Then, of course, comes the confrontation with the outside world. *Ma* is the idealization of the eternal mother, her bliss, renunciation and inescapable tragedy.

Except for her book on sexual love, *Eroticism*, which Martin Buber urged her to write, she turned out only a variety of reviews and minor essays during the first decade of this century. By then she had established herself as an essayist and novelist of some importance in the literary world of Central Europe. However, it was a period in which she increasingly felt the need to be with people and to exchange the isolation of work at a desk for what she later called "vital activity," in other words, to wed psychology to life. One can readily see that her desire to join the psychoanalytic fraternity was less the "Christmas present" she wanted with a childlike naïveté, as Freud first thought, than something that very naturally grew on and with her in the course of her life experience.

To say that Lou's life was never boring would be a gross understatement. She had a way of attracting, absorbing and discarding human beings with an innate drive; of squeezing the last drop of life out of existence, a feat which she performed sometimes nonchalantly, sometimes with ruthless and an always compulsive unconsciousness. It is difficult and daring to conjecture how men bore the impact Lou had on them, from Richard Beer-Hofmann—who seemingly eschewed the issue by quickly marrying a rather simpleminded, uncomplicated facsimile of Lou—to Paul Reé and Viktor Tausk, two men who, in their encounter with Lou, became the victims of their weaknesses and her strength.

Reé had a fatal accident in 1901 while living estranged from the world—that is, Lou—in his Swiss mountain retreat. To avoid the word "suicide," we can say that Reé's accident was undoubtedly a deliberate challenge to fate; Dr. Tausk's suicide was a demonstrative act against his loneliness and frustration. Lou met Tausk when she started her career as a lay analyst and began to work with Freud. Although he played an important part in her life, he was not even mentioned in her autobiography. This repression and her "scientific" reaction to his suicide are puzzling facets of this many-faceted woman.

Tausk had a brilliant mind and wild temperament. Sigmund Freud, with whom he worked enthusiastically, considered him a threat to psychoanalysis because of his deviant ideas. Lou's great interest in man's—and particularly in her own—narcissistic tendencies, was complemented by Tausk's study of narcissism, and they became intimate friends. After some time, it became apparent that he needed her, and he asked her to marry him. She remained adamant in refusing him.

In her *Freud Journal* she said about him:

He is deceiving himself about me with his fantasies. In the long run no helpful relationship is possible; there can be none when reality is cluttered by the wraiths of unabreacted primal reminiscences. An impure tone resonates through everything, buzzing as it were with murmurings from within. Yet from the very beginning I realized it was this very struggle in Tausk that most deeply moved me—the struggle of the human creature. Brother-animal. You.

A few years after this was written Viktor Tausk committed suicide. "He returned worn out from the horrors of war," as Freud wrote her; he faced difficulties in building up his practice in Vienna, intended to marry someone else, but, a week before his wedding, killed himself. In his farewell letters he "insisted on his clarity of mind, blamed only his own inadequacy and his failure in life." Lou's reply to Freud was analytical rather than compassionate: "Your news about poor Tausk came as a complete surprise to me. I was fond of him, thought I knew him and yet I would never have thought of suicide in connection

with him. . . . It is true that I have no idea what method he chose (as
a doctor he would have had very easy access to poison). If he shot
himself, I can imagine that his death represented a last supreme
libidinal satisfaction, namely, an act of violence and of suffering at
one and the same time. For this was Tausk's problem, his danger,
which at the same time constituted his charm (in nonpsychoanalytic
language it amounted to a frenzied soul with a tender heart)."

Even the one great platonic relationship of her life, that with
Sigmund Freud, was subjected to an analysis by the historian of
psychoanalysis, Paul Roazen, who came up with the hypothesis that
Freud too succumbed to her sexual attraction and was in love with
her.

At the risk of repeating a truism, I must emphasize that no purely
platonic love is possible between men and women of relatively
normal heterosexual inclinations. We are attracted to one another
with an unfailing animal instinct, just as we may also reject a person
because of certain, often undefinable, physical expressions. Even a
seemingly tender relationship of platonic description in which the
carnal contact is reduced to an occasional kiss on the cheek or hand
or a brief hug (and perhaps not even these), may expose man and
woman to pleasurable experiences which the emotional and only very
private seismograph registers. If Freud did not come physically close
to Lou, he certainly walked her home late at night, invited her to stay
in his home, gave her money when she was in financial distress, and
expressed his admiration for her in his letters in a variety of ways.
Though they certainly found pleasure in each other on several levels,
this does not mean that Freud had "fallen" in love with Lou, though
he may have loved her. Moreover, he did not reject Viktor Tausk, one
of his many wayward disciples, out of jealousy because he realized
that Lou had "for some time favored" him with her friendship, as he
euphemistically said in one of his letters (when he knew only too well
that they were lovers). He treated Tausk as a rebellious son since he
disagreed with his theories and probably disliked his temperamental
stance and independent thinking.

Soon after Lou left Rilke she learned of Paul Reé's accidental death in the Engadine "where we used to spend our summers together and where he has been living alone, summer and winter." Lou immediately suspected that it may have been suicide, but no proof for this assumption exists. Nevertheless, she was full of remorse. She felt guilty and may unwittingly have dramatized her guilt because it strengthened the contours of her mirror image as *femme fatale*. True, Reé had lived many years in seclusion. He may have hinted at doing away with himself at a morose moment when he realized that Lou would never be his. We may presume that he would not have committed suicide (if he did) had Lou stayed with him. By the same token we could say that she would have saved Tausk's life and would have made happier people of Zemek and Rilke if she had continued to live with them—and with many others who succumbed to the "Lou temptation." In a Freudian sense, we run into accidents. If Lou had stayed with Reé, it might have prevented his suicide but not his accident. He died because he was a philosopher of minor stature and could not take his failure, living, as he did, in the shadow of giants like Nietzsche.

Lou accepted her guilt in Reé's death and sought self-punishment through illness. She developed a severe heart disease. She knew no other way out than to consult her Viennese physician Dr. Pineles, a decision that started her on the road to new bliss and calamities. Dr. Pineles cured her by being Zemek, the man who loved her with passionate sincerity, who gave her a child and, at that time, had only one goal in life: to marry her. He intended to see Lou's husband and to insist on a divorce, but Lou prevented him from doing so and forced him to interrupt the pregnancy. It was a highly dramatic episode in both their lives, one in which they could easily have lost their heads. It is probably to these events that Freud referred when he spoke in his obituary for Lou that "the most moving event of her feminine fate took place in Vienna."

Zemek did not commit suicide. He remained her physician and lover for a few more years until he found the situation unbearable and humiliating. He left her and, although this brilliant physician was a very desirable man, he never married. He seems to have refused to live with a lie and subject another woman to a constant comparison with Lou. He died in 1936 of natural causes, one year before Lou's death. He did not die of a broken heart since he knew how to live with it.

Among Lou's several lovers was the Swedish psychotherapist Poul Bjerre who was married to an invalid woman. He lived and traveled with Lou for two years and was very happy with her. He was intrigued by the combination of her unusual intuition and intellect, as he said, of the passionate woman and rare listener who was a philosopher and scholar. He described his experiences with her when he was an old man:

One noticed at once that Lou was an extraordinary woman. She had the gift of entering completely into the mind of the man she loved. Her enormous concentration fanned, as it were, her partner's intellectual fire. I have never met anyone else in my long life who understood me so quickly, so well, and so completely, as Lou did. . . . She discussed her most intimate and private affairs with the greatest nonchalance . . . she did seem unconcerned about the consequences of her actions and was in this respect more like a force of nature than a human being. Her unusually strong will liked to triumph over men. She could be very passionate, but only momentarily so, and with a strange cold passion. I think Nietzsche was right when he said that Lou was a thoroughly evil woman. Evil, however, in the Goethean sense: evil that produces good. She hurt me much but she also gave me much. When I met her I was working on the foundations of my psychotherapy which is based, in contrast to Freud's, on the principle of synthesis. In my talks with Lou things became clear to me that I might not have found by myself. Like a catalyst she activated my thought processes. She may have destroyed lives and marriages but her presence was exciting. One felt the spark of genius in her. One grew in her presence.

Lou described Bjerre about a year after she had left him. It was at a time when she thought of Rilke. It was Whitsun again. Rilke had not written her since "his winter letters." He wrote her from time to time, sometimes only a desperate card with words of longing. After having worked with and inspired Bjerre, she attended many seminars with Freud, and after having met Tausk, Lou could not help thinking of Rainer and comparing him with Bjerre. She was undoubtedly longing for Rainer while dissecting both him and Bjerre in her journal, May 11, 1913:

B . . . has his origins in the world of reality, even banality . . . he himself is somewhat given to the banal and brutal, which he has corrected by means of another brutality—the complete personal revolution that made him a noble "helper" and savior, but on account of his lack of inner freedom paralyzed his creative talent. He appears a many-sided man, a bit of a dilettante, determined to attain in every respect his "own" spiritual goal—to *rise*.

. . . even his marriage and his wife fit the pattern in an unusually frightful way, with him acting as his wife's nurse, her helper, and the savior of her life. Only thus was love allowed to him and only thus was it possible for him to have anyone at his side, a "loneliness for two."

And as if Bjerre would have wanted to retaliate, we read in his account of her:

She told me that she had been pregnant once but that she could not, or did not want to, become a mother. There may have been deeper reasons, however, for her refusal to accept motherhood. . . . A woman who becomes a mother sacrifices herself in a certain sense to her child. But that was precisely what Lou could not do. She could never, not even during the most passionate embrace, and then she was by no means cold, give herself completely. She always talked about it but she could not do it. Intellectually she could merge into her partner but not humanly. Perhaps this was the real tragedy in Lou's life. She longed for deliverance from her strong personality but did not find it. In the deepest meaning of the word, Lou was the unredeemed woman.

Poul Bjerre, who always remained at odds with Freud, introduced or reintroduced Lou to the master. Her close relationship with Bjerre, their discussions and interpretations of psychic phenomena gave Lou the knowledge and insight into the major aspects of Freud's ideas. Her former link with Nietzsche also helped her to be respected and to gain entrance to Freud's inner circle. This skeptical, rather pessimistic man must have been puzzled by the buoyant spirit and energy of this woman who showed a surprising understanding of the most difficult problems and whose remarks proved her intelligence. Freud may have felt the intensity of her interest in his thoughts and theories as a reassuring messenger coming from the outside world as unexpected as was Lou's participation at the Weimar Congress.

She immediately plunged into psychoanalytic studies by herself and, to some extent, still with the help of Bjerre. But at the end of

1911 she could say, like someone who had been shipwrecked and suddenly saw land: "Psychoanalysis—with ever increasing admiration for Freud's unreservedness, rectitude, objectivity. I am getting deeper into it than through Bjerre . . ."

In September, 1912, she wrote Freud from Göttingen that the study of psychoanalysis continued to preoccupy her and that she would like to come to Vienna to attend his lectures and seminars. Freud replied:

Dear Frau Andreas, When you come to Vienna we shall all do our best to introduce you to what little of psycho-analysis can be demonstrated and imparted. I have already interpreted your attendance at the Weimar Congress as a favorable omen. Yours faithfully, Freud

The phrase that he interpreted her presence at Weimar as a favorable omen reveals the feeling of wonder that must have struck him upon meeting her. Of course, he could not surmise that this woman who had never been analyzed would one day make a great analyst.

"The Father-Face"

"The father-face which [has] presided" over her life in her later years was that of Freud. The manner in which she came to Freud was that of innocent curiosity about the mechanism of the human psyche and with a spotty knowledge of what was then scientifically known. The most fundamental preparation she brought to him was the treasure of her life experiences.

These experiences helped to heighten her interest in psychoanalysis, but what triggered her passionate embrace of its study must have been her dissatisfaction with her creative writing. She was an ambitious woman, a perfectionist in many ways. Freud remarked on the modesty that kept her from mentioning her literary work. But this was less modesty than her determination to be considered by him as a writer on psychoanalytic themes solely. She never found full gratification in creating fictional characters which, in her case, were always shadows of her own experiences with people who had passed through her life. Even when she created herself as the heroine in her memoirs, she fictionalized the events to the extent that poetry was given as much space as truth. The experience was always more exciting to her than its re-creation on paper. What absorbed her were people and their inner struggles. What made her write was the fascination of visualizing a human being in his nakedness, of blending his problems with her imagination of his real conflicts.

Writing in her *Journal* about a visit to Freud on February 2, 1913, she reported that Freud also discussed her reasons for becoming so deeply interested in psychoanalysis. It was not only a neutral, objective interest or the fascination to stand in the presence of a new science, it was from a far more personal reason. ". . . Psychoanalysis bestowed a gift on me personally, its radiant enrichment of my own life that came from slowly groping the way to the tools by which it is embedded in the totality. When Freud said laughingly, 'I really think you look on analysis as a sort of Christmas present,' I could only agree, since for me it was not a question of resolving conflicts between the depth and the surface." After a visit at Freud's house on April 6, 1913, she wrote in her *Journal* as if in love with her happiness: "As I set out home with his roses, I rejoiced that I had met with him on my journey and was permitted to experience him—as the turning point of my life."

When the two met at the Weimar Congress in 1911 she was, in spite of her fifty years, a radiant personality. Freud, only five years older, was at the height of his faculties and fame. When his biographer, Ernest Jones, described Freud's temperament as that of "a conquistador—an adventurer if you want to translate the word—with the curiosity, the boldness, and the tenacity that belongs to that type of being," he also adumbrated what characterized Lou. There were many levels on which these two strong personalities were close to one another, points of instinctive attraction that explain the tacit interaction between them. He was undoubtedly impressed by the unburdened freedom with which she approached psychoanalysis, never allowing him to doubt how devoted she was to him. But even the greatest man is not free of certain weaknesses, and Freud's shortcomings are well known. Despite his strictly scientific thinking he was superstitious and, in a partly serious, partly self-mocking manner, may have believed in Lou as a spirit sent to him at the right moment, the moment when he was struggling with many of his disciples turned renegade. At this point, he may have needed an intelligent yes-sayer.

But she was far from being a sycophant. She had her own opinions, mostly based on her ability to penetrate and interpret reactions in herself and in those whom she encountered. Their correspondence over many years offers great insight into their relationship; it was one of mutual respect, understanding and love. Even if her sometimes cumbersome elaborations on case histories—she often asked him for advice—called forth a brief or admonishing reply, his tone was never impolite or annoyed. He recognized the struggling but enthusiastic beginner and, at one point, told her not to get personally involved in her cases ("You are no legal friend or helpful aunt, but a therapist . . ."). Later when she was more accomplished, he advised her not to overwork or accept too many analytic sessions. There was always a very personal, friendly and sometimes fatherly tone to his letters, the undeniable note of someone who cared.

Freud seemed to be interested in her reactions to his works, and over the years there was a constant exchange of opinions. As early as May, 1916, Lou worried in one of her letters that she might interpret "anything amiss. . . . I am particularly anxious to avoid any sort of misunderstanding as to your meaning. That at least is my honest and sincere endeavor." And Freud's reply: "I cannot believe that there is any danger of your misunderstanding any of our arguments; if so it must be our, in this case, my fault. After all, you are an 'understander' *par excellence* [a remark echoing a similar statement made by Nietzsche]; and in addition your commentary is an amplification and improvement on the original."

In July, 1917, she sent him her comments on his work on the *General Theory of the Neuroses* and asked him whether he would write "yes" or even just a question mark, where appropriate. Freud replied: "I have to disappoint you. I am not going to say 'yes' or 'no,' nor shall I deal out question marks, but I shall do what I have always done with your comments; enjoy them and let them have their effect on me. It is quite evident from them how you anticipate and complement me each time, how you strive prophetically to unite my fragments into a structural whole."

On the 6th of January, 1935, Freud wrote Lou a long account—as a matter of fact, several pages long—of his ideas on Moses in particular, and religion in general, from which he fashioned his last book, *Moses and Monotheism*, published four years later. He confided to Lou his thoughts about his new concept: "What you have heard about my last piece of work I can now explain in greater detail. It started out from the question as to what has really created the particular character of the Jew, and I came to the conclusion that the Jew is the creation of the man Moses." But Freud's Moses was not the Moses of the Bible; he was not a Jew, but a well-born Egyptian who left his fatherland and decided to create a new nation out of a Semitic tribe upon whom he imposed a monotheistic faith, the spiritualized religion of Aten. Moses was probably killed in a popular uprising, and his people united with kindred tribes who worshiped Jahve, a volcano god living on Mount Sinai. Gradually the repressed god of Moses became Jahve.

Freud concluded this long letter:

Religions owe their compulsive power to the *return of the repressed;* they are reawakened memories of very ancient, forgotten, highly emotional episodes of human history. I have already said this in *Totem and Taboo;* I express it now in the formula: the strength of religion lies not in its *material,* but in its *historical* truth.

And now you see, Lou, this formula, which holds so great a fascination for me, cannot be publicly expressed in Austria today, without bringing down upon us a state prohibition of analysis on the part of the ruling Catholic authority. And it is only this Catholicism which protects us from the Nazis. And furthermore the historical foundations of the Moses story are not solid enough to serve as a basis for these invaluable conclusions of mine. And so I remain silent. It suffices me that I myself can believe in the solution of the problem. It has pursued me throughout the whole of my life.

Forgive me, and with cordial greetings from your

Freud

He probably wrote Lou such a detailed plan of his book because he knew of her deep-seated interest in religion. She hardly knew how to thank him, she answered a few days later. She had been carrying the letter around with her for three days and realized that her reply would be little more than "a brief exclamation." Actually, it was an enthusiastic exclamation of some length. Lou realized the importance of Freud's idea that religions owe their compulsive power to the "return of the repressed," but she was also aware of the importance of "the very fact *that* you have written to me and allowed me to share in this . . ." It was her only letter ever signed with: "In deep gratitude."

Lou was sincerely impressed by Freud's vision. Although since childhood she had been preoccupied with religion, which held her interest with mystical power, she felt that whatever she might analytically intellectualize about it, it was dwarfed by Freud's conceptions. Her first psychoanalytic essay, "Of Early Divine Service" ("*Vom frühen Gottesdienst*"), published in *Imago* in 1913, dealt with the psychology of religion.

The mysticism to which she subscribed and which had lost the basis of any traditional faith had been shifted onto an intellectual basis in the framework of the unconscious. By objectifying the gods, men make them manlike. Through their projection into a fictionalized existence, the gods—or man's belief in them—serve as a crutch for feelings of insecurity and inferiority. We shape out of our own image a perfect one to whom we can pray and submit. Thus, the love of God turns into the highest form of self-love. Believing in a primal union of all that exists, love becomes the rediscovery of the other—the lost—part of the self.

In her *Freud Journal*, in November, 1913, she explained that:

In the God-father concept, the self and the other once more form an unbroken unity for the believer out of which we just emerge at birth—for we do not come out of duality but only enter it in our conscious existence. Perhaps in that way the father did not gradually become God, but the divine totality still glowed around the father who represented it, as our immediate environment. One might at heart believe that it is on account of the force of conscious experience alone, the dualistic cleavage into human existence, into ego and world, that God was somehow for primitive man the first and only certainty; God was, so to speak, his recollection.

The idea of unity prevailing in all her concepts meant that man's ability and tendency to act imaginatively "preserved the lost unity in the god." Her stress on unity and synthesis had often placed Lou and Freud at opposite poles. On July 30, 1915, he wrote her: "Every time I read one of your letters of appraisal I am amazed at your talent for going beyond what has been said, for completing it and making it converge at some distant point. Naturally I do not always agree with you. I so rarely feel the need for synthesis . . . I am of course an analyst and believe that synthesis offers no obstacles once analysis has been achieved. . . . Your letter also contains a precious promise. I should very much like to read 'Anal and Sexual,' and if our periodicals can still carry on, I will see that it gets printed."

Among her psychoanalytic writings were several works which also had Sigmund Freud's special approval. In his *Three Essays on Sexuality* Freud referred to Lou's "Anality and Sexuality," published in 1916, as "a paper which has given us a very much deeper understanding of the significance of anal erotism." When the child is deprived of taking pleasure in anal activity, the world's hostility to his impulses becomes established, Lou explained. In its consequences, this realization leads to the repression of a vital part of the self and the separation of self from the environment. As far as sexuality is concerned, Lou came to the conclusion that, with the anal zone and the genital in close proximity, particularly with woman, more than a romantic gesture of love is needed to create a liberating atmosphere to overcome shame and guilt.

Apparently, Lou became aware of her real self as Narcissus did. She did not drown in the water as did the legendary Greek; she was able to love and embrace, to understand and penetrate the beguiling mirror image looking back at her. Long before she embarked on putting into words the somewhat distorted reflection of herself in her memoirs, she wrote an autobiographical sketch in 1911, published in *Literary Echo*. She could not have chosen a more revealing title than "In the Mirror" in which she told about her imagination in childhood always running away with her. When she described experiences in those early years, they seemed wild fantasies and lies to others. To her they were the realities of her imagination. She always wanted to visualize the poetic truth about people and encounters that could never be identical with the factual truth.

She could not help seeing herself and the world reflected in the water: ". . . One must remember that the Narcissus of the legend does not stand in front of an artificial mirror but before one of nature. Perhaps he does not only see himself reflected in the water but, in addition to himself, everything else as well, otherwise would he have stayed?" Again her idea of the unity of being is expressed by this thought. Had Narcissus not seen himself "as still everything," he would not have lingered but fled, he would have been horrified to realize that he was alone and no longer united with nature.

Side by side with the concept of the original unity of being, narcissism as something very basic in life had an almost manic fascination for her. In both these respects Freud disagreed with her, but recognized how the two were interrelated. As Lou explained in her 1913 diary notes, "Freud admitted that ultimately this quest for unity stems from narcissism from where, however, by his own surmise, our joy in living also comes to us." Lou seems to have felt the need to justify and explain her thirst for life, for intellectual and physical adventures, philosophically and psychologically.

She disagreed with Freud's "overemphasis of consciousness, as if everything infantile were pathological by reason of its immaturity." This ran counter to her own basic feelings. However magnificent her mind was—and no one ever doubted her cerebral capacities—she knew only too well of the raw powers and dark forces in her, of how important man's "archaic" beginnings were that he never outgrows, even though he may grow out of them. Her optimism and vivacity made her also distinguish between pathological and natural repression as a life-inhibiting and life-enhancing process. She saw in culture not an impediment, but something that man in his way of progressing would have to assimilate and master. Although Lou thought that, later on, Freud came closer to her point of view, he remained in fact the pessimist who did not believe that man was fit for culture. Freud could never accept any euphoric state or visualize a "definitive unity of things," as Lou did, and he condemned such beliefs as childish and unscientific. "The unity of this world," he wrote her, "seems to me so self-evident as not to need emphasis. What interests me is the separation and breaking up into its component parts."

Undoubtedly, Lou was in love with her own narcissistic tendency and therefore ready to accept it as a source for many potent forces, such as creativity and a positive outlook on life. In her essay, "The Dual Orientation of Narcissism," she concluded that "in the ecstasy enduring narcissistically behind everything, the optimist is ever in the right; in his disregard for this inner 'nonobjective' presupposition, the pessimist—libidolessly, lovelessly judging—is ever in the wrong."

In the year 1916 Freud celebrated his sixtieth birthday. The First World War was in its second year. Freud wrote Lou: "Even in the happiest of times it would be but a melancholy event." The pupil proved to be the master of life in her reply: "You say that it would have been but a melancholy event at any time—but when each year that passes is rich and momentous, and where one would not miss a single product of mind, there can be no melancholy, and at the end of another ten years there will be yet another joyous celebration."

Over the years their respective roles as an optimist and a pessimist ran like a natural thread through their correspondence, with Freud varying as salutation the phrase: ". . . may your faith in life persist wherever you are!" After the third month of the war in 1914 he stated that for him the world would never again be a happy place. "It is too hideous. And the saddest thing about it is that it is exactly the way we should have expected people to behave from our knowledge of psychoanalysis. Because of this attitude to mankind I have never been able to agree with your blithe optimism." And five days earlier he had written Lou a brief note whose four lines ended with: "In the hope of a word of comfort from you."

At the beginning of their friendship Freud may have seen in her the only real bond between himself and Nietzsche. But this tenuous and vicarious link from Lou to Nietzsche could not explain Freud's very personal feeling for her, his respect for her integrity and ethical ideals, which he thought far transcended his own. (How else can we understand his view of her as being superior "over all of us"?) Through the years she was one of his first and favorite readers. We cannot assume that he was merely polite when he assured her that she always gave more than she received. They differed in many ways and on various issues, as I have stressed. But in spite of it their friendship lasted from 1912 when Lou joined Freud and his circle until her death in 1937.

Freud best summed up their essential differences in one of his letters. It was at the beginning of the last decade of their lives when both had learned to endure the physical insults of their weakening natures. Freud apologized for not having written sooner. He complained that work and visitors kept him from writing to her, but above all, "the difficult task of maintaining what measure of health is left to me allows me no free time at all." This mood of defiant despair led to the following paragraph:

But now that I am writing you at last I am delighted to observe that nothing has altered in our respective ways of approaching a theme, whatever it may be. I strike up a—mostly very simple—melody; you supply the higher octaves for it; I separate the one from the other, and you blend what has been separated into a higher unity; I silently accept the limits imposed by our objectivity, whereas you draw express attention to them. Generally speaking we have understood each other and are at one in our opinions. Only, I tend to exclude all opinions except one, whereas you tend to include all opinions together.

Freud could not have had a bad opinion about her skill as a psychoanalyst because he sent her many patients and even hoped she might help free his daughter Anna from her father-fixation. Anna Freud and Lou became intimate friends. He told Lou how glad he was about her fond feeling for his daughter ("I know she will not be stranded as long as you are alive, but she is so much younger than the two of us . . ."). A year later, on May 3, 1925, Lou wrote on the occasion of Freud's birthday that she felt as if she belonged to his family: "Dear Professor, I cannot express in words all that I wish and hope for you in the way of happiness. I feel only too acutely how completely I am identified with you all, as though I were a fragment of some age-old Anna, and somehow inseparable from you all."

To one of her many birthday congratulations Freud replied (May 11, 1927): "My dear indomitable friend! I read your birthday letter with the same feeling that one gets when sitting by the fireside in winter and basks in its warmth." It was a wonderful and, in many ways, surprising relationship between Lou and Freud who, in a letter to Arnold Zweig only six days after her death, reassured his friend and, no doubt, himself that he was very fond of her, "curiously enough without a trace of sexual attraction." Ernest Jones attests that Freud was one of the most monogamous males he knew of.

"Curiously enough," at the very beginning of their friendship Freud reacted twice in writing to the fact that she had missed his lecture, or rather he had missed her at his lecture. On November 10, 1912: "I have adopted the bad habit of always directing my lecture to a definite member of the audience, and yesterday I stared as if spellbound at the vacant chair reserved for you." And the same sentiment was repeated on March 2, 1913: "I am very sorry that I have to answer your letter in writing, i.e., that you were not at my lecture on Saturday. I was thus deprived of my point of fixation and spoke uncertainly! Fortunately it was the last lecture." That he had chosen Lou as a point of fixation may have been curious chance. But that he spoke uncertainly because he was deprived of his point of fixation is, if nothing else, a frank admission that Freud's "Lou-fixation" began when she started to sit in on his lectures.

Ernest Jones asserted that there is little doubt that Freud found the psychology of women more enigmatic than that of men, and quoted Freud: "The great question that has never been answered and which I have not yet been able to answer, despite my thirty years of research into the feminine soul, is 'What does a woman want?' "

Lou, on the other hand, was very positive in her attitude toward what a woman is and wants. She thought of man as the seeker and dreamer, pursuing the unattainable in romantic lostness as his Faustian archetype, while the woman was the Eternal Feminine that, in the Goethean sense, leads men on—as a point of attraction and, beyond this, as an image of inspiration. Thus, the woman presents herself to Lou as a desired goal, but, at the same time, she remains a free agent, self-determined and self-reliant.

Woman is far more self-contained than man, Lou thought. Reality is deeply anchored in her, while revelation of life is a part of what she receives, not what she has to seek, like man. Therefore, this childbearing creature is creative in reproducing an image or part of herself in the same way that the artist creates with each work a mirror image of himself. His sexuality is synchronized to his search and dream, therefore of necessity aggressive. Her sexuality is indicative of her closeness to total and eternal union. Being the one who receives and conceives, she is the antithesis of Faustian man.

Lou's ideal of womanhood had all the earmarks of contemporary feminism without ever permitting it to be categorized as such. Out of her personal experiences she shaped concepts in which narcissism, femininity and creativity are closely interrelated. She was such a strong personality that she could convincingly present the gained wisdom from her experiences as a solidly built philosophy. Spirituality and sensuality were totally integrated in her, and what she considered an important developmental goal, namely, the unity of sex and ego, was fully reflected in the reality of her life as much as in her philosophy.

Most of these ideas went back to the year 1899, when she published a long essay, "Woman as a Human Being" (*"Der Mensch als Weib"*), and were written without any psychoanalytic knowledge. Clinical scientists may reproach her for having been inclined to interpret "life in the language of the dream" instead of relating dreams to life. She was a poet of life, and the poetic scope in her writings distinguished her from all other Freudian disciples. Freud himself thought that she was the poet of psychoanalysis, whereas he was writing prose.

In spite of her excellent record as an analyst for almost three decades, every case was for her a *roman à clef*. This was to be expected from someone who wanted to find the key to the secret of life—that remained her first and greatest passion. She referred in one of her later papers to her "intoxication with life—a little of which beneficially circulates in the blood and brain of healthy man."

In her autobiography she tells of Freud's reaction to an early poem of hers, "Hymn to Life," which Freud first took to be a poem by Nietzsche who wrote the music for it at a time when the poet-philosopher thought of himself as a composer. In this poem Lou expressed the wish to live forever regardless of the pain life might force her to endure. Freud, who suffered a great deal from head colds, replied laconically: "A bad cold could already cure me of such a desire."

A Destiny Fulfilled

Most lives are lived in a marginal manner; some of them are full of forays at the heart of an illusive matter and absorb and reflect as much as their will and desires permit. Lou's life was lived from the very center of her existence, dominated by an excessive will and insatiable desires. Wherever she went and whatever she did, it always was the matter of her heart that drove her to experience the hidden secrets of life. She unraveled plenty of them. But when the revelation of a secret yielded little gain for her, her restless imagination created the excitement of a magnified disclosure until she got tired of all illusions and charades and dropped it as an active child does with a boring toy. But she never gave up seeing and hoping with an almost naïve, and therefore disarming, optimism, with an ever-surprising belief in herself and life. At the age of sixty-six she wrote Sigmund Freud (May 4, 1927) that she was "all eagerness about the surprises still in store for me from the wonder packet 'life.' "

Her incredible life force can only be understood if we can visualize a person who has embraced life in a demonstratively whole-hearted fashion, driven by the impulse of an explorer. Essentially, she wanted to discover herself by way of experiencing and probing others. She was surely puzzled by her own complexities and thought she would find a way to her real self during her many detours through other people. She was fully aware of the many contradictions in herself, but no one appears to have noticed the hardships she must have endured to reconcile these conflicts. Perhaps she hardly knew it herself, because her tremendous willpower made her ride the crest of her feelings all the time. She could be concerned and domineering, passionate and cold. She might extol motherhood in one of her novels, but in real life she violently rejected the idea of giving birth, primarily because she could not bear the thought of giving up her personal freedom.

How different was Lou's reaction from Alma Mahler's! For her, childbearing was a part of being a total woman, who thought of it as an experience that she would not have liked to miss. In this respect Lou was certainly not only too involved in the pursuit of her own being; she simply could not have faced the fact that another creature with a life and will of its own would bear some or most of her features, be another and yet different Lou.

Do Lou's contrasts not suggest a theoretically determined mind pitted against the wild cries of her emotions? Undoubtedly, she was profound in her thinking, and her brilliant mind could quickly absorb whatever task it undertook. And yet she was able to wear profundity lightly and create the impression of total ease. She had the rare gift of making people feel at home with themselves, even though she may have been going through a period of great anxiety from which she was far from free. She was often seen in the mysterious light of someone spending freely of her warmth and intellect and doing it with self-evident grace.

However, she was never sure of herself and her actions. How could we otherwise explain that she asked most of her lovers—when she closed the chapter of an affair—to return her letters or to burn them? Why did she fictionalize her memoirs, hiding from posterity her most important love encounters? Neither Zemek nor Poul Bjerre appears on the pages that supposedly sum up her recollections. And why were her feelings for Richard Beer-Hofmann repressed? Even Freud remarked about her utter discretion. Did she fear being too blunt with reality in accounting for experiences that weighed heavily in her life? The word "discretion" was certainly missing from Alma

Mahler's dictionary, and Gertrude Stein loved to talk about herself with liberal frankness, perhaps whimsically hiding directness behind the convolutions of her language.

One paragraph in Lou's *Lebensrückblick* (Reflections on My Life) may give us a clue to the reasoning behind her feelings when she wrote: "What is elemental and intimate does not speak of itself, and therefore the essential as such may remain unsaid." But, so she continued to philosophize, when the positive about oneself is silenced, it can still become a confession through its negative viewpoint. The contours can be drawn with its shortcomings and wantings, the spots left empty can condition its outlines.

Lou must have been able to create "the strongest impression of the genuineness and harmony of her nature," because Freud mentioned it in her obituary, written by him for the *Zeitschrift*. He undoubtedly spoke from his own observation and experience. But Lou can be quoted as saying about herself: "Strange: whenever I most firmly believed that what I was doing was perfectly sensible and natural, that I was on the straight and narrow path, I brought about the worst catastrophes. How come?"

We might also ask with her: how come? When Freud wrote about her in a letter addressed to his family that Lou "is altogether an outstanding woman," he may have recognized that her reactions and behavior in general ignored and violated social conventions and taboos all the time. Without the benefit of psychoanalysis she always gave in to her instincts and drives, never permitting anything to stand in her way while unfolding all her potentialities. She never repressed her desires. In one of her early essays contributed to the psychoanalytic journal *Imago*, she admitted that she had an "inborn prejudice against all consciousness of guilt."

It seems she did not feel the slightest guilt at hurting someone who loved her dearly. To be sure, a great deal remained unresolved between her subconscious drives and conscious actions. However, she accepted herself and faced the truth of her nature. Freud alluded to this remarkable accomplishment—achieved without having gone through analysis—when he wrote her in May, 1931, of her "superiority over all of us—in accord with the heights from which you descended to us."

Freud may have genuinely been awed by Lou's ability to live with herself the way she did, undisturbed and untouched by her inner conflicts, by the grace of her mind, which did not tolerate any pangs of conscience. If conscience is a part of our fear that someone may be watching us, Lou cared little about it. She had a strong distaste for sharing the secrets of her private life with others. Only Gertrude Stein may have had an even stronger contempt for the world's opinion about the way she was and lived, although both were human enough to have relished being appreciated by others. Gertrude Stein had fits of fury over being better known than her works, but the image she created for herself was more legible than her literary work.

Alma's escape into a feeling of superiority was different. Her romantic spirit dominated her actions throughout her life and had that German touch of being lost in dreams, a condition alien to either Lou Salomé or Gertrude Stein. Alma's emotional life was keyed to finding her own reflection in the mirror image of great men. The greater the achievement, she admitted, the more I must love a man. A built-in emotional thermostat apparently regulated her feelings, and she was distressed about her daughter's choice of men. "There," she noted in her diary about Anna, "she tends to go wrong because she does not seek—and therefore will not find—the superior type." Alma was very conscious of what she was doing, but in her romantic lostness she felt pangs of guilt and even spoke of having committed spiritual adultery.

Lou felt totally tied to and interrelated with the world of phenomena, of flowers and animals. For her, the force of love was an elemental experience to which everything else had to be subjected, a feeling she certainly shared with Alma. Nature has no regard for petty considerations; it is driven by an enigmatic, mysterious power. Lou once wrote: "Life is only true life when it signifies not comfort, but procreation, a synthesis of pain and happiness, misery and bliss." Did Lou see herself as an elemental power, a storm sweeping along a mystically predetermined path? She had only one aim in life: to fulfill herself and her destiny. She had a certain image of herself and, with fanatic determination, pursued that image.

Her life was a series of conquests. She could not help captivating and capturing anyone who crossed her path. She may have brought unhappiness to some, but not before giving of herself with profusion. Their unhappiness seemed to have been intolerable to men like Reé and Tausk, to Zemek or Bjerre, because of the vast emptiness that engulfed them after Lou's departure and the realization that nothing would ever be able to fill the void left by her. She saw in her relationships—however short and however physical they may have been—something alive that was her very personal creation. She tended and cultivated them like flowers in a garden and felt that she had the right to let them die or struggle along alone by their own natural laws. And did not Alma feel the same when she divorced her feelings from Oskar Kokoschka, who for many years hoped for her return; or Walter Gropius, who only slowly accepted life without Alma Mahler?

The most important conquest, the crowning of Lou's mature years, was psychoanalysis. Even though Sigmund Freud was the very real image she revered, the conquest was a whole world of adventures for her, with the poetry of man's soul being the supreme subject; it was the only platonic, in fact abstract, love affair in her life which, in its infinite variety, always surprised her, always kept her without the faintest sign of ennui.

Lou was always far ahead of her time, a facsimile of that rare creature best summed up as a Renaissance figure. She was possessed by an insatiable intellectual curiosity and the feeling of having plunged herself in a sea of total freedom in which the creative impulse had free reign and nothing else mattered than to savor the joys of life. After Reé's death Lou remarked to one of her friends: "Too much! I have had too much! too much of what is good and rich for one human life!"

Freud stressed in her obituary that she was devoid of "all feminine, perhaps most human frailty." But the most appropriate epitaph that can be found for her is: "Whoever came close to her succumbed to the magic of her personality."

In the last analysis, it was the magic of personality that distinguished Lou Salomé, Gertrude Stein and Alma Mahler. To them, all the world was a stage, and all the men and women they met merely players who made their entrances and exits to give them their cues. But being good actresses, these three women knew where and how to find the luminaries of their time, brightening established lights with their own. Even the extras they engaged became stars in the aura of their brilliance. If their life experiences were to be acted out upon a stage—paraphrasing Shakespeare in *Twelfth Night*—we could condemn them as improbable fiction. But these master magicians of their own and their co-players' destinies knew how to live the fiction of their lives as the poetic truth of reality.

Supporting Cast

(Personalities who played an important part in the protagonists' lives or in the development of the arts between 1880 and World War II)

ANDERSON, SHERWOOD (1876–1941): American author who was greatly inspired and influenced by Gertrude Stein and whose most important book, *Winesburg, Ohio*, strongly affected the technique of the American short story. A superb storyteller, who portrayed life in the small towns of the American Midwest with poetic realism.

ANDREAS, FRIEDRICH CARL (1846–1930): Spent most of his early years in the Orient where he accumulated a wealth of linguistic and cultural knowledge of various peoples. He was an erudite scholar, and the only man who actually succeeded in marrying Lou Salomé, even though in name only. Late in his life he received a professorship at the University of Göttingen; he left a few scholarly books behind him.

APOLLINAIRE, GUILLAUME (1888–1918): French poet, dramatist, short-story writer, and influential art critic. He was a leading figure in the avant-garde movements early in this century. He was the first to use the term "surrealism." Gertrude Stein admired his work, particularly his *Calligrammes*, which she felt were closest to cubism and very much akin to her own work.

APPIA, ADOLPHE (1862–1928): Swiss stage designer who, together with Gordon Craig, changed the visual image of the theater from realism to illusion. In 1899 he wrote *Die Musik und die Inscenierung* (Music and Staging), followed by *L'Oeuvre d'art vivant* (The Work of the Living Art) in 1921, in which he expanded his theories on movement, spatial projection and mobile light. His ideas revolutionized modern stage concepts.

BALL, HUGO (1886–1927): Writer and actor, he was one of the co-founders of dadaism in Zürich's Café Voltaire. His writings are characterized by a strong critical spirit. Among his works were a Hermann Hesse biography and such books of essays as *Die Flucht aus der Zeit* (Flight from Time).

BEER-HOFMANN, RICHARD (1866–1945): Austrian playwright, poet and novelist whose work was mainly founded on the heritage of the Old Testament. He became well-known for a few of his poems, such as the "Lullaby for Miriam," or his play, *The Count of Charolais*.

BERENSON, BERNARD (1865–1959): American art critic, recognized as an authority on Italian Renaissance art. For most of his mature life he lived in his famous villa "I Tatti" near Florence. He advised some of the most famous art collectors and wrote books, such as *The Italian Painters of the Renaissance* and *Rumor and Reflection*, which belong to the most illuminating works about art and the artist in the Renaissance.

BERG, ALBAN (1885–1935): Austrian composer and disciple of Arnold Schönberg. He transmuted his master's more radical concepts into a somewhat more conventional and harmonic idiom. He combined a sense of drama *(Wozzeck, Lulu)* with a flair for lyrical flow *(Lyric Suite)*.

BROD, MAX (1884–1968): An intimate friend of Franz Werfel and Franz Kafka, he edited Kafka's works, and authored several novels, poems and essays. He emigrated to Israel and became the head of the Habimah Theatre in Tel Aviv.

BURCKHARDT, MAX EUGEN (1854–1912): Although a minor poet and essayist, he made a name for himself as the director of the Burgtheater, Vienna's leading playhouse. There, against the wishes of the royal clique, he produced the avant-garde playwrights of those days, Ibsen and Hauptmann.

COCTEAU, JEAN (1891–1963): Versatile French poet, protean man, novelist, playwright, movie director and draughtsman, Cocteau ushered in a new experimental era with the ballet *Parade* in 1917. He went through most "isms" of the twentieth century and was often associated with surrealism. Although he was the *enfant terrible* of French letters, he was elected to the Académie Française in 1955. A poet at heart in whatever art form he expressed himself, he remained unconventional in all his varied activities.

EBNER-ESCHENBACH, MARIE (1830–1916): A leading novelist of her time, she lived most of her life in Vienna. Her writings were essentially realistic, rooted in liberal Catholicism, distinguished by a strong feeling of social consciousness.

FITZGERALD, F. SCOTT (1896–1940): Well-known American novelist who wrote about the rich and what money did to them. He dealt with the cynicism, confusion and tragedies of young people in the Jazz Age. Among his best-known books are *The Great Gatsby, This Side of Paradise* and *Tender Is the Night.*

FREUD, SIGMUND (1856–1939): The famous founder of psychoanalysis, his thinking and intellectual courage led to striking discoveries that gave our century its awareness of man's inner mechanism. He wrote many books of which his *Interpretation of Dreams* is the most accessible; *Moses and Monotheism* was his last one, finished in exile in London at the age of eighty-three, the year he died.

FRIEDELL, EGON (1878–1938): One of Vienna's unique personalities, philosopher, playwright, actor, critic and cultural historian. His best-known play was *The Jesus Problem*, a play on Judas. He wrote an erudite, fascinating work in three volumes, *Cultural History of Modern Times.*

GILLOT, HENDRIK (1836–1916): As minister of the Dutch Reformed Church in St. Petersburg, Russia, he was a captivating orator and a man of great learning, tutoring the Czar's children as well as Lou Salomé.

GRIS, JUAN (1887–1927): One of the major Spanish cubist painters, he was associated with Picasso and Braque and was helped by Gertrude Stein. Gris combined intuition with mathematical calculation and developed an increasingly lyrical style in cubist fashion, freeing himself from synthetic severity and achieving lightness and colorfulness, giving his objects more volume and a bold roundness.

GROPIUS, WALTER (1883–1969): One of the foremost architects of our time, born in Berlin, founder of the famous *Bauhaus* art school at Weimar in 1919; he directed it until 1928. A voluntary exile from Hitler's Germany, he came to the United States where he continued his influential work, teaching at Harvard University. He died in Boston in 1969.

HAAS, WILLY (1891–1973): German writer and editor, born in Prague. He became famous as the editor of the once leading periodical, *Die Literarische Welt* (The Literary World), and as an essayist who wrote mainly on literary personalities and epochs. He wrote a preface to the German edition of Alma Mahler-Werfel's autobiography.

HAUPTMANN, GERHART (1862–1946): Began as a sculptor and became one of Germany's greatest playwrights. He wrote realistic plays of social protest, such as *The Weavers*, as well as romantic plays of poetic mysticism. He won the Nobel Prize for literature in 1912.

HEMINGWAY, ERNEST (1898–1961): One of America's foremost novelists, who received the Nobel Prize for literature in 1954. He began writing in Paris in the 1920s with Gertrude Stein as his mentor. He is considered a leading exponent of the tough vernacular school of American fiction. Virility and violence, daring and death are his most frequent themes. His most popular novels are *For Whom the Bell Tolls, A Farewell to Arms, Death in the Afternoon.*

HOFMANNSTHAL, HUGO VON (1874–1929): Austrian poet, playwright, novelist, essayist, descendant of a Spanish-Jewish family. He wrote librettos for Richard Strauss *(Elektra, Der Rosenkavalier)*, a modern version of *Everyman* and Calderon's *The Great World Theatre*. In most of his works dreams are a higher form of reality, and realities are the foil of a true dream. He seemed to have been born with the wisdom of the ages, as he showed particularly in his *Letter of Lord Chandos*, a record of the fall of man stated in modern terms.

JAMES, WILLIAM (1842–1910): One of the leading American psychologists and philosophers of the last century. He was best known as one of the founders of pragmatism. He had great influence on his students, among whom was Gertrude Stein.

KAFKA, FRANZ (1883–1924): Almost unknown during his lifetime, particularly after World War II Kafka's stories were recognized as the work of a great modern writer. Such books as *The Trial, The Castle, Metamorphosis* anticipated the horrors of our time, man's search for acquittal from unknown offenses, his paralyzed impotence and futile efforts for redemption in a world full of despair and guilt, of torment and anxiety.

KAHLER, ERICH VON (1885–1970): German writer and lecturer who emigrated to the United States after Hitler seized power. As a historian and literary man he published such books as *The German Character in the History of Europe; The Orbit of Thomas Mann; The Tower and the Abyss*, an inquiry into the transformation of the individual.

KAMMERER, PAUL (1880–1926): Controversial Austrian biologist whose thesis on *The Inheritance of Acquired Characteristics* created a stir among the biologists at the beginning of this century.

KLIMT, GUSTAV (1862–1918): Founder of the Viennese *Sezession*, the *Jugendstil* or Art Nouveau group that turned against traditionalism and on whose works early expressionism was based. He began with an illustrative style both naturalistic and symbolistic as it is mainly found in his monumental murals. His style became very ornamental.

KOKOSCHKA, OSKAR (1886–   ): Leading exponent of the psychological portrait during the first decade of this century. As a painter of landscapes and townscapes he began to work in the style of Art Nouveau *(Jugendstil)* and turned to a very personal expressionistic and lyrical concept. His early writings broke new ground and heralded expressionism and surrealism, which came into being much later.

KRAUS, KARL (1874–1936): Austrian poet and satirist. Erich Heller called him "the Swift of our time." He was the editor and sole contributor to the satiric periodical *Die Fackel* (The Torch), in which he lampooned the demonic possibilities of mediocrity. He equated journalism with the decline of man's morals and foresaw the decline and doom of Western civilization long before Oswald Spengler. His monumental work, *The Last Days of Mankind*, a documentary play about World War I, an 800-page satire, is a frightful mosaic of human stupidity and callousness.

KRENEK, ERNST (1900–   ): Austrian composer, was a pupil of Franz Schreker and later adopted Arnold Schönberg's twelve-tone method of composition. His jazz-influenced opera, *Jonny spielt auf*, has often been produced. He came to the United States in 1939, taught at several universities and, producing a wide range of chamber, choral and orchestral works, has continued to experiment with many techniques and styles.

MAASS, JOACHIM (1901–1972): German novelist and essayist, lived in the United States after World War II. He published several books in Germany and some of them were translated, such as *The Magic Year*.

MAHLER, GUSTAV (1860–1911): One of the great Austrian composers and conductors of his time. He wrote ten symphonies, the last unfinished. His forty songs are not really lieder but rather abbreviated symphonic movements. He inherited a romantic conception of music and searched for the expression of spiritual reality. He also inherited Jewish intellect and skepticism, the drive to surpass himself, to overcome the dread of the meaninglessness of life. This made him into a taskmaster as conductor and *Direktor* of the Vienna Opera, which, however, reached its climactic period under him.

MATISSE, HENRI EMILE BENOÎT (1869–1954): One of the leading French painters of the twentieth century. Early in his career he joined the avant-garde and became famous when, in 1905, he exhibited a portrait of his wife, *Woman with a Hat*, at the Salon des Indépendants, a painting bought by Leo Stein. His inventiveness, his daring use of colors, his ability to create an image to the point of intricate abstraction helped him to bring forth a great number of masterpieces. Retiring to Vence in the hills behind Nice, he designed the entire decoration of the Chapel of the Rosary, brilliant stained-glass windows, furniture and murals. Matisse referred to this chapel as his crowning masterpiece.

MEYSENBURG, MALWIDA VON (1816–1903): Friend of Nietzsche and Wagner, she was known as the social conscience of her time, as one of the great idealists and fighters for woman's emancipation. She became involved in the 1848 Revolution, had to flee her native Berlin, settled first in London and then in Rome. Her best-known book was *Memoirs of an Idealist.*

MOLL, CARL (1861–1945): Pupil of Emil Schindler, but never reached his master's skill. He painted a great many landscapes and still lifes and was, at the beginning of this century, strongly influenced by the Art Nouveau *(Jugendstil)* movement. He married Mrs. Schindler after his master's death, and thus became Alma Mahler-Werfel's stepfather.

NIETZSCHE, FRIEDRICH (1844–1900): One of the most influential thinkers of the last century; Martin Heidegger said that he was the last great metaphysician and the final point of a development that began with Plato. This poet-philosopher has become best known for his work, *Thus Spake Zarathustra,* his concept of superman, of man overcoming himself.

PFITZNER, HANS (1869–1949): Was active as a conductor, composer, teacher and writer. He stressed romanticism of German provenience in most of his works with a highly nationalistic gesture. The only opera that survived him and is occasionally produced at German opera houses is *Palestrina.*

PICASSO, PABLO (1881–1973): Spanish painter, one of the artistic giants of this century; lived in France most of his mature life. He began as a post-impressionist and is, together with Braque, considered the co-founder of cubism. He worked in many media and styles, but remains a titan of the visual arts. He also wrote poetry and plays in which he was also radically avant-garde but less successful. He was an intimate friend of Gertrude Stein.

PINELES, FRIEDRICH (1868–1936): Emigrated to Vienna from Galicia which, until 1918, was a part of the Austro-Hungarian monarchy. He came from an old, respected Jewish family, studied medicine and was one of the seven students who registered for Freud's famous seminar on neuroses in the winter semester 1895–1896. It was at that time that he met Lou Salomé whose friend and lover he became. He never married and died as one of Vienna's great physicians to whose clientèle belonged the city's high society and artist colony.

REÉ, PAUL (1849–1901): German philosopher, known for his positivism, which originally impressed Nietzsche. He became Nietzsche's and Lou Salomé's friend. Among his works are *On the Sources of Moral Sentiment* (1877), *The Origin of Conscience* (1885), and *The Illusion about Man's Freedom of Will* (1885).

REINHARDT, MAX (1873–1943): World-famous Austrian stage director. His stage conceptions were imaginative, colorful and swift. He staged more than six hundred plays during his lifetime and, since he believed that every play demands its own style, his methods were eclectic, reaching from the symbolic and suggestive to the most naturalistic and realistic. He became especially famous—also in America—for his spectacular productions with gigantic crowd scenes (*The Miracle*, 1911; *The Eternal Road*, 1937).

RILKE, RAINER MARIA (1875–1926): Born in Prague and, with the help of Lou Andreas-Salomé, became one of the greatest German poets, a saint of sensibility, a tragic-heroic figure and at the same time an egotistical weak one. He impressed the world with his characteristically Rilkean style and poetic cadences. Some of his most famous books are: *The Book of Hours, Duino Elegies, The Sonnets to Orpheus, The Notebook of Malte Laurids Brigge*.

RODIN, AUGUSTE (1840–1917): A giant in the history of sculpture. His bas-reliefs representing scenes from *Dante's Divine Comedy*, his sculptural images of *The Thinker, Balzac* or *Victor Hugo, John the Baptiste Preaching* or *The Burghers of Calais* are monumental works. With his *Hands* and *The Hands of God*, or the *Cathedrale* he created the monument of his own dream-fulfilled greatness. These hands became the revelation of a man who lived all his life with the hand of God pointed at him.

ROLLER, ALFRED (1864–1935): One of the great Viennese scenic designers. He transposed Gordon Craig's and Adolphe Appia's ideas into practical stage images. His motto was: "Each work of art carries within it the law of its staging." He attempted a simplification and artistic suggestiveness of the stage design. He became famous for the use of the so-called "Roller" towers which were movable corner pieces. His designs for the Vienna Opera made a strong impression on press and public. Later he worked for Max Reinhardt and designed many décors for him (*Faust, Oedipus Rex, Everyman*).

SCHINDLER, EMIL JAKOB (1842–1892): Viennese landscape painter of great renown who could rightfully be called the Schubert of painters. He was bohemian in his outlook on life. Alma Mahler-Werfel was his daughter.

SCHNITZLER, ARTHUR (1862–1931): Austrian physician, playwright and novelist, best known for his witty psychological studies of love-lost souls, mainly of the Viennese species. He visualized the world as a clinic and made gentle X-ray studies of his patients' hopes and doubts, joys and frustrations. His prescriptions were pleasure and tenderness to be taken in small doses. He was a misunderstood moralist who showed evil for the sake of good, as in his play, *Reigen* (La Ronde).

SCHÖNBERG, ARNOLD (1874–1951): One of the iconoclastic modern composers whose writing on a twelve-tone system revolutionized music in the twentieth century. He began writing in the atonal style in 1908. A refugee from Hitler's Germany, he came to the United States in 1933 and lived in California until his death. He also painted well, wrote poetically, and was a great teacher. Alban Berg and Anton von Webern were among his outstanding disciples.

SCHREKER, FRANZ (1878–1934): Conductor, composer and teacher. His most successful opera was *Der Schatzgräber* (1920). His musical style had Wagnerian features mingled with Debussyian impressionism. Like Wagner, he wrote his own librettos, which were full of mysticism, naturalism, and had touches of sexual psychology. His influence as a teacher was profound.

STEIN, LEO (1872–1947): Gertrude's brother, who exerted great influence on her. He was an aesthete and art connoisseur, a brilliant conversationalist who, however, was a failure as a writer and painter. He wrote two books: *Journey Into Self* and *Appreciation: Painting, Poetry and Prose.*

STIEGLITZ, ALFRED (1864–1946): American pioneer in artistic photography, editor of *Camera Work.* He was the husband of Georgia O'Keefe and a great friend and admirer of Gertrude Stein.

TAUSK, VIKTOR (1877–1919): One of the more brilliant Freudian disciples and an intimate friend of Lou Andreas-Salomé. His main work was about narcissism. Freud rejected him because of his daring psychoanalytic approaches. His attachment to Lou was very strong. He committed suicide.

THOMSON, VIRGIL (1896–   ): Composer, critic and intimate friend of Gertrude Stein. He set her *Four Saints in Three Acts* (1934) and *The Mother of Us All* (1947) to music. He has also written several books on music.

TOKLAS, ALICE B. (1877–1967): Most famous for having been Gertrude Stein's companion and secretary. She seems to have had great influence on Gertrude Stein. She wrote her autobiography, *What Is Remembered*, in 1963.

TOLSTOI, LEO (1828–1910): One of the most formidable writers and thinkers of Russia in the mid-nineteenth century. When he later broke his ties with his family and the government he was looked upon as a saint by the peasantry. A great moralist and reformer, he was also one of the world's greatest novelists (*Anna Karenina, War and Peace, The Kreutzer Sonata*); a creative essayist ("What Is Art?", "How Much Land Does a Man Need?"), as well as an impressive dramatist (*The Power of Darkness, The Living Corpse*). Tolstoi is universally accepted as a man of wisdom and action.

TRAKL, GEORG (1887–1914): One of the great poets writing in the German language during the first decade of our century. Born at Salzburg, he died in Galicia while with the Austrian army. His poetry is somewhat obscure, but full of evocative imagery, dynamic metaphors, great sensibility and a beautiful autumnal rhythm.

URZIDIL, JOHANNES (1896–1970): German poet and novelist born in Prague; he emigrated to the United States as a refugee from Nazism. An expert on Goethe, he wrote *Goethe in Böhmen* (Goethe in Bohemia), and published novels and several books of poetry. Most of his stories deal with Kafka's Prague and are written with great warmth and humor. Only one of his many books was translated: *There Goes Kafka*.

VAN VECHTEN, CARL (1880–1964): Novelist and essayist, known for his witty, satirical and sophisticated writing of life among New York society people and aesthetes of the 1920s. He was also a music and drama critic for New York newspapers for a number of years. He was a great friend of Gertrude Stein, who appointed him executor of her works.

WASSERMANN, JAKOB (1873–1934): Austrian novelist. Among his many books are two that are outstanding: *Caspar Hauser* and *Christian Wahnschaffe*.

WEDEKIND, FRANK (1864–1918): Began his career as a journalist and publicist, but soon discovered his dramatic gifts and became a forerunner of expressionism. He was a great moralist who criticized the hypocrisy of social conventions and was the first to fight for a new sex morality, particularly with his play *Spring's Awakening* in 1891. He played the main parts in many of his dramas and also became a well-known *Kabaretist*.

WERFEL, FRANZ (1890–1945): Austrian poet, novelist and playwright, born at Prague. Most of his works express a semi-mystical belief in the brotherhood of man. He published many volumes of poetry, novels and plays. Among his best-known works are *The Forty Days of Musa Dagh*, *Verdi*, and *The Song of Bernadette*; his most popular play was *Jacobowsky and the Colonel*, adapted by S. N. Behrman, which was also turned into a movie. He emigrated to the United States with his wife, Alma Mahler-Werfel, in 1940.

WEININGER, OTTO (1880–1903): Viennese philosopher. A genius who committed suicide after having written a then sensational book, *Sex and Character*.

WHITEHEAD, ALFRED NORTH (1861–1947): One of the leading and most influential philosophers and mathematicians of our era. His most popular book, published in 1925, was *Science and the Modern World*

He viewed philosophy from the standpoint of mathematics and called it the philosophy of organism. His views are idealistic rather than materialistic and have a touch of mysticism. Religious experience and the concept of a God seen as an impersonal image and the ultimate good play a principal role in his thinking.

WILDER, THORNTON (1897–   ): American playwright and novelist who gave the middle-class theater a new poetic impetus, a wider dimension and new stage ideas, in such plays as *Our Town* and *The Skin of Our Teeth*. Some of his novels *(The Bridge of San Luis Rey* and *The Ides of March)* are full of ideas and structurally complex, but have also a characteristic charm.

ZEMLINSKY, ALEXANDER VON (1872–1942): Known first as a conductor of operas. He was conductor at the opera houses of Vienna, Prague and Berlin. In 1938 he emigrated to the United States where he died four years later. He is less remembered for his six operas than for being one of the most outstanding teachers. Among his students were Arnold Schönberg, Erich Korngold and also Alma Mahler.

ZUCKERKANDL, BERTA (1863–1945): Famous journalist and great society lady of her time. She wrote three books, the best known of which is *Oesterreich Intim,* her memoirs covering the period 1892–1942. She translated 120 plays and wrote innumerable features for newspapers, mainly for the *Neues Wiener Journal.* She also furthered the careers of many young artists, mainly Viennese, among them the painters Klimt and Kokoschka. She was on very good terms with Alma and Gustav Mahler.

Bibliography and Sources

Alma Mahler-Werfel: Body and Mind

BERG, ALBAN. *Briefe an seine Frau.* Herausgegeben von Helene Berg. München: Albert Langen, 1965.

BLAUKOPF, KURT. *Gustav Mahler oder der Zeitgenosse der Zukunft.* Wien-München-Zürich: Verlag Fritz Molden, 1969.

GIEDION, SIEGFRIED. *Walter Gropius. Mensch und Werk.* Stuttgart: Verlag Gerd Hatje, 1954.

GROPIUS, WALTER. *Apollo in der Demokratie.* Mainz: Kupferberg Verlag, 1967.

———. *Internationale Architektur.* München: Albert Langen, 1925.

———. *Die neue Architektur und das Bauhaus.* Mainz: Kupferberg Verlag, 1965.

KLIMT, GUSTAV. *Dokumentation.* Herausgegeben von Christian M. Nebehay. Wien: Nebehay Verlag, 1969.

KOKOSCHKA, OSKAR. *Mein Leben.* München: Bruckman Verlag, 1971.

———. *My Life.* Translated by David Britt. London: Thames and Hudson, 1974. New York: Macmillan Publishing Co., 1974.

MAHLER-WERFEL, ALMA. *Gustav Mahler.* Erinnerungen und Briefe. Amsterdam: Bermann-Fischer/Querido Verlag, 1949.

———. *Mein Leben.* Vorwort von Willy Haas. Frankfurt am Main: S. Fischer Verlag, 1960.

MAHLER-WERFEL, ALMA, and ASHTON, E. B. *And the Bridge Is Love.* New York: Harcourt Brace Jovanovich, Inc. 1958. London: Hutchinson & Co., Ltd., 1958.

SCHNITZLER, ARTHUR. *Gesammelte Werke.* 5 Bände. Berlin: S. Fischer Verlag, 1922–23.

SORELL, WALTER. "For Art's Sake." Essay on Gustav Mahler. In *Opera News*, New York. Vol. 24, March 5, 1960.

TRAKL, GEORG. *Die Dichtungen.* Gesamtausgabe. Mit einem Anhang. Zürich: Verlag der Arche, 1946.

WERFEL, FRANZ. *Jacobowsky und der Oberst.* Komödie einer Tragödie. Stockholm: Bermann-Fischer Verlag, 1944.

———. *Das Lied von Bernadette.* Stockholm: Bermann-Fischer Verlag, 1942.

———. *Paulus unter den Juden.* Dramatische Legende. Berlin-Wien: Paul Zsolnay, 1926.

———. *Spiegelmensch.* Magische Trilogie. München: Kurt Wolff, 1920.

———. *Die Vierzig Tage des Musa Dagh.* Berlin-Wien: Paul Zsolnay, 1933.

———. *Wir sind.* Gedichte. Leipzig: Kurt Wolff, 1917.

Gertrude Stein: A Mind Is A Mind Is A Mind

BRIDGMAN, RICHARD. *Gertrude Stein in Pieces.* New York: Oxford University Press, 1970.

BRINNIN, JOHN MALCOLM. *The Third Rose: Gertrude Stein and Her World.* Boston: Little, Brown, 1959.

FULLER, EDMUND (ed.). *Journey Into the Self: Being the Letters, Papers and Journals of Leo Stein.* New York: Crown Publishers, 1950.

ROGERS, W. G. *When This You See Remember Me: Gertrude Stein in Person.* New York: Rinehart and Company, Inc., 1948.

SPRIGGE, ELIZABETH. *Gertrude Stein: Her Life and Her Work.* New York: Harper & Row, Publishers, Inc., 1957. London: Hamish Hamilton, 1957.

STEIN, GERTRUDE. *The Autobiography of Alice B. Toklas.* New York: Random House, Inc., 1936.

———. *Brewsie and Willie.* New York: Random House, Inc., 1946.

———. *Everybody's Autobiography.* New York: Random House, Inc., 1947.

———. *Four in America.* New Haven: Yale University Press, 1947.

———. *The Geographical History of America.* New York: Random House, Inc., 1936.

———. *Geography and Plays.* New York: Haskell House Publishers, 1967.

———. *Last Operas and Plays.* New York: Rinehart and Company, Inc., 1949.

———. *Lectures in America.* New York: Random House, Inc., 1935.

———. *The Making of Americans.* New York: Harcourt Brace Jovanovich, Inc., 1934.

———. *Picasso.* New York: Charles Scribner's Sons, 1939.

————. *Portraits and Prayers.* New York: Random House, Inc., 1934.
————. *Tender Buttons.* New York: Claire Marie, 1914.
————. *Things As They Are.* Pawlet, Vt.: Banyan Press, 1950.
————. *Three Lives.* New York: The Grafton Press, 1910.
————. *Wars I Have Seen.* New York: Random House, Inc., 1945.
————. *What Are Masterpieces and Why Are There So Few of Them?* New York: Pitman Publishing Co., 1969.
STEIN, LEO. *Appreciation: Painting, Poetry, and Prose.* New York: Crown Publishers, 1947.
SUTHERLAND, DONALD. *Gertrude Stein: A Biography of Her Work.* New Haven: Yale University Press, 1951.
TOKLAS, ALICE B. *What Is Remembered.* New York: Holt, Rinehart and Winston, 1963.
VAN VECHTEN, CARL (ed.). *Selected Writings of Gertrude Stein.* New York: Random House, Inc., 1934.

Lou Andreas-Salomé: Mind and Body

ANDREAS-SALOMÉ, LOU. *Aus fremder Seele.* Stuttgart: Cotta, 1896.
————. *Drei Briefe an einen Knaben.* Leipzig: Kurt Wolff, 1917.
————. *Drei Stunden ohne Gott.* Jena: Eugen Diederichs, 1922.
————. *Die Erotik.* Frankfurt am Main: Rütten & Loening, 1910.
————. *Fenitschka. Eine Ausschweifung.* Stuttgart: Cotta, 1898.
————. *Henrik Ibsens Frauen-Gestalten.* Jena: Eugen Diederichs, 1910.
————. *Im Zwischenland.* Stuttgart-Berlin: Cotta, 1902.
————. *In der Schule bei Freud.* Herausgegeben von Ernst Pfeiffer. Zürich: Max Niehaus Verlag, 1958. *The Freud Journal of Lou Andreas-Salomé.* Translated and with an introduction by Stanley A. Leavy. New York: Basic Books, Inc. Publishers, 1964.
————. *Lebensrückblick.* Grundriss einiger Lebenserinnerungen. Aus dem Nachlass herausgegeben von Ernst Pfeiffer. Zürich: Max Niehaus Verlag, 1951. Wiesbaden: Im Insel-Verlag, 1951.
————. *Ma.* Stuttgart-Berlin: Cotta, 1901.
————. *Mein Dank an Freud.* Wien: Internationaler Psychoanalytischer Verlag, 1931.
————. *Menschenkinder.* Stuttgart-Berlin: Cotta, 1899.
————. *Rainer Maria Rilke.* Leipzig: Im Insel-Verlag, 1928.
————. *Rodinka.* Jena: Eugen Diederichs, 1923.
————. *Ruth.* Stuttgart: Cotta, 1895.
————. *Der Teufel und seine Grossmutter.* Jena: Eugen Diederichs, 1928.

BERNOULLI, CARL ALBRECHT. *Nietzsches Lou-Erlebnis.* Zürich: Raschers Jahrbuch I, 1910.

BINION, RUDOLPH. *Frau Lou. Nietzsche's Wayward Disciple.* Foreword by Walter Kaufmann. Princeton, N.J.: Princeton University Press, 1968.

BUTLER, E. M. *Rainer Maria Rilke.* Cambridge: At the University Press, 1941.

JONES, Ernest. *The Life and Work of Sigmund Freud.* 3 vols. New York: Basic Books Inc., 1953.

KUTSCHER, ARTUR. *Frank Wedekind. Sein Leben und seine Werke.* München: Georg Müller, 1922.

NIETZSCHE, FRIEDRICH. *Friedrich Nietzsches Briefwechsel mit Franz Overbeck.* Herausgegeben von Dr. Richard Oehler und Carl Albrecht Bernoulli. Leipzig: A. Kröner, 1916.

————. *Friedrich Nietzsches Gesammelte Werke.* Leipzig: A. Kröner, 1910.

PETERS, H. F. *My Sister, My Spouse.* A Biography of Lou Andreas-Salomé. New York: W. W. Norton & Company, Inc., 1962.

PFEIFFER, ERNST. *Notes to: Rainer Maria Rilke, Lou Andreas-Salomé. Briefwechsel.* Zürich: Max Niehaus Verlag, 1952.

————. (ed.) *Sigmund Freud and Lou Andreas-Salomé Letters.* Translated by William and Elaine Robson-Scott. New York: A Helen and Kurt Wolff Book. Harcourt Brace Jovanovich, Inc., 1966.

PODACH, ERICH F. *Friedrich Nietzsche und Lou Salomé. Ihre Begegnung 1882.* Zürich und Leipzig: Max Niehaus Verlag. No date.

RILKE, RAINER MARIA. *Briefe.* 6 Bände. Herausgegeben von Ruth Sieber-Rilke und Carl Sieber. Leipzig: Insel-Verlag, 1929–1937.

————. *Briefe 1902–1906.* Herausgegeben von Ruth Sieber-Rilke und Carl Sieber. Leipzig: Insel-Verlag, 1929.

————. *Sämtliche Werke.* Leipzig: Insel-Verlag, 1955.

Index